Emily Bronte

WUTHERING HEIGHTS

Emily Bronte

WUTHERING HEIGHTS

[Edited with Introduction, Author's Information, Criticism, Study Questions and Bibliography]

Aditya Nandwani
B.A. English (Hons) , Delhi University;
M.A. (English), IGNOU; Print Journalism (English) YMCA

ANMOL PUBLICATIONS PVT. LTD.
NEW DELHI - 110 002 (INDIA)

ANMOL PUBLICATIONS PVT. LTD.

H.O.: 4374/4B, Ansari Road, Darya Ganj,
New Delhi-110 002 (India)
Ph.: 23278000, 23261597

B.O.: No. 1015, Ist Main Road, BSK IIIrd Stage
IIIrd Phase, IIIrd Block
Bangalore - 560 085 (India)
Visit us at: www.anmolpublications.com

Wuthering Heights

First Published, 2009

PRINTED IN INDIA

Printed at Mehra Offset Press, Delhi.

Contents

Preface

Emily Brontë was one of the six children born to Reverend Patrick Brontë and Maria Branwell Brontë. She was born in Thornton, Yorkshire, England, on July 30, 1818. Her popular Bronte sisters were Maria, Elizabeth, Charlotte, Anne, and Branwell. In the age of two, her family moved to Haworth and experienced the moors, a part of the Pennine Chain of mountains, and here she lived until she died 30 years later.

Wuthering Heights is one her most popular and renowned works. Interestingly, this book has received neither critical praise nor any local popularity during its initial publication. However, Wuthering Heights received a lot of popularity both publicly as well as critically after 1847. Victorian society was not ready to accept the violent characters as well as harsh realities of Wuthering Heights.

Charlotte Bronte was the first person to praise publicly Wuthering Heights and wrote a preface and introduction for the second publication of the novel in 1850. She was the first and foremost critic of Wuthering Heights and was the sister of Emily Bronte. Yet Charlotte herself was not entirely convinced of all its merits.

Author

Chapter 1

Introduction of Wuthering Heights

Although Wuthering Heights received neither critical praise nor any local popularity during its initial publication, the reading public has changed substantially since 1847, and now both critical and popular opinion praise Emily Brontë's singular work of fiction. Victorian society would not accept the violent characters and harsh realities of Wuthering Heights, but subsequent audiences are both more understanding and accepting of the use of unsavory aspects of human life in literature.

The first person to praise publicly Wuthering Heights was Charlotte Brontë, Emily's sister, who wrote a preface and introduction for the second publication of the novel in 1850 and became the novel's first and foremost critic. Yet Charlotte herself was not entirely convinced of all its merits. Commenting upon the advisability of creating characters such as Heathcliff, Charlotte states, "I scarcely think it is [advisable]." Charlotte's comments may be a direct concession and appeal to Victorian audiences to accept and respect Wuthering Heights without having to accept completely everything within the text. In addition to having difficulty with the content, the Victorian audience's view of women could not allow anyone of that period to accept that Wuthering Heights was the creation of a female (it had been published originally under the pseudonym Ellis Bell). After its initial publication, both critical and popular audiences ended up embracing Wuthering Heights, and it remains one of the classic works still read and studied.

Wuthering Heights is an important contemporary novel

for two reasons: Its honest and accurate portrayal of life during an early era provides a glimpse of history, and the literary merit it possesses in and of itself enables the text to rise above entertainment and rank as quality literature. The portrayal of women, society, and class bear witness to a time that's foreign to contemporary readers. But even though society is different today than it was two centuries ago, people remain the same, and contemporary readers can still relate to the feelings and emotions of the central characters—Heathcliff and Catherine—as well as those of the supporting characters. Because Brontë's characters are real, they are human subjects with human emotions; therefore, Wuthering Heights is not just a sentimental romance novel. It is a presentation of life, an essay on love, and a glimpse at relationships. Many critics, praising Brontë's style, imagery, and word choice, contend that Wuthering Heights is actually poetry masquerading as prose.

This lyrical prose has a distinct structure and style. Significantly, Wuthering Heights is about ordered pairs: two households, two generations, and two pairs of children. Some critics dismiss the plot of the second-generation characters as being a simple retelling of the first story; however, in doing so, they are dismissing the entire second half of the book. Each of the two main story lines of the two generations comprises 17 chapters. Clearly, in order to appreciate fully Wuthering Heights, attention must be paid to the second half, particularly noting that the second half is not just a retelling but rather a revising—a form of renewal and rebirth.

These ordered pairs more often than not, are pairs of contrast. The most noticeable pair is that of the two houses: Wuthering Heights and Thrushcross Grange. Wuthering Heights has the wild, windy moors and its inhabitants possess the same characteristics. Opposite this are the calm, orderly parks of Thrushcross Grange and its inhabitants. Each household has a male and female with a counterpart at the other. Readers gain insight into these characters not only by observing what they think, say, and do but also by comparing them to their counterparts, noticing how they do not think, speak, and act. Much is learned by recognizing what one is not.

Structurally, the narrative is also primarily told from a paired point of view. Lockwood frames the initial story, telling the beginning and ending chapters (with minor comments within). Within the framework of his story, Nelly relates the majority of the action from her outsider's point of view. In essence, readers are eavesdropping rather than experiencing the action. And embedded within Nelly's narrative are chapters told primarily from another character's point of view that has been related to Nelly. This technique allows readers to experience more than would with any one narrator, enabling readers to gain an insider's perspective.

The role of the outsider should not be overlooked because the setting of Wuthering Heights is one of complete isolation; therefore, only those with first- or second-hand experiences are able to relate them to others. The moors connecting Wuthering Heights and Thrushcross Grange serve a dual purpose—linking the two households while simultaneously separating them from the village and all others.

This isolated setting is important for Brontë's combination of realism and gothic symbolism. Brontë took conventions of the time and instead of merely recreating them in a work of her own, used them as a springboard to write an entirely original tale, creating characters who are simultaneously real and symbolic archetypes.

Brontë uses these characters to explore themes of good versus evil, crime and punishment, passion versus rationality, revenge, selfishness, division and reconciliation, chaos and order, nature and culture, health and sickness, rebellion, and the nature of love. These themes are not independent of each other; rather, they mix, mingle, and intertwine as the story unfolds. Wuthering Heights is also a social novel about class structure in society as well as a treatise on the role of women. Brontë illustrates how class mobility is not always moving in one direction. For Catherine, representing a lower class, social class plays a major role when deciding to get married. That is why she cannot marry Heathcliff and agrees, instead, to marry Edgar. For Isabella, however, just the opposite is true. She is drawn to the wild, mysterious man, regardless of the fact that he is beneath her social standing. Because of her infatuation, she loses everything that is dear to her. Readers must therefore look not only to social class when judging and analyzing characters; they must determine what decisions are made by members of a certain class and why these characters made the decisions they did.

On the surface, Wuthering Heights is a love story. Delving deeper, readers find both a symbolic and psychological novel. (Contemporary audiences, for example, easily relate to issues of child abuse and alcoholism.) In fact, Wuthering Heights cannot be easily classified as any particular type of novel—that is the literary strength that Brontë's text possesses. The novel told from multiple points of view is easily read and interpreted from multiple perspectives, also.

Like other literary masterpieces, Wuthering Heights has spawned dramatic productions, a musical retelling, movies, and even a novel that fills in the gaps of Heathcliff's three missing years. Emily Brontë's novel has overcome its initial chilly reception to warm the hearts of romantics and realists worldwide.

Chapter 2

Emily Bronte and Her Works

"Wuthering Heights is a strange sort of book—baffling all regular criticism; yet, it is impossible to begin and not finish it; and quite as impossible to lay it aside afterwards and say nothing about it." This review, from Douglas Jerrold's Weekly Newspaper, was one of the first receptions to Emily Brontë's novel, and concluded with the line, "we must leave it to our readers to decide what sort of a book it is." The conclusion in this review, which is the extent of praise the novel received on its publication, pertains not only to the novel Wuthering Heights but to Emily Brontë herself; it is up to readers to determine what type of writer Brontë was: Besides Wuthering Heights, only a few poems of hers exist and precious little of her personal history exists to complement those writings. Thus, in order to ascertain what type of writer Brontë was, critics must speculate based on a limited family history, some poems, and one excellent novel.

Brontë was one of six children born to Reverend Patrick Brontë and Maria Branwell Brontë. Born in Thornton, Yorkshire, England, on July 30, 1818, she was the sister of Maria, Elizabeth, Charlotte, Anne, and Branwell. Her family moved to Haworth when she was two years old, and here she first experienced the moors, a part of the Pennine Chain of mountains, andhere she lived until she died 30 years later.

A variety of conflicting influences shaped her life. Her father, of Irish descent, was known for his poetry and imagination even though he was the cleric. Her mother, a staunch Methodist, died when Emily was only three years old, so what she knew of her she learned from her siblings and her

Aunt Elizabeth (Maria's sister), who raised the children after Maria's death. Elizabeth brought a religious fervor to the house that Brontë soon rejected. Brontë's environment shaped her life and her work. The village of Haworth was isolated and surrounded by moors; thus, the one world she knew and lived in became the setting for her only novel. Paralleling her own life, she creates motherless characters in Wuthering Heights.

Writing was a means of amusement for the Brontë children. After the two oldest sisters died, the remaining siblings began writing plays and poems, creating a world called Angria and Gondal. These worlds became little books and the sources for later poetry and prose. Emily Brontë went to school, but she was unable to stay there. Possessing a reclusive nature, she had longings and desires for her home on the moors, which prompted her return home after a scant three months.

In the following year, 1837, she attempted to teach school. This endeavor lasted eight months, but she could not handle the stress and again returned home. In 1842 she went with Charlotte to Brussels to study foreign languages and school management in order to open a school in Haworth. Brontë had success there. One of her professors stated that she "had a head for logic and a capability for argument, unusual in a man, and rare indeed in a woman," but she returned to Haworth when her aunt died in 1843. Living with her father at the parsonage in Haworth, this became a period of creativity. Although the earliest dated poem is from 1836, the majority of her poetry that survives was written during this time.

Like most authors, Emily Brontë was a product of her environment, and this directly influenced her writing. During her life she had no close friends, was interested in mysticism, and enjoyed her solitude outdoors. All of these elements grace both her poems and Wuthering Heights. In fact, many contemporary critics praise Emily Brontë first and foremost as a poet, marveling at the poetic nature of Wuthering Heights.

In 1845 Charlotte found some of the poetry that Emily had been writing and eventually persuaded her sister to attempt to publish her work. Charlotte and Emily, along with their sister Anne, eventually published a collection of poems under the male names of Currer, Ellis, and Acton Bell. Each pseudonym begins with the same consonant as the writer's name. The sisters paid to have the collection published, and even though it only sold two copies, they were undaunted and continued to write. This time each sister wrote a novel.

Evidence suggests that Emily Brontë began writing Wuthering Heights in December 1845 and completed it the next year. A year after that, in July of 1847, Wuthering Heights was accepted for publication; however, it was not printed until December, following the success of Jane Eyre.

Although Wuthering Heights did not meet with the critical success Jane Eyre received, contemporary critics tend to consider Emily the best writer of the Brontë sisters. Emily Brontë's highly imaginative novel of passion and hate was too savage and animal-like and clumsy in its own day and time, but contemporary audiences consider it mild.

The fall following publication, Emily Brontë left home to attend her brother's funeral. She caught a severe cold that spread to her lungs, and she died of tuberculosis on December 19, 1848. Following the publication of poems, Jane Eyre, Wuthering Heights, and Anne's novel Agnes Grey, audiences considered all three "Bells" to be one author. Confusion continued as Anne published The Tenant of Wildfell Hall. Wuthering Heights was reissued with poems and a biographical notice by Charlotte. By this time, both Emily and Anne had died, and Charlotte succinctly stated how and why she and her sisters assumed the name of Bell. Charlotte Brontë also provided insight into the life of her sister.

Long after its initial publication and subsequent death of its author, Wuthering Heights has become one of the classics of English literature. After the reissue of Emily Brontë's text, the editors of the Examiner commented upon Charlotte's introduction. Their words and sentiments are often echoed by admirers of Wuthering Heights: "We have only most unfeignedly to deplore the blight which fell prematurely on sure rich intellectual promise, and to regret that natures so rare and noble should so early have passed away."

Her Works

Fiction/Novel Category

Wuthering Heights

Poem Category

Anticipation
Bluebell, The
Day Dream, A
Death
Death-Scene, A
Elder's rebuke, The
Encouragement
Faith and Despondency
Honour's Martyr
Hope
Lady to her guitar, The
Last Words
Little While, a Little While, A
Loud without the wind was roaring
Love and Friendship
My Comforter
Night-Wind, The
No coward soul is mine
Old Stoic, The
Philosopher, The
Plead for me
Prisoner, The
Self-Interogation
Shall earth no more inspire thee
Stars
Sympathy
To Imagination
Two children, The
Visionary, The
Wanderer from the Fold, The
Warning and Reply

Chapter 3

Background and Analysis of Major Characters

Background

Wuthering Heights was published 1847, the only novel written by Emily Bronte. It was published under the 'pen name' of Ellis Bell. Her life had been largely confined to the village of Haworth, Yorkshire, where her father was a local vicar. Mrs. Bronte died when the children were quite young and were reared by maiden aunts and housekeepers. Very little formal education was experienced by the Brontes until they decided on careers. All three sisters became published writers. Charlotte; "Jane Eyre", Anne; "The Tenant of Wildfell Hall" and Emily; "Wuthering Heights". The novel was written between 1845 and 1847 and its first edition succeeded in selling only 7 copies. The death of Emily in 1949 prompted Charlotte to write a preface to the second edition, published in 1951. As Charlotte was a well known author in this height, the book gained popularity and by the 20th century, the love story of Heathcliff and Catherine became a classic of literature. The novel was influenced by the two styles of the late 18th and early 19th centuries.

The late 18th century was dominated by the Gothic novel, in which the supernatural played the role. This reached its highest point with the publication of "Dracula" by Brahm Stoker. This also influenced Mary Shelly to write "Frankenstein". The early 19th century was dominated by the novels of Sir Walter Scott and Jane Austin. These novelists were influenced by the romantic movement of Wordsworth and Colderidge. Both of these influences are seen in "Wuthering Heights", where the house itself and its inhabitants, the servants and the dogs are typical of the Gothic novel, where Thrushcross Grange by contrast is more typical of the world of Jane Austin.

Therefore Wuthering Heights can be interpreted as a compendium as both the Gothic and romantic novels of the periods immediately proceeding 1847. Emily Bronte herself was the youngest of six children. Her father was born Patrick Prunty on the 17 March 1777 in Co. Down. He was ambitious and won a place at Cambridge, a magnificent achievement for the son of a story-teller. He changed the spelling of his name to Bronte in about 1799, after Nelson was created Duke of Bronte. When he left Cambridge he became a Church of England clergyman and he married Marie Branwell in 1812. She was from Penzance in Cornwall, they had 6 children, 5 girls and 1 boy, Branwell.

In 1820, the family moved to Haworth Parsonage in Yorkshire, which was located on the edge of the Yorkshire moors, the family lived there until he died in 1861. In 1821, tragedy struck the family with the death of Marie, and the task of raising the family was then taken on by the mother's sister. Her personality is reproduced in the character of Joseph in Wuthering Heights. In 1824, 4 of the girls were sent to Cowanbridge Boarding School, to begin their education, within a month 2 were dead due to the inhumane regime. The others, Emily and Charlotte, returned home to be educated by their father. He had inherited his fathers story-telling talents and he entertained his children in the Parsonage.

In 1826, Branwell received a present of a box of toy soldiers, the children gave each soldier a name, invented a land where these characters would live, called Angria, while Emily and Anne in turn invented another place called, Gondal, a practice then began of the children writing chronicles of their own fabled country. In 1835, Emily was again sent to the school of RoeHead, where Charlotte was a teacher, however she returned home after 3 months. In 1837, she spent 6 months as a teacher in

Halifax. Charlotte was of the opinion that the sisters should open their own school, so in 1842, they went to Brussels to approve their proficiencies in European languages, however they soon had to return home for the funeral of their aunt and Emily never left Haworth again. Charlotte then published a collection of their poems which sold only two copies.

The sisters then each decided to write a novel, Emily's Wuthering Heights seemed to be both a commercial and literature failure when it was published in 1847. Meanwhile, their brother Branwell died in September 1848 and while attending his funeral, Emily caught a chill and it developed into consumption, she refused all medical aid and died on 19 December 1848. In 1850, Charlotte published a second edition of Wuthering Heights to which she had written a preface, on this occasion it met with both critical and commercial success, and by the end of the century it was regarded as one of the greatest novels ever written.

Analysis of Major Characters

Analysis of Catherine Earnshaw

If Heathcliff can be considered the main protagonist of the novel then Catherine Earnshaw is the dominant female spirit which prevails the novel. She is a character dominated by obsession and her single greatest obsession is her love for Heathcliff. It is this which gives food to her soul, which controls her life and gives a sense of meaning, purpose and direction to her existence.

The love which she professes for Heathcliff is not mere romantic love; neither is it based on mere physical attraction, it is an identification, a union of souls-: "Without Heathcliff" she says "the universe would turn to a mighty stranger". She contrasted the love that she professes for Heathcliff with that she publicly exclaimed for Edgar-: "My love for Edgar is like the foliage in the woods: time will change it, I'm well aware, as winter changes the trees. My love for Heathcliff resembles the eternal rocks beneath: a source of little visible delight, but necessary. Nelly, I am Heathcliff". Catherine's relationship with Heathcliff was established in childhood, Nelly remarked-: "The greatest punishment we could invent for her, was to keep her separate from him". Catherine possesses a wild, passionate nature which initially is presented when she spat at Heathcliff on discovering that he was the reason for her father loosing the whip she was to get. Further evidence of Catherine's wildness can be seen from the pledge she and Heathcliff made-: "promised fair to grow up as rude as savages" in response to the terinay of Hindley.

It was as Nelly said-: "one of their chief amusements, to run away to the moors in the morning and to remain there all day, and the after punishment grew a mere thing to laugh at." Catherine is defiant of authority and seemed to enjoy the wrath of others-: "she was never so happy as when we were all scalding her at once" Catherine's passionate nature, evident throughout her childhood, seemed not to exist in her early months of her marriage to Edgar. Her passion was described as-: "gunpowder which lay as harmless as sand because no fire came near to explode it".

While Catherine is wild, wilful and passionate, she also possesses a double character. Her five week sojourn at the grange awakens in her an appreciation of the civilised world. When she returns to the Heights, both manner and appearance have changed and is shocked in appearance of Heathcliff and Edgar. From then on, Catherine adopts a split personality - an amusing lady-like disposition in the company of the Lintons and returning to her wild passionate self when accompanied by Heathcliff.

She declared her wish to be 'the greatest lady in the neighbourhood" as the materialistic side to her personality begins to assert itself. For the first time in the novel, Catherine worries how others see her and she confesses to Nelly it would degrade her to marry Heathcliff. The duality of Catherine's character revealed a crisis point with her marriage to Edgar - the one event in the novel above all others which determines the futures of the central characters. Catherine's marriage to him is a betrayal of her nature. Not only has she broken with her kindred spirit, Heathcliff, but she has physically removed herself from the wildness and freedom from the Heights and the crags. This choice made by Catherine favoured wealth, civilisation and social position over her natural affinity with the untamed, uncivilised world represented by Heathcliff.

Catherine's marriage to Edgar and her rejection of Heathcliff is a rejection of herself. In going to the Grange, she has turned her back, not only on Heathcliff, but on the carefree lifestyle she enjoyed at the Heights. In comparing their souls, she said of Heathcliff-: "his and mine are the same and Linton's is as different as is moon from lightning or frost from fire." Before she died, she came to terms with her error, recognised she would only be at peace-: "not among the Linton's,...under the Chapel roof, but in the open air". The error committed by Catherine in marring Edgar is one of which she was fully aware-: "I'm convinced I'm wrong - I've no more business to marry Edgar than I have to be in heaven" She also recognises that her heaven is not a traditional one but rather one out on the moors with Heathcliff.

In the delirium she suffered before death, she longs for that freedom-: "I wish I were a girl again, half savage, hardy and free" However, it is then too late. The return of Heathcliff after a three year absence is a catalyst which arouses her true nature. On his visits to the Grange, it is noticeable that a table was set for he a Catherine, and another for Isabella and Edgar, symbolising the gulf between them and the fact that Catherine occupied an unnatural position in this civilised world.

A significant feature of Catherine's character is her wish to dominate both situations and people. When she wants to be alone with Edgar on one of his visits to the Heights, she pinches Nelly in exasperation and then delivers her a stinging blow when Nelly refuses to leave the room. When Heraton cries put in fear of Catherine, her response was to shake him-: "'till the poor child waxed livid" She refuses to allow Edgar to leave after witnessing this event-: "I should be miserable all night, and I won't be miserable for you" Nelly recalled that Edgar-: "possessed the power to depart as much as a cat possesses the power to leave a mouse half killed" Later on, she orchestrates a fight between Edgar and Heathcliff and throws the key into the fire when Edgar attempts to leave. She described Edgar, her husband, as 'a sucking leveret'. Catherine's domineering personality resulted in her every whim being catered to at the Grange. Nelly recalled that Edgar had-: "an inept rooted fear of ruffling her humour" The author uses nature imagery to emphasis the extent of her dominance-: "it was not the thorn bending to the honeysucles, but the honeysucles embracing the thorns" Although Catherine is a domineering, wilful, she displays a certain naiveté throughout the novel.

The main example of this is of course the self deception that is her marriage to Edgar. She is naive because she believes that her marriage will actually advance her relationship with Heathcliff. The position she will have as mistress of the Grange and Mrs. Linton will allow her to raise Heathcliff up from his lowly position and -: "place him out of my brothers power" In her innocence, Catherine believes she can keep both men, on Heathcliff's return believing that he and Edgar could be friends. Catherine's illness and death represent perhaps a natural and predictable result of her movement from the Heights to the Grange, by not staying true to her nature and by swapping the outdoor life that she had with Heathcliff for the role as the lady of the manor. She has in a sense cut off her own oxygen supply, instead of the wild air of the moors she now breaths the stifled air of the Grange, like a flower without light she eventually withers and dies, a situation entirely of her own making.

Having rejected Heathcliff in favour of marriage to Edgar, she was found by the society in which she lived, once this course was chosen there was no going back, although she realised the error of her ways, she had placed herself in a situation in which death could only extricate her, therefore she was buried at the edge of the kirkyard where the border between it and the surrounding moors was ill-defined. In death, she had returned to nature and regained her freedom, the dire consequences of her failure to remain loyal to her true self. A significant feature of Catherine's character is the influence she continues to have after her death, like Heathcliff she has a troubled spirit which torments Heathcliff to the point of madness and even to his own death.

Analysis of Cathy Clinton

The Cathy we meet at the beginning of the ovel is the result of a number of years living under the influence of Heathcliff. As with Hareton the better side of her nature and personility has been subdued and she is presented to us as unmannerly, ill-tempered, unhospitable and shrewdish. Her treatment of Lockwood in the opening chapters exemplifies the depths to which she has sunk, she snaps at im when he attempts to help her with the cannisters and flings the tea back when she discovers he has not been invited. In contrast with this behaviour and the character once described by Nelly is striking. Nelly saw her as having a "capacity for intense attatchment, reminding me of her mother, and still she did not resemble her: for she could be soft and mild as a dove". Nelly also suggested that "her anger was never furious, her love never fierce".

Her marriage to Linton was the turning point in Cathy's development as prior to that Nelly had been somewhat a surrogate mother to her and her childhood revolved around the enclosed pastures of Thrushcross Grange. She had the constant care and love of her father and the undivided attention of Nelly and lived in a world where Wuthering Heights did not exist. Despite this protection and her civilsed background she displayed something of her mother's willful personality as she constantly sought to explore the world beyond the Grange.

For her, the distant peak of Pennistone Crag symbolised the outside world and when she finally envagled Nelly to allow her to take her pony beyond the Grange she stumbled upon the world of Wuthering Heights and into the realm of Heathcliff.

Her courtship with her cousin Linton brought to the surface many sides of her personility. She displayed pity, patience and genuine care for Linton but was not above the mockery of Hareton. There is evidence in the novel that Cathy and Linton were not well matched. This is clearly demonstrated in their contrasting descriptions of a perfects summer's day. Cathy, like her mother, sees the outside world of nature as presenting her with an idyllic experience.

Her marriage to Linton was short-lived, thereafter her position in society and within the household of Wuthering Heights deterioated rapidly to the point where we meet her at the beginning of the novel.

Analysis of Edgar Linton

Edgar is the son of Mr. and Mrs. Linton, the heir to the estate of Thrushcross Grange and most importantly a foil to Heathcliff, everything about the two boys/men is different and their one common denominator, being their love for Catherine Earnshaw. Edgar's world is one of pampered, comfort and wealth, his home, Thrushcross Grange, is "a splendid place carpeted with crimson and crimson covered chairs and tables" - "white ceiling bordered by gold" - "glass drops hanging from silver chains". The mode of Edgar's dress on his childhood visits to the Heights suggests this rich and pampered lifestyle, he and his sister are smothered in furs, a metaphorical protection against the society which exists within the Heights and its wild and natural surroundings.

Edgar is portrayed as a petty and precocious child. His attitude to Heathcliff's first visit to the Grange reflects his sense of superiority, he is petty and sullen and is seen weeping as a result of a quarrel over a little dog. Heathcliff's reaction to this "To quarrel over who should hold a heap of warm hair" projects Edgar as a weak and petty individual from the outset of the novel. In her recollections, Nelly Dean portrayed Edgar as a weak and soft individual, she recalled that "he wanted spirit in general" and she referred to him as a "soft thing". Physically and emotionally, he quickly comes under Catherine's spell and is unable to leave the Heights after witnessing a quarrel between Hareton, Nelly and Catherine in which the latter's violent behaviour strikes fear into Edgar, "He possessed the power to depart as much as a cat possess the power to leave a mouse half killed".

Although he becomes the master of the Grange, the local magistrate, the husband of Catherine and in many eyes, the greatest man in the neighbourhood, is generally cowardly when faced with Heathcliff, so much so that Catherine refers to him as a "sucking leveret".

Another feature of Edgar's character is his fear of Catherine's temper, and in the light of this, his willingness to cater to her every whim. Nelly suggests that he had "a deep rooted fear of ruffling her humour". It was this fear that forced him to give in to Catherine's request that Heathcliff be allowed to visit at the Grange.

His fear is again evident as he gives in to Catherine's request that two tables be set up in the dining room rather than have Heathcliff eat in the servant's quarters which is what Edgar would have liked. Catherine speaks of his passive love saying "I have such faith in Linton's love that I believe I might kill him and he wouldn't wish to retaliate". Edgar's ultimatum to Catherine to choose between he and Heathcliff "I absolutely require to know which you choose" comes to nothing in the face of Catherine's anger. One of the few occasions on which Edgar proves to be decisive is when he warns Isabella that he will have nothing to do with her if she marries Heathcliff - this is a threat that he maintained till the end. Edgar is naive in believing that Cathy could grow up at the Grange without discovering the existence of the Heights.

Despite this naivety there is much to admire in the character of Edgar Linton. Much of this is associated with his civilised living, gentle nature and pleasant manner. His devotion to Catherine during her illness is an admirable aspect of his character. His love and devotion to her is beyond question. His willingness to take responsibility for young Linton after Isabella's death shows his generous nature particularly as Heathcliff, who he abhors, is the boy's father. He is willing to allow Cathy marry Linton if it would allow her to be consoled after his own death. Her chance of possible happiness is more important to him than Heathcliff gaining control of Linton. Edgar, like Heathcliff, is affected by Catherine's death and looks forward to a reunion with her after his own death, however the intervening 17 years for Edgar are marked by resignation rather than torment as was the case with Heathcliff.

Analysis of Hareton

For the most part of the novel Hareton strikes us as a mirror image of the younger Heathcliff. He is bad tempered, uncivilised and vicious. It would it seems have proved Heathcliff's own theory "That one tree would grow as crooked as another with the same wind to twist it". Under Heathcliff's tutelage Hareton has grown up almost as savage like. On Nelly's return to the Heights she is shocked by the greeting she receives from her former care. He hurls a stone at her and follows with a string of curses.

The Hareton met by Lockwood in the opening chapters is gruff and uncommunicative and he easily angered or disturbed by Lockwood's misunderstanding of the household relationships. His innate decency and his better self are merely submerged beneath this brutal mask "Good things lost amid a wilderness of weeds". None recognises this fact more so than Heathcliff himself who describes Hareton as "gold put to the use of paving stones" and delights that Hareton "takes pride in his brutishness". Heathcliff recognises Hareton's intelligence "If he were born a fool I should not enjoy it half as much but he's no fool".

Heathcliff clearly delineates between Hareton and Linton desribing the comparison as that between "gold" and "tin polished to ape a service of silver". In the novel it is most ironic that Hareton grows "damnably fond" of Heathcliff despite Heathcliff's attempts to usurp his rights of succession and to destroy everything positive about him. However Heathcliff is unable to get below the surface and while his outward brutishness might suggest little of substance beneath, his fundamental decency is untouched and he responds to Cathy's beauty and love by striving heroically to improve his mind. Despite this latent development and a recognition of his rightful place in society he is the only mourner who weeps by Heathcliff's corpse and genuinely grieves his death. An explanation of this is that both Hareton and Cathy are portrayed in the novel as children of love and so combine the positive and good qualities of their respective parents.

A mind as noble as that possessed by Hareton would have recognised in Heathcliff the unfortunate results of mistreatment. His own experience at the hands of Heathcliff has allowed him to view the world from Heathcliff's position. The character of Hareton is important in portraying the idea that the natural savagery of man is hidden by but a thin veneer of civilisation and that that human beings can easily become bestial in outlook and nature (behaviour). Ultimately, however, Hareton exemplifies the power of love and kindness and the conquest of hate and the supreme Christian virtue of returning good for evil.

Analysis of Heathcliff

Heathcliff is introduced in Nelly's narration as a seven year old Liverpool foundling (probably an Irish famine immigrant) brought back to Wuthering Heights by Mr. Earnshaw. His story, in the words of Nelly, is "a cuckoo's story", Heathcliff is the usurper. His presence in Wuthering Heights overthrows the prevailing habits of the Earnshaw family, members of the family soon become involved in turmoil and fighting and family relationships become spiteful and hateful.

Even on his first night, he is the reason Mr. Earnshaw breaks the toys he had bought for his children. Nelly recorded "From the very beginning he bred bad feelings in the house". Heathcliff usurps the affections of Mr. Earnshaw to the exclusion of young Hindley-: "The young master had learnt to regard his father as an oppressor rather than a friend". Such is the extent of Heathcliff's usurpation, that Hindley is sent off to boarding school. As an adult, Heathcliff repeats the process, as he usurps the affections of Hareton and takes pride in the fact that he would be defended by the son in a fight with the father. Ultimately, Heathcliff parallels the cuckoo in taking over ownership of the Heights, thereby dispossessing the rightful heir, Hareton. Heathcliff destroys the natural familial emotional bonds which previously existed in the Earnshaw household. His presence results in a polarisation within the family, at first Mr. Earnshaw and the Catherine become his allies, whereas Hindley becomes his enemy.

The role of the usurper leads to Heathcliff's suffering at the hands of Hindley and it is the treatment neated out by Hindley to Heathcliff after the death of Mr. Earnshaw, that arouses in Heathcliff a deep and abiding hatred and an all consuming passion for revenge. Heathcliff never forgot an injury inflicted on him during childhood and on his return to Wuthering Heights, after a three year absence, the impulse to revenge himself on all those he regards as having wronged him becomes his overpowering passion.

He ruins Hindley by encouraging his excessive drinking and gambling and with him aside he then turns his attention to Hareton-: "We'll see if one tree won't grow as crooked as another with the same wind to twist it". His revenge is also directed towards Edgar Linton, whom he sees as having stolen Catherine from him. He devises a series of schemes to wrest the ownership of the Grange from the Linton family and secure it for himself. He marries Isabella to "gain a foothold in the Grange" and to reek revenge on Edgar-: "Edgar's proxy in suffering". He forces the marriage between his son Linton and Cathy to secure the ownership of the Grange, his revenge on Edgar is complete, he having lost his sister, wife daughter, estate and in the final analysis, the closest companionship of Catherine in death. Heathcliff's role as an avenger is helped by his intelligence and understanding, not just of his own motivations, but of the motivations of others.

He recognises the source of Isabella's infatuation that-: "she abandoned this under a delusion" - "picturing in me a hero of romance". He also capitalises on Linton's poor health by inviting the pity of Cathy so that her affection and sympathy would facilitate a marriage that would leave he, Heathcliff, as master of the Grange.

As Heathcliff seeks his revenge, he becomes fiendish and is constantly associated with diabolical feelings, images and actions. The use of the imagery reinforces the inhuman aspect of

Heathcliff. He regrets saving the infant Hareton. Nelly recalled that his face bore the greatest pain at he being the instrument that thwarted his own revenge. He takes perverse pleasure in the fact that Hareton was born with a sensitive nature which Heathcliff has corrupted and degraded. Heathcliff's pleasure at this corruption is increased by the fact that-: "Hareton is damnably fond of me". Heathcliff's cruelty is also evident when he hangs Isabella's dog despite her protestations.

His attitude is devoid of fatherly feeling. He sees him only as a pawn in his revenge and his main consideration lies in calculating whether Linton lives long enough to have married Catherine so having acquired Thrushcross Grange-: "We calculate it will scarcely last 'till it's eighteen." Once the marriage has taken place, Linton's life is seen as worthless by Heathcliff-: "His life is not worth a farthing, and I won't spend a farthing on him" His cruel treatment of Isabella is, for him, a source of enjoyment. He tells Nelly-: "The more the worms writhe, the more I yearn to crush the entrails" Isabella recognises the sadistic treatment by Heathcliff and asks- "Is Mr. Heathcliff a man - is he the devil?"

There is, however, another side of the novels leading character. At no point in the novel can we doubt Heathcliff's eternal faithfulness to Catherine. His love survives her rejection of him-: "It would degrade me to marry Mr. Heathcliff" and despite her marriage to Edgar, Heathcliff's love for her continues undaunted. Heathcliff suffers much emotional rejection, but at no point does he waiver in his loyalty to her-: "I seek no revenge on you...the tyrant grinds down his slaves and they don't turn against him, they crush those beneath them" His genuine concern for Catherine prevents him from exacting direct revenge from Edgar. He says to Catherine-: "I would of died by witches before I would have touched a single hair of his head." When hearing of Catherine's illness, he exclaims-: "Existence after loosing her would be hell" In this statement, we can see the extent of Heathcliff's dedication and loyalty to Catherine and the sense of desolation her death would bring to him.

At times in the novel, Heathcliff is portrayed as a tormented spirit. After the death of Catherine, Heathcliff's lust for love is gone. His existence is then focused totally on exacting revenge. As his death approaches, he confesses to Nelly the extent of Catherine's hold over him, though she's now been dead 18 years-: "I cannot look down into the floor, her features are shaped in the flags...in every cloud, in every tree." The degree in which Heathcliff is tormented by Catherine is reflected when he said-: "Why did you betray your own heart, Cathy?...you love me, what right had you to leave me?" The sense of despair following news of Catherine's death is a good example of Heathcliff's tormented spirit-: "I cannot live without my life, I cannot live without my soul" He, said Nelly, howled not like a man, but like a savage beast getting goaded to death with knives and spears.

Life for Heathcliff after Catherine's death is an unnatural existence. He feels he belongs with her both in body and in spirit and has already arranged with the Sexton to be buried beside her. Life for him is "like bending back a stiff spring". The young Cathy recognises that Heathcliff has rejected all society although she doesn't realise that his attachment remains to her late mother-: "Mr. Heathcliff, you have nobody to love you...your cruelty arises from your greater misery."

From the beginning of the novel and most likely from the beginning of his life, he has suffered pain and rejection. When he is brought to Wuthering Heights by Mr. Earnshaw, he is viewed as a thing rather than a child. Mrs. Earnshaw was ready to fling it out of doors, while Nelly put it on the landing of the stairs hoping that it would be gone the next day. Without having done anything to deserve rejection, Heathcliff is made to feel like an outsider, following the death of Mr. Earnshaw, suffers cruel mistreatment at the hands of Hindley. In these formative years, he is deprived of love, sociability and education, according to Nelly, Hindley's treatment of Heathcliff was "enough to make a fiend of a saint". He is separated from the family, reduced to the status of a servant, forced to become a farm hand, undergoes regular beatings and is forcibly separated from Catherine. Personality that Heathcliff develops in his adult life has been formed in response to the deprivation of his childhood.

Heathcliff received constant reminder of his lesser status e.g. on his first visit to the Grange, Catherine is taken into the Linton household, whereas Heathcliff is rejected, made fun of, and alienated. Later, when Catherine returns to Wuthering Heights, her changed appearance further alienates Heathcliff, a point emphasised during the visits of the Linton children, Heathcliff was not considered fit to join the party. The final sense of alienation and the most damning occurs with Catherine's marriage to Edgar, this he considers a betrayal of his love for her, in favour of the social status and civilised existence of the Grange.

Heathcliff is however proud and determined and does not cower when confronted by those who consider themselves to be superiors, his determination was evident when taking advantage of Mr. Earnshaw's favouritism and exchanging horses with young Hindley, though his situation and position is somewhat worsened after the death of Mr. Earnshaw, Heathcliff's pride nevertheless remains intact. When Catherine returned to the Heights after her five week stay at the Grange, she is much changed in appearance and makes fun of the ragged Heathcliff, when ordered to shake hands with Catherine by Hindley, Heathcliff refuses, saying-: "I shall not stand to be laughed at, I shall not hear it". Similarly, when insulted by Edgar during one of his visits to the Heights, Heathcliff empties a toureen of applesauce over him. Finally, when the realisation dawns on him that Catherine has chosen status, wealth and position in preference to him, he disappears for three years and returns in the guise of a gentleman.

Part of Heathcliff's survival mechanism during the period that he is being terrorised by Hindley, is the thought and prospect of revenge, he is determined to have is own back and confesses to Nelly-: "I don't care how long I wait, if I can only do it at last, I hope he will not die before I do".

As Heathcliff approaches death and a reunion of Catherine, his resolve for revenge weakens until he no longer has an interest in that former preoccupation-: "I have lost the faculty of enjoying their destruction". This dousing of the flames of Heathcliff's revenge is a catalyst not just in the novel but in the histories of the Earnshaw and Linton families. Hareton and Cathy are spared, the sense of evil visited upon them by Heathcliff is removed and there occurs a spiritual renaissance within Wuthering Heights.

Heathcliff is a many faced character, in his early years he is characterised somewhat by his fiery temper, his sulleness, his proud nature, his fierce attachment to Catherine, his spitefulness and his capacity for hatred. The adult Heathcliff, who returns to Wuthering Heights after a three year absence, is a super-human villain driven by revenge, distorted by the sense of the wrongs done to him and made emotionally unstable by Catherine's marriage. This later Heathcliff is characterised by callousness by an incapacity to love and eventually by an all consuming passion for revenge against those who have wronged him and for unification with his beloved Catherine.

Stages in Heathcliff's Development:

- Arrival in Wuthering Heights and favoured child of Mr. Earnshaw, beginnings of relationship with Catherine.
- Mistreatment under Hindley, loss of social position, rejection by Catherine.
- Three year absence from the Heights.
- Returned in the guise of a gentleman, re-establishment of relationship with Catherine, execution of plan of revenge.
- Weakening of resolve, approach of death, admission of failure, burial beside Catherine.

Chapter 4

Plot Synopsis and Major Characters

Context

Wuthering Heights is a series of flashbacks and narrations from different characters in the book. At the end of this précis is a chronological list of the main events of the story.

The book starts in the year 1801 and tells us about a man, Lockwood, who has taken on the tenancy of Thrushcross Grange in the isolated moors of North England. The landlord of the Grange is a moody, brooding man called Heathcliff who lives in Wuthering Heights.

After two frightening and disturbing visits to Wuthering Heights, Lockwood manages to persuade Heathcliff's housekeeper, Nelly Dean, to tell him the story of Heathcliff and explain his encounter with an apparent ghost while spending the night at Wuthering Heights. Nelly is in a good position to do this because she has known the family since she was a young girl.

The head of the family was Mr. Earnshaw and he had two children, Hindley and Catherine (called Cathy). One day, Earnshaw brings home an orphan boy from Liverpool and although the two Earnshaw children both dislike this newcomer, Cathy quickly grows to love him. The two become inseparable and spend many happy times on the moors.

Hindley continues to resent this interloper whom Earnshaw treats as one of his own children, and in fact prefers him to Hindley. On the death of Mrs. Earnshaw, Hindley becomes even more alienated from his father, and treats Heathcliff cruelly. Hindley is sent away to college while Heathcliff is kept at home. On the death of Mr. Earnshaw, Hindley inherits Wuthering Heights and together with his wife, Frances, they take control of the farm. Heathcliff is treated as a common laborer, forced to work in the fields. Cathy and Heathcliff remain close, and one night they wander to Thrushcross Grange to tease the spoilt Linton children, Edgar and Isabella. Cathy is bitten by a dog and is forced to stay at the Grange in order to recuperate. Heathcliff is unceremoniously ushered from the house.

Mrs. Linton strives to turn Cathy, the wild girl, into a proper young lady. Cathy is in awe of her wealthy surroundings and is smitten with Edgar. This complicates her relationship with Heathcliff for whom she still has passionate feelings. Frances gives birth to a baby boy who is named Hareton and she dies shortly afterwards. Hindley becomes a heavy gambler and an alcoholic after this event and continues to treat Heathcliff badly. Despite her passionate love for Heathcliff, Cathy wishes to improve her position socially and becomes engaged to Edgar. Unaware of Cathy's strong feelings for him, Heathcliff runs away from Wuthering Heights when he learns that Cathy cannot marry him.

Cathy and Edgar marry and shortly afterwards, Heathcliff returns, a very wealthy man. He fuels Hindley's gambling and drinking habits to the extent that he has to sign over Wuthering Heights to Heathcliff. Heathcliff feels wronged by Cathy and the Lintons and seeks revenge on them all. His aim is to inherit Thrushcross Grange by marrying Isabella Linton. This will also make Cathy jealous. She realizes that she has made a mistake in marrying Edgar because Heathcliff is not willing to share her with anybody else.

She gives birth to a daughter, Catherine and then dies. She had sought forgiveness from Heathcliff, but he curses her spirit to remain on earth and haunt him; anything as long as she does not leave him alone. Isabella is unable to take Heathcliff's cruelty any longer and flees to London where she gives birth to Heathcliff's son, named Linton.

Thirteen years pass, during which time Nelly is Catherine's nursemaid at Thrushcross Grange. She has her mother's beauty and is also headstrong, but this is tempered by her father's more peaceful influence. Edgar protects her from the knowledge of Wuthering Heights and the two cousins that she has. It is only now that she becomes aware of Hareton, and they start to play together. Also at this time Isabella dies and Linton comes to live at the Grange, but is soon collected by Heathcliff to stay at Wuthering Heights. Linton is a sickly child and Heathcliff treats him cruelly.

A further three years elapse and one day while Catherine is out of the watchful eyes of her father and nursemaid, she meets Heathcliff. He is anxious for Catherine to marry Linton so that he can be sure of securing Thrushcross Grange on the death of the sickly Edgar.Edgar forbids Catherine to meet with Linton and so they exchange letters.

When Nelly discovers this she destroys the letters so Catherine begins to sneak out at night to spend time with Linton. It is clear that Linton is pursuing Catherine, only because Heathcliff is forcing him in order to have his revenge on Edgar Linton. Heathcliff needs to force the situation and he lures Nelly and Catherine to Wuthering Heights where he holds them prisoner. Catherine marries Linton and Edgar dies shortly afterwards. The sickly Linton dies soon after this, and now Heathcliff has both Wuthering Heights and Thrushcross Grange. He forces Catherine to remain at Wuthering Heights and she is treated like a servant.

Thrushcross Grange is rented to Lockwood. This is the story as told to Lockwood by Nelly. He is appalled and ends his tenancy at the Grange and returns to London. Six months elapse and Lockwood returns and is curious to know how the story has developed. Although Catherine had teased Hareton about his illiteracy, she has now mellowed and feels guilty for this earlier treatment. She now has grown to love Hareton and they live quite happily at Wuthering Heights.

Heathcliff has lost the desire to see his vengeful schemes to an end for he is now totally haunted by the memory of Cathy, so much so that he speaks to her ghost. Everything he sees in Wuthering Heights reminds him of Cathy and what he has lost. The fact that between them Hareton and Catherine have so much in common with Cathy, and also that there is a growing love between them, means that Heathcliff has to divorce himself from the world in order to obtain some sort of peace. Eventually after spending a night on the moors where he presumably met Cathy's ghost, he returns to Wuthering Heights more contented. Partly through starvation, Heathcliff dies.

Hareton and Catherine inherit Wuthering Heights and Thrushcross Grange and plan to be married on the next New Year's Day. Lockwood goes to visit the graves of Cathy and Heathcliff; whose spirits roam the moors. Wuthering Heights is the name of the family home of the Earnshaws, being completed in the year 1500 by presumably Hareton Earnshaw. This is marked on the stone above the main door. Nelly, who was born in 1758, three years before Heathcliff and Cathy, tells the majority of the story. Nelly becomes a servant at Wuthering Heights and grows up with our two main characters. Mr. Earnshaw brings Heathcliff to Wuthering Heights in 1767, and he soon replaces Hindley, Cathy's older brother in Mr. Earnshaw's affections.

Initially, Hindley and Cathy treat Heathcliff cruelly, she considers him to be coarse and rough, but soon the two become great friends. They spend much of their time playing on the moors inventing stories and pretending to be kings and queens. There they have a special place. Earnshaw sends Hindley away to college. Hindley marries Frances and on the death of Mr. Earnshaw in 1777, takes possession of Wuthering Heights. Heathcliff's education is cut short and he becomes the farm laborer. In this year, Cathy has her first visit to Thrushcross Grange where she is attacked by a guard dog and is forced to recuperate in the Grange where Mrs. Linton endeavors to transform her from a wild girl into a socialite.

In 1778, Hareton is born to Hindley and Frances, and she dies shortly afterwards. Hindley grieved at his loss, turns to alcohol and gambling in order to escape his grief. Two years later, Heathcliff overhears Nelly and Cathy talking him. Cathy reveals that she is attracted to the wealth and glamour of Thrushcross Grange and could never marry Heathcliff. He leaves Wuthering Heights and doesn't hear the remainder of the conversation where Cathy reveals her undying love for Heathcliff.

Cathy becomes engaged to Edgar Linton and they are married in 1783. Shortly after this, Heathcliff arrives back at Wuthering Heights. He now has a vast fortune and he starts to put into motion his plan for revenge on all those that have hurt and humiliated him.

Cathy is clearly excited at Heathcliff's return and Edgar realizes that she still has strong feelings for Heathcliff. Cathy realizes that she has made a mistake in marrying Edgar, but still thinks that she can enjoy the best of both worlds, her status with Edgar and her freedom and love with Heathcliff.

Heathcliff is hurt by Cathy's marriage and wishes to exact revenge on her. He also hopes to obtain Thrushcross Grange for himself and, therefore, takes advantage of Isabella Linton, Edgar's sister's infatuation for him. Heathcliff wants to use her in order to inherit the Grange and make Cathy jealous.

In 1784 Heathcliff and Isabella elope. Cathy is taken ill and just prior to her death, she gives birth to Catherine. The next year Isabella can no longer take the cruelty from Heathcliff and she moves to London where she gives birth to Linton. In 1785, Hindley dies and Heathcliff inherits Wuthering Heights as he holds the mortgage on the property, brought about by Hindley's spiraling debt to him.

Twelve years elapse and it is now 1797, and Edgar has been extremely protective of Catherine, and she does not know about her cousins Hareton and Linton. Catherine finally meets Hareton and visits Wuthering Heights for the first time. She teases him about his lack of education. A year later, Isabella dies in London, and Linton is brought back to the Grange where Edgar hopes to continue his upbringing. However, Heathcliff insists that his son is returned to him at Wuthering Heights.

In 1800, Heathcliff is anxious that Catherine and Linton should marry. In this way, he will be able to achieve his goal by obtaining control of Thrushcross Grange. Heathcliff is anxious that the marriage takes place before the failing Edgar dies, and in order to secure this he abducts Catherine and Nelly who are kept prisoner at Wuthering Heights. On Edgar's death, Heathcliff obtains control of the Grange. Nelly stays at the Grange and is given permission to rent it out, hence Lockwood's entrance on the scene. When Lockwood hears all the details of the story, he decides that he no longer wishes to take on the tenancy of the Grange.

However, in 1802 he returns, where he finds out that Heathcliff has died. Catherine and Hareton are in love. They plan to marry.

Major Characters

Heathcliff The main character

Orphaned as a child, he is constantly on the outside, constantly losing people. Although he and Catherine Earnshaw profess that they complete each other, her decision to marry Edgar Linton almost destroys their relationship. He spends most of his life contemplating and acting out revenge. He is abusive, brutal, and cruel.

Catherine Earnshaw

The love of Heathcliff's life. Wild, impetuous, and arrogant as a child, she grows up getting everything she wants. When two men fall in love with her, she torments both of them. Ultimately, Catherine's selfishness ends up hurting everyone she loves, including herself.

Edgar Linton Catherine's husband and Heathcliff's rival

Well-mannered and well-to-do, he falls in love with and marries Catherine. His love for her enables him to overlook their incompatible natures.

Cathy Linton Daughter of Catherine and Edgar

A mild form of her mother, she serves as a reminder of her mother's strengths and weaknesses. (Note: For the purpose of clarity, the younger Catherine is referred to as "Cathy" in this Note, and her mother is referred to as "Catherine." This convention is not used in the original text.)

Linton Heathcliff Son of Heathcliff and Isabella

Weak and whiny (both physically and emotionally), he serves as a pawn in Heathcliff's game of revenge. He marries Cathy.

Hareton Earnshaw Catherine's Nephew, Son of Hindley

Although uneducated and unrefined, Hareton has a staunch sense of pride. He is attracted to Cathy but put off by her attitude. His generous heart enables the two of them to eventually fall in love and marry. Hareton is the only person to mourn Heathcliff's death.

Ellen (Nelly) Dean The Primary Narrator and Catherine's servant

Although she is one person capable of relating the majority of the events that occurred, she is not without bias.

Lockwood Heathcliff's tenant at Thrushcross Grange and the impetus for Nelly's narration

Although he serves primarily as the catalyst for the story, Lockwood's role is an outsider who happens to gain inside information. His visit to Wuthering Heights and subsequent actions directly affect the plot.

Mr. Earnshaw Catherine's Father

He brings Heathcliff into his family and soon favors the orphan over his own son, Hindley.

Mrs. Earnshaw Catherine's mother

Not much is known about her, except that she favors her own son to Heathcliff, whom she does not like.

Hindley Earnshaw Catherine's Brother

Jealous of Heathcliff, he takes a bit of revenge on Heathcliff after his father dies. He proves to be no match for

Heathcliff, however, eventually losing his son and his family's home.

Frances Earnshaw Hindley's Wife

A sickly woman who dies soon after Hareton is born.

JOseph Servant at Wuthering Heights

A hypocritical zealot who possesses a religious fanaticism that most find wearisome.

Mr. and Mrs. Linton Edgar's Parents

They welcome Catherine into her home, introducing her to the life in upper society. They die soon after nursing Catherine back to health.

Isabella Edgar's sister

Her infatuation with Heathcliff causes her to destroy her relationship with her brother. She experiences Heathcliff's brutality first hand. She flees to London where she gives birth to Heathcliff's son, but her attempts to keep her son from his father fail.

Zillah Heathcliff's Housekeeper

She saves Lockwood from a pack of dogs and serves as Nelly's source of information at Wuthering Heights.

Chapter 5

An Emily Bronte Chronology

1818	July 30, Emily Jane Bronte born at Thornton, near Bradford, Yorkshire.
1820	April, the Bronte family moves to Haworth.
1821	September, Mrs. Bronte dies.
1824	November, Emily Bronte enrolls at the Cowan Bridge School.
1825	May 6, Maria Bronte dies; June 1, Charlotte and Emily leave Cowan Bridge; June 15 Elizabeth Bronte dies.
1826	June, Mr. Bronte brings home twelve wooden soldiers for Branwell—the start of the Btontes' oral literature and imaginative games.
1831	Emily and Anne begin the Gondal saga.
1834	November 24, the earliest dated Emily Bronte manuscript—mentions the Gondals discovering Caaldine.
1835	July—Octobet, a pupil in Miss Wooler's school at Roe Head; is sent home after alarming Charlotte with her physical decline.
1836	July 12, the earliest dated poem.
1837	September, goes to teach at Law Hill School, near Halifax; remains there for about six months—the exact dates of the Law Hill period are disputed.
1838-42	Over half of Bronte's surviving poems written.
1842	February—November, at school in Brussels with Charlotte to study music and foreign languages; writes the essays in French; returns to Haworth after the death of Aunt Branwell.

1843 Alone at Haworth with her father; a time of creativity and freedom.

1844 Begins to arrange her poems into two notebooks, dividing the Gondalan from the non-Gondalan material.

1845 The Brontes give up hopes for a school of their own; Branwell, working on a novel, tells his sisters of the profitable possibilities of novel writing; Emily's birthday note shows her hearty and content, reunited with Anne and as enthusiastic as ever about the Gondalans; October, Charlotte discovers Emily's poems and convinces her sister to collaborate on a volume of poems; December, Wuthering Heights begun.

1846 May, Poems by Currer Ellis, and Acton Bell published, with the Brontes paying for costs; July, Wuthering Heights finished and begins to make the round of publishers, along with Agnes Grey by Anne Bronte and The Profrssor by Charlotte; September 14, last dated complete poem.

1847 July, T. C. Newby accepts Wuthering Heights and Agnes Grey but delays publishing until the success of Jane Eyre arouses interest in the "Bells"; December, Wuthering Heights and Agnes Grey published.

1848 Confusion in the literary world over the identity and number of the Bells; Anne publishes The Tenant of Wildftll Hall; Emily withdraws more resolutely into herself; September 24, Branwell dies; October 1, Emily leaves home for the last time to attend Branwell's funeral service—catches a severe cold which develops into inflammation of the lungs; December 19, Emily Bronte dies.

1850 Wuthering Heights reissued, with a selection of poems, and a biographical notice by Charlotte.

1893 The Bronte Society established.

1941 Hatfield's edition of The Complete Poems of Emily Jane Bronte published.

Chapter 6

Selected Chapters: Wuthering Heights

Volume 1

Chapter

1801. — I have just returned from a visit to my landlord — the solitary neighbour that I shall be troubled with. This is certainly a beautiful country. In all England I do not believe that I could have fixed on a situation so completely removed from the stir of society — a perfect misanthropist's heaven; and Mr. Heathcliff and I are such a suitable pair to divide the desolation between us. A capital fellow! He little imagined how my heart warmed towards him when I beheld his black eyes withdraw so suspiciously under their brows, as I rode up, and when his fingers sheltered themselves, with a jealous resolution, still further in his waistcoat, as I announced my name.

"Mr. Heathcliff?" I said.

A nod was the answer.

"Mr. Lockwood, your new tenant, sir. I do myself the honour of calling as soon as possible after my arrival, to express the hope that I have not inconvenienced you by my perseverance in soliciting the occupation of Thrushcross Grange. I heard yesterday you had had some thoughts — — "

"Thrushcross Grange is my own, sir," he interrupted, wincing. "I should not allow any one to inconvenience me, if I could hinder it. Walk in!"

The "walk in" was uttered with closed teeth, and expressed the sentiment, "Go to the deuce." Even the gate over which he leant manifested no sympathizing movement to the words; and I think that circumstance determined me to accept the invitation. I felt interested in a man who seemed more exaggeratedly reserved than myself. When he saw my horse's breast fairly pushing the barrier, he did put out his hand to unchain it, and then sullenly preceded me up the causeway, calling, as we entered the court, "Joseph, take Mr. Lockwood's horse, and bring up some wine."

"Here we have the whole establishment of domestics, I suppose," was the reflection suggested by this compound order. "No wonder the grass grows up between the flags, and cattle are the only hedge-cutters." Joseph was an elderly, nay, an old man — very old, perhaps, though hale and sinewy. "The Lord help us!" he soliloquized in an undertone of peevish displeasure, while relieving me of my horse, looking, meantime, in my face so sourly that I charitably conjectured he must have need of divine aid to digest his dinner, and his pious ejaculation had no reference to my unexpected advent.

Wuthering Heights is the name of Mr. Heathcliff's dwelling, "wuthering" being a significant provincial adjective, descriptive of the atmospheric tumult to which its station is exposed in stormy weather. Pure, bracing ventilation they must have up there at all times, indeed. One may guess the power of the north wind blowing over the edge by the excessive slant of a few stunted firs at the end of the house, and by a range of gaunt thorns all stretching their limbs one way, as if craving alms of the sun. Happily the architect had foresight to build it strong. The narrow windows are deeply set in the wall, and the corners defended with large jutting stones. Before passing the threshold, I paused to admire a quantity of grotesque carving lavished over the front, and especially about the principal door; above which, among a wilderness of crumbling griffins and shameless little boys, I detected the date "1500," and the name "Hareton Earnshaw." I would have made a few comments, and requested a short history of the place from the surly owner; but his attitude at the door appeared to demand my speedy entrance or complete departure, and I had no desire to aggravate his impatience previous to inspecting the penetralium.

One step brought us into the family sitting-room, without any introductory lobby or passage. They call it here "the house" pre-eminently. It includes kitchen and parlour generally. But, I believe, at Wuthering Heights the kitchen is forced to retreat altogether into another quarter — at least I distinguished a chatter of tongues and a clatter of culinary utensils deep within; and I observed no signs of roasting, boiling, or baking about the huge fireplace, nor any glitter of copper saucepans and tin cullenders on the walls. One end, indeed, reflected splendidly both light and heat from ranks of immense pewter dishes, interspersed with silver jugs and tankards, towering row after row, on a vast oak dresser, to the very roof.

The latter had never been underdrawn; its entire anatomy lay bare to an inquiring eye, except where a frame of wood laden with oatcakes and clusters of legs of beef, mutton, and ham concealed it. Above the chimney were sundry villainous old guns and a couple of horse-pistols, and, by way of ornament, three gaudily painted canisters disposed along its ledge. The floor was of smooth, white stone; the chairs, high-backed, primitive structures painted green, one or two heavy black ones lurking in the shade. In an arch under the dresser reposed a huge liver-coloured bitch pointer surrounded by a swarm of squealing puppies, and other dogs haunted other recesses.

The apartment and furniture would have been nothing extraordinary as belonging to a homely, northern farmer with a stubborn countenance and stalwart limbs set out to advantage in knee-breeches and gaiters. Such an individual seated in his armchair, his mug of ale frothing on the round table before him, is to be seen in any circuit of five or six miles among these hills, if you go at the right time after dinner. But Mr. Heathcliff forms a singular contrast to his abode and style of living. He is a dark-skinned gipsy in aspect. in dress and manners a gentleman — that is, as much a gentleman as many a country squire; rather slovenly, perhaps, yet not looking amiss with his negligence, because he has an erect and handsome figure, and rather morose. Possibly, some people might suspect him of a degree of underbred pride; I have a sympathetic chord within that tells me it is nothing of the sort. I know, by instinct, his reserve springs from an aversion to showy displays of feeling, to manifestations of mutual kindliness. He'll love and hate equally under cover, and esteem it a species of impertinence to be loved or hated again. No, I'm running on too fast. I bestow my own attributes over liberally on him. Mr. Heathcliff may have entirely dissimilar reasons for keeping his hand out of the way when he meets a would-be acquaintance to those which actuate me. Let me hope my constitution is almost peculiar. My dear mother used to say I should never have a comfortable home, and only last summer I proved myself perfectly unworthy of one.

While enjoying a month of fine weather at the sea coast, I was thrown into the company of a most fascinating creature — a real goddess in my eyes, as long as she took no notice of me. I "never told my love" vocally; still, if looks have language, the merest idiot might have guessed I was over head and ears. She understood me at last, and looked a return — the sweetest of all imaginable looks. And what did I do? I confess it with shame — shrank icily into myself, like a snail; at every glance retired colder and farther, till finally the poor innocent was led to doubt her own senses, and, overwhelmed with confusion at her supposed mistake, persuaded her mamma to decamp.

By this curious turn of disposition I have gained the reputation of deliberate heartlessness; how undeserved I alone can appreciate. I took a seat at the end of the hearthstone opposite that towards which my landlord advanced, and filled up an interval of silence by attempting to caress the canine mother, who had left her nursery, and was sneaking wolfishly to the back of my legs, her lip curled up, and her white teeth watering for a snatch.

My caress provoked a long, guttural gnarl. "You'd better let the dog alone," growled Mr. Heathcliff, in unison, checking fiercer demonstrations with a punch of his foot.

"She's not accustomed to be spoiled — not kept for a pet." Then, striding to a side door, he shouted again, "Joseph!" Joseph mumbled indistinctly in the depths of the cellar, but gave no intimation of ascending; so his master dived down to him, leaving me vis-a-vis the ruffianly bitch and a pair of grim shaggy sheep-dogs, who shared with her a jealous guardianship over all my movements. Not anxious to come in contact with their fangs, I sat still; but, imagining they would scarcely understand tacit insults, I unfortunately indulged in winking and making faces at the trio, and some turn of my physiognomy so irritated madam that she suddenly broke into a fury and leapt on my knees. I flung her back, and hastened to interpose the table between us. This proceeding roused the whole hive. Half a dozen four-footed fiends, of various sizes and ages, issued from hidden dens to the common centre. I felt my heels and coat-laps peculiar subjects of assault; and parrying off the larger combatants as effectually as I could with the poker, I was constrained to demand, aloud, assistance from some of the household in re-establishing peace.

Mr. Heathcliff and his man climbed the cellar steps with vexatious phlegm. I don't think they moved one second faster than usual, though the hearth was an absolute tempest of worrying and yelping. Happily, an inhabitant of the kitchen made more dispatch. A lusty dame, with tucked-up gown, bare arms, and fire-flushed cheeks, rushed into the midst of us flourishing a frying-pan, and used that weapon and her tongue to such purpose that the storm subsided magically, and she only remained, heaving like a sea after a high wind, when her master entered on the scene.

"What the devil is the matter?" he asked, eyeing me in a manner that I could ill endure after this inhospitable treatment. "What the devil, indeed!" I muttered. "The herd of possessed swine could have had no worse spirits in them than those animals of yours, sir. You might as well leave a stranger with a brood of tigers!" "They won't meddle with persons who touch nothing," he remarked, putting the bottle before me, and restoring the displaced table. "The dogs do right to be vigilant. Take a glass of wine."

"No, thank you."

"Not bitten, are you?"

"If I had been, I would have set my signet on the biter."

Heathcliff's countenance relaxed into a grin.

"Come, come," he said; "you are flurried, Mr. Lockwood. Here, take a little wine. Guests are so exceedingly rare in this house that I and my dogs, I am willing to own, hardly know how to receive them. Your health, sir!" I bowed and returned the pledge, beginning to perceive that it would be foolish to sit sulking for the misbehaviour of a pack of curs; besides, I felt loath to yield the fellow further amusement at my expense, since his humour took that turn.

He — probably swayed by prudential consideration of the folly of offending a good tenant — relaxed a little in the laconic style of chipping off his pronouns and auxiliary verbs, and introduced what he supposed would be a subject of interest to me — a discourse on the advantages and disadvantages of my present place of retirement. I found him very intelligent on the topics we touched; and before I went home I was encouraged so far as to volunteer another visit to-morrow. He evidently wished no repetition of my intrusion. I shall go, notwithstanding. It is astonishing how sociable I feel myself, compared with him.

Chapter

Yesterday afternoon set in misty and cold. I had half a mind to spend it by my study fire, instead of wading through heath and mud to Wuthering Heights. On coming up from dinner, however, (N.B. I dine between twelve and one o'clock; the housekeeper, a matronly lady taken as a fixture along with the house, could not, or would not comprehend my request that I might be served at five), — on mounting the stairs with this lazy intention, and stepping into the room, I saw a servant-girl on her knees, surrounded by brushes and coal-scuttles, and raising an infernal dust as she extinguished the flames with heaps of cinders. This spectacle drove me back immediately; I took my hat, and, after a four miles walk, arrived at Heathcliff's garden gate just in time to escape the first feathery flakes of a snow shower. On that bleak hill top the earth was hard with a black frost, and the air made me shiver through every limb. Being unable to remove the chain, I jumped over, and, running up the flagged causeway bordered with straggling gooseberry bushes, knocked vainly for admittance, till my knuckles tingled and the dogs howled.

"Wretched inmates!" I ejaculated, mentally, "you deserve perpetual isolation from your speciesfor your churlish inhospitality. At least, I would not keep my doors barred in the day time — I don'tcare — I will get in !"

So resolved, I grasped the latch, and shook it vehemently. Vinegar-faced Joseph projected hishead from a round window of the barn. "What are ye for?" he shouted. "T' maister's down i' t' fowld. Go round by th' end ut' laith, if ye went to spake to him." "Is there nobody inside to open the door?" I hallooed responsively. "There's nobbut t' missis, and shoo'll not oppen't an ye mak yer flaysome dins till neeght." "Why? Cannot you tell her who I am, eh, Joseph?" "Nor-ne me! I'll hae noa hend wi't," muttered the head, vanishing.

The snow began to drive thickly. I seized the handle to essay another trial, when a young man without coat, and shouldering a pitchfork, appeared in the yard behind. He hailed me to follow him; and, after marching through a wash-house, and a paved area containing a coal-shed, pump, and pigeon-cot, we at length arrived in the huge, warm, cheerful apartment where I was formerly received.

It glowed delightfully in the radiance of an immense fire, compounded of coal, peat, and wood; and near the table, laid for a plentiful evening meal, I was pleased to observe the "missis," an individual whose existence I had never previously suspected. I bowed and waited, thinking she would bid me take a seat. She looked at me, leaning back in her chair, and remained motionless and mute.

"Rough weather!" I remarked. "I'm afraid, Mrs. Heathcliff, the door must bear the consequence of your servants' leisure attendance. I had hard work to make them hear me." She never opened her mouth. I stared — she stared also. At any rate, she kept her eyes on me in a cool, regardless manner, exceedingly embarrassing and disagreeable. "Sit down," said the young man gruffly. "He'll be in soon." I obeyed, and hemmed, and called the villain Juno, who deigned, at this second interview, to move the extreme tip of her tail, in token of owning my acquaintance. "A beautiful animal!" I commenced again. "Do you intend parting with the little ones, madam?" "They are not mine," said the amiable hostess, more repellingly than Heathcliff himself could have replied. "Ah, your favourites are among these?" I continued, turning to an obscure cushion full of something like cats. "A strange choice of favourites!" she observed scornfully.

Unluckily it was a heap of dead rabbits. I hemmed once more, and drew closer to the hearth, repeating my comment on the wildness of the evening. "You should not have come out," she said, rising and reaching from the chimney-piece two of the painted canisters.

Her position before was sheltered from the light; now, I had a distinct view of her whole figure and countenance. She was slender, and apparently scarcely past girlhood; an admirable form, and the most exquisite little face that I have ever had the pleasure of beholding; small features, very fair; flaxen ringlets, or rather golden, hanging loose on her delicate neck; and eyes, had they been agreeable in expression, that would have been irresistible. Fortunately for my susceptible heart, the only sentiment they evinced hovered between scorn and a kind of desperation, singularly unnatural to be detected there. The canisters were almost out of her reach. I made a motion to aid her. She turned upon me as a miser might turn if any one attempted to assist him in counting his gold. "I don't want your help," she snapped. "I can get them for myself." "I beg your pardon," I hastened to reply.

"Were you asked to tea?" she demanded, tying an apron over her neat black frock, and standing with a spoonful of the leaf poised over the pot. "I shall be glad to have a cup," I answered. "Were you asked?" she repeated. "No," I said, half smiling. "You are the proper person to ask me." She flung the tea back, spoon and all, and resumed her chair in a pet. Her forehead corrugated, and her red under-lip pushed out, like a child's ready to cry. Meanwhile, the young man had slung on to his person a decidedly shabby upper garment, and, erecting himself before the blaze, looked down on me from the corner of his eyes, for all the world as if there were some mortal feud unavenged between us. I began to doubt whether he were a servant or not.

His dress and speech were both rude, entirely devoid of the superiority observable in Mr. and Mrs. Heathcliff. His thick brown curls were rough and uncultivated, his whiskers encroached bearishly over his cheeks, and his hands were embrowned like those of a common labourer. Still his bearing was free, almost haughty, and he showed none of a domestic's assiduity in attending on the lady of the house. In the absence of clear proofs of his condition, I deemed it best to abstain from noticing his curious conduct; and, five minutes afterwards, the entrance of Heathcliff relieved me, in some measure, from my uncomfortable state.

"You see, sir, I am come, according to promise," I exclaimed, assuming the cheerful; "and I fear I shall be weather-bound for half an hour, if you can afford me shelter during that space."

"Half an hour?" he said, shaking the white flakes from his clothes. "I wonder you should select the thick of a snowstorm to ramble about in. Do you know that you run a risk of being lost in the marshes? People familiar with these moors often miss their road on such evenings; and I can tell you there is no chance of a change at present."

"Perhaps I can get a guide among your lads, and he might stay at the Grange till morning. Could you spare me one?"

"No, I could not."

"Oh, indeed! Well, then, I must trust to my own sagacity."

"Umph!"

"Are you going to mak th' tea?" demanded he of the shabby coat, shifting his ferocious gaze from me to the young lady.

"Is he to have any?" she asked, appealing to Heathcliff.

"Get it ready, will you?" was the answer, uttered so savagely that I started. The tone in which the words were said revealed a genuine bad nature. I no longer felt inclined to call Heathcliff a capital fellow. When the preparations were finished, he invited me with — "Now, sir, bring forward your chair." And we all, including the rustic youth, drew round the table, an austere silence prevailing while we discussed our meal. I thought, if I had caused the cloud, it was my duty to make an effort to dispel it.

They could not every day sit so grim and taciturn; and it was impossible, however ill-tempered they might be, that the universal scowl they wore was their everyday countenance.It is strange," I began, in the interval of swallowing one cup of tea and receiving another — "it is strange how custom can mould our tastes and ideas.

Many could not imagine the existence of happiness in a life of such complete exile from the world as you spend, Mr. Heathcliff; yet, I'll venture to say, that surrounded by your family, and with your amiable lady as the presiding genius over your home and heart — " "My amiable lady!" he interrupted, with an almost diabolical sneer on his face. "Where is she — my amiable lady?"

"Mrs. Heathcliff, your wife, I mean."

"Well, yes — Oh! you would intimate that her spirit has taken the post of ministering angel, and guards the fortunes of Wuthering Heights, even when her body is gone. Is that it?" Perceiving myself in a blunder, I attempted to correct it.

I might have seen there was too great a disparity between the ages of the parties to make it likely that they were man and wife. One was about forty, a period of mental vigour at which men seldom cherish the delusion of being married for love, by girls: that dream is reserved for the solace of our declining years. The other did not look seventeen.

Then it flashed upon me — "The clown at my elbow, who is drinking his tea out of a basin and eating his bread with unwashed hands, may be her husband. Heathcliff, junior, of course. Here is the consequence of being buried alive: she has thrown herself away upon that boor, from sheer ignorance that better individuals existed! A sad pity — I must beware how I cause her to regret her choice."

The last reflection may seem conceited; it was not. My neighbour struck me as bordering on repulsive. I knew, through experience, that I was tolerably attractive.

"Mrs. Heathcliff is my daughter-in-law," said Heathcliff, corroborating my surmise. He turned, as he spoke, a peculiar look in her direction, a look of hatred, unless he has a most perverse set of facial muscles that will not, like those of other people, interpret the language of his soul.

"Ah, certainly — I see now; you are the favoured possessor of the beneficent fairy," I remarked, turning to my neighbour.

This was worse than before: the youth grew crimson, and clenched his fist with every appearance of a meditated assault. But he seemed to recollect himself, presently, and smothered the storm in a brutal curse, muttered on my behalf, which however, I took care not to notice.

"Unhappy in your conjectures, sir!" observed my host; "we neither of us have the privilege of owning your good fairy; her mate is dead. I said she was my daughter-in-law, therefore, she must have married my son."

"And this young man is — "

"Not my son, assuredly."

Heathcliff smiled again, as if it were rather too bold a jest to attribute the paternity of that bear to him.

"My name is Hareton Earnshaw," growled the other; "and I'd counsel you to respect it!"

"I've shown no disrespect," was my reply, laughing internally at the dignity with which he announced himself.

He fixed his eye on me longer than I cared to return the stare, for fear I might be tempted either to box his ears or render my hilarity audible. I began to feel unmistakably out of place in that pleasant family circle. The dismal spiritual atmosphere overcame, and more than neutralized, the glowing physical comforts round me; and I resolved to be cautious how I ventured under those rafters a third time.

The business of eating being concluded, and no one uttering a word of sociable conversation, I approached a window to examine the weather. A sorrowful sight I saw —

dark night coming down prematurely, and sky and hills mingled in one bitter whirl of wind and suffocating snow.

"I don't think it possible for me to get home now without a guide," I could not help exclaiming. "The roads will be buried already; and, if they were bare, I could scarcely distinguish a foot in advance."

"Hareton, drive those dozen sheep into the barn porch. They'll be covered if left in the fold all night. And put a plank before them," said Heathcliff.

"How must I do?" I continued, with rising irritation.

There was no reply to my question; and on looking round I saw only Joseph bringing in a pail of porridge for the dogs, and Mrs. Heathcliff leaning over the fire, diverting herself with burning a bundle of matches which had fallen from the chimney-piece as she restored the tea-canister to its place. The former, when he had deposited his burden, took a critical survey of the room, and in cracked tones grated out, —

"Aw woonder how yah can faishion to stand thear i' idleness un war, when all on 'em's goan out! Bud yah're a nowt, and it's no use talking; yah'll niver mend o' yer ill ways, but goa raight to t' divil, like yer mother afore ye!"

I imagined for a moment that this piece of eloquence was addressed to me; and, sufficiently enraged, stepped towards the aged rascal with an intention of kicking him out of the door. Mrs. Heathcliff, however, checked me by her answer.

"You scandalous old hypocrite!" she replied. "Are you not afraid of being carried away bodily, whenever you mention the devil's name? I warn you to refrain from provoking me, or I'll ask your abduction as a special favour. Stop! Look here, Joseph," she continued, taking a long, dark book from a shelf; "I'll show you how far I've progressed in the black art. I shall soon be competent to make a clear house of it. The red cow didn't die by chance, and your rheumatism can hardly be reckoned among providential visitations!"

"Oh, wicked, wicked!" gasped the elder; "may the Lord deliver us from evil!""No, reprobate; you are a castaway. Be off, or I'll hurt you seriously. I'll have you all modelled in wax and clay; and the first who passes the limits I fix shall — I'll not say what he shall be done to, but you'll see! Go! I'm looking at you."

The little witch put a mock malignity into her beautiful eyes, and Joseph, trembling with sincere horror, hurried out, praying and ejaculating "wicked" as he went. I thought her conduct must be prompted by a species of dreary fun; and, now that we were alone, I endeavoured to interest her in my distress. "Mrs. Heathcliff," I said earnestly, "you must excuse me for troubling you. I presume, because, with that face, I'm sure you cannot help being good-hearted. Do point out some landmarks by which I may know my way home. I have no more idea how to get there than you would have how to get to London."

"Take the road you came," she answered, ensconcing herself in a chair, with a candle, and the long book open before her. "It is brief advice, but as sound as I can give." "Then, if you hear of me being discovered dead in a bog or a pit full of snow, your conscience won't whisper that it is partly your fault?" "How so? I cannot escort you. They wouldn't let me go to the end of the garden wall."

"You! I should be sorry to ask you to cross the threshold for my convenience on such a night," I cried. "I want you to tell me my way, not to show it, or else to persuade Mr. Heathcliff to give me a guide." "Who? There is himself, Earnshaw, Zillah, Joseph, and I. Which would you have?"

"Are there no boys at the farm?"

"No; those are all."

"Then, it follows that I am compelled to stay."

"That you may settle with your host. I have nothing to do with it." "I hope it will be a lesson to you to make no more rash journeys on these hills," cried Heathcliff's stern voice from the kitchen entrance. "As to staying here, I don't keep accommodations for visitors. You must share a bed with Hareton or Joseph, if you do."

"I can sleep on a chair in this room," I replied.

"No, no! A stranger is a stranger, be he rich or poor. It will not suit me to permit any one the range of the place while I am off guard!" said the unmannerly wretch.

With this insult, my patience was at an end. I uttered an expression of disgust, and pushed past him into the yard, running against Earnshaw in my haste. It was so dark that I could not see the means of exit; and, as I wandered round, I heard another specimen of their civil behaviour amongst each other. At first the young man appeared about to befriend me.

"I'll go with him as far as the park," he said.

"You'll go with him to hell!" exclaimed his master, or whatever relation he bore. "And who is to look after the horses, eh?" "A man's life is of more consequence than one evening's neglect of the horses. Somebody must go," murmured Mrs. Heathcliff, more kindly than I expected. "Not at your command!" retorted Hareton. "If you set store on him, you'd better be quiet."

"Then I hope his ghost will haunt you; and I hope Mr. Heathcliff will never get another tenant till the Grange is a ruin!" she answered sharply.

"Hearken, hearken; shoo's cursing on 'em!" muttered Joseph, towards whom I had been steering.

He sat within earshot, milking the cows by the light of a lantern, which I seized unceremoniously, and calling out that I would send it back on the morrow, rushed to the nearest postern. "Maister, maister, he's staling t' lanthern!" shouted the ancient, pursuing my retreat. "Hey, Gnasher! Hey, dog! Hey, Wolf, holld him, holld him!"

On opening the little door, two hairy monsters flew at my throat, bearing me down and extinguishing the light; while a mingled guffaw from Heathcliff and Hareton put the copestone on my rage and humiliation.

Fortunately, the beasts seemed more bent on stretching their paws and yawning, and flourishing their tails, than devouring me alive; but they would suffer no resurrection, and I was forced to lie till their malignant masters pleased to deliver me. Then, hatless and trembling with wrath, I ordered the miscreants to let me out — on their peril to keep me one minute longer — with several incoherent threats of retaliation that, in their indefinite depth of virulency, smacked of King Lear.

The vehemence of my agitation brought on a copious

bleeding at the nose; and still Heathcliff laughed, and still I scolded. I don't know what would have concluded the scene had there not been one person at hand rather more rational than myself and more benevolent than my entertainer. This was Zillah, the stout housewife, who at length issued forth to inquire into the nature of the uproar. She thought that some of them had been laying violent hands on me; and, not daring to attack her master, she turned her vocal artillery against the younger scoundrel.

"Well, Mr. Earnshaw," she cried, "I wonder what you'll have agait next! Are we going to murder folk on our very door-stones? I see this house will never do for me. Look at t' poor lad; he's fair choking! — Wisht, wisht! you munn't go on so. Come in, and I'll cure that. There now, hold ye still."

With these words she suddenly splashed a pint of icy water down my neck, and pulled me into the kitchen. Mr. Heathcliff followed, his accidental merriment expiring quickly in his habitual moroseness.

I was sick exceedingly, and dizzy and faint, and thus compelled perforce to accept lodgings under his roof. He told Zillah to give me a glass of brandy, and then passed on to the inner room; while she condoled with me on my sorry predicament, and having obeyed his orders, whereby I was somewhat revived, ushered me to bed.

Chapter

While leading the way upstairs, she recommended that I should hide the candle, and not make a noise; for her master had an odd notion about the chamber she would put me in, and never let anybody lodge there willingly.

I asked the reason.

She did not know, she answered; she had only lived there a year or two; and they had so many queer goings on, she could not begin to be curious.

Too stupified to be curious myself, I fastened my door and glanced round for the bed. The whole furniture consisted of a chair, a clothes-press, and a large oak case, with squares cut out near the top resembling coach windows.

Having approached this structure, I looked inside, and perceived it to be a singular sort of old-fashioned couch, very conveniently designed to obviate the necessity for every member of the family having a room to himself. In fact, it formed a little closet, and the ledge of a window, which it enclosed, served as a table.

I slid back the panelled sides, got in with my light, pulled them together again, and felt secure against the vigilance of Heathcliff, and every one else.

The ledge, where I placed my candle, had a few mildewedbooks piled up in one corner; and it was covered with writing scratched on the paint. This writing, however, was nothing but a name repeated in all kinds of characters, large and small — Catherine Earnshaw, here and there varied to Catherine Heathcliff and then again to Catherine Linton.

In vapid listlessness I leant my head against the window, and continued spelling over Catherine Earnshaw — Heathcliff — Linton, till my eyes closed. But they had not rested five minutes when a glare of white letters started from the dark as vivid as spectres — the air swarmed with Catherines; and rousing myself to dispel the obtrusive name, I discovered my candle-wick reclining on one of the antique volumes, and perfuming the place with an odour of roasted calf-skin. I snuffed it off, and, very ill at ease under the influence of cold and lingering nausea, sat up and spread open the injured tome on my knee. It was a Testament, in lean type, and smelling dreadfully musty.

A fly-leaf bore the inscription, "Catherine Earnshaw, her book," and a date some quarter of a century back. I shut it, and took up another, and another, till I had examined all. Catherine's library was select, and its state of dilapidation proved it to have been well used, though not altogether for a legitimate purpose. Scarcely one chapter had escaped a pen-and-ink commentary — at least, the appearance of one — covering every morsel of blank that the printer had left. Some were detached sentences; other parts took the form of a regular diary, scrawled in an unformed, childish hand. At the top of an extra page (quite a treasure, probably, when first lighted on) I was greatly amused to behold an excellent caricature of my friend Joseph, rudely yet powerfully sketched. An immediate interest kindled within me for the unknown Catherine, and I began forthwith to decipher her faded hieroglyphics.

"An awful Sunday!" commenced the paragraph beneath. "I wish my father were back again. Hindley is a detestable substitute — his conduct to Heathcliff is atrocious — H. and I are going to rebel — we took our initiatory step this evening.

"All day had been flooding with rain. We could not go to church, so Joseph must needs get up a congregation in the garret; and while Hindley and his wife basked downstairs before a comfortable fire — doing anything but reading their Bibles, I'll answer for it — Heathcliff, myself, and the unhappy plough-boy were commanded to take our prayer-books and mount. We were ranged in a row on a sack of corn, groaning and shivering, and hoping that Joseph would shiver too, so that he might give us a short homily for his own sake. A vain idea! The service lasted precisely three hours; and yet my brother had the face to exclaim, when he saw us descending,

"'What! done already?'

On Sunday evenings we used to be permitted to play, if we did not make much noise; now a mere titter is sufficient to send us into corners!

" 'You forget you have a master here,' says the tyrant. 'I'll demolish the first who puts me out of temper! I insist on perfect sobriety and silence. O boy! was that you? — -Frances darling, pull his hair as you go by. I heard him snap his fingers.' Frances pulled his hair heartily, and then went and seated herself on her husband's knee; and there they were, like two babies, kissing and talking nonsense by the hour — foolish palaver that we should be ashamed of. We made ourselves as snug as our means allowed in the arch of the dresser. I had just fastened our pinafores together, and hung them up for a curtain, when in comes Joseph on an errand from the stables. He tears down my handiwork, boxes my ears, and croaks, —

" 'T' maister nobbut just buried, and Sabbath no o'ered, und t' sound o' t' gospel still i' yer lugs, and ye darr be laiking!

Shame on ye! Sit ye down, ill childer; there's good books eneugh if ye'll read 'em. Sit ye down, and think o' yer sowls!'

"Saying this, he compelled us so to square our positions that we might receive from the far-off fire a dull ray to show us the text of the lumber he thrust upon us. I could not bear the employment. I took my dingy volume by the scroop, and hurled it into the dog-kennel, vowing I hated a good book. Heathcliff kicked his to the same place. Then there was a hubbub!

" 'Maister Hindley!' shouted our chaplain. 'Maister, coom hither! Miss Cathy's riven th' back off "Th' Helmet o' Salvation," un Heathcliff's pawsed his fit into t' first part o' "T' Brooad Way to Destruction!" It's fair flaysome that ye let 'em go on this gait. Ech! th' owd man wad ha' laced 'em properly; but he's goan!'

"Hindley hurried up from his paradise on the hearth, and seizing one of us by the collar, and the other by the arm, hurled both into the back kitchen, where, Joseph asseverated, 'owd Nick' would fetch us as sure as we were living; and, so comforted, we each sought a separate nook to await his advent.

"I reached this book, and a pot of ink from a shelf, and pushed the house-door ajar to give me light, and I have got the time on with writing for twenty minutes; but my companion is impatient and proposes that we should appropriate the dairy woman's cloak, and have a scamper on the moors, under its shelter. A pleasant suggestion — and then, if the surly old man come in, he may believe his prophesy verified — we cannot be damper, or colder, in the rain than we are here." I suppose Catherine fulfilled her project, for the next sentence took up another subject; she waxed lachrymose.

"How little did I dream that Hindley would ever make me cry so!" she wrote. "My head aches, till I cannot keep it on the pillow; and still I can't give over. Poor Heathcliff! Hindley calls him a vagabond, and won't let him sit with us, nor eat with us any more; and he says, he and I must not play together, and threatens to turn him out of the house if we break his orders.

"He has been blaming our father (how dared he?) for

treating H. too liberally; and swears he will reduce him to his right place — "

I began to nod drowsily over the dim page; my eye wandered from manuscript to print. I saw a red ornamented title — "Seventy Times Seven, and the First of the Seventy-First. A Pious Discourse delivered by the Reverend Jabes Branderham, in the Chapel of Gimmerden Sough." And while I was, half consciously, worrying my brain to guess what Jabes Branderham would make of his subject, I sank back in bed, and fell asleep.

Alas, for the effects of bad tea and bad temper! what else could it be that made me pass such a terrible night? I don't remember another that I can at all compare with it since I was capable of suffering.

I began to dream, almost before I ceased to be sensible of my locality. I thought it was morning, and I had set out on my way home, with Joseph for a guide. The snow lay yards deep in our road; and, as we floundered on, my companion wearied me with constant reproaches that I had not brought a pilgrim's staff, telling me I could never get into the house without one, and boastfully flourishing a heavy-headed cudgel, which I understood to be so denominated.

For a moment I considered it absurd that I should need such a weapon to gain admittance into my own residence. Then a new idea flashed across me. I was not going there. We were journeying to hear the famous Jabes Branderham preach from the text, "Seventy Times Seven," and either Joseph the preacher or I had committed the "First of the Seventy-First," and were to be publicly exposed and excommunicated.

We came to the chapel. I have passed it really in my walks twice or thrice. It lies in a hollow between two hills — an elevated hollow, near a swamp, whose peaty moisture is said to answer all the purposes of embalming on the few corpses deposited there. The roof has been kept whole hitherto; but as the clergyman's stipend is only twenty pounds per annum, and a house with two rooms, threatening speedily to determine into one, no clergyman will undertake the duties of pastor, especially as it is currently reported that his flock would rather let him starve than increase the living by one penny from their own pockets. However, in my dream, Jabes had a full and attentive congregation, and he preached — good God! what a sermon, divided into four hundred and ninety parts, each fully equal to an ordinary address from the pulpit, and each discussing a separate sin! Where he searched for them, I cannot tell. He had his private manner of interpreting the phrase, and it seemed necessary the brother should sin different sins on every occasion. They were of the most curious character — odd transgressions that I never imagined previously.

Oh, how weary I grew! How I writhed, and yawned, and nodded, and revived! How I pinched, and pricked myself, and rubbed my eyes, and stood up, and sat down again, and nudged Joseph to inform me if he would ever have done! I was condemned to hear all out. Finally, he reached the "First of the Seventy-First." At that crisis, a sudden inspiration descended on me. I was moved to rise and denounce Jabes Branderham as the sinner of the sin that no Christian need pardon.

"Sir," I exclaimed, "sitting here within these four walls, at one stretch, I have endured and forgiven the four hundred and ninety heads of your discourse. Seventy times seven times have I plucked up my hat and been about to depart; seventy times seven times have you preposterously forced me to resume my seat. The four hundred and ninety-first is too much. — Fellow-martyrs, have at him! Drag him down, and crush him to atoms, that the place which knows him may know him no more!"

"Thou art the man!" cried Jabes, after a solemn pause, leaning over his cushion. "Seventy times seven times didst thou gapingly contort thy visage; seventy times seven did I take counsel with my soul. Lo, this is human weakness; this also may be absolved! The 'First of the Seventy-First' is come. Brethren, execute upon him the judgment written. Such honour have all His saints!"

With that concluding word, the whole assembly, exalting their pilgrim's staves, rushed round me in a body; and I, having no weapon to raise in self-defence, commenced grappling with Joseph, my nearest and most ferocious assailant, for his. In the confluence of the multitude several clubs crossed; blows aimed at me fell on other sconces. Presently the whole chapel resounded with rappings and counter-rappings. Every man's hand was against his neighbour; and Branderham, unwilling to remain idle, poured forth his zeal in a shower of loud taps on the boards of the pulpit, which responded so smartly that at last, to my unspeakable relief, they woke me. And what was it that had suggested the tremendous tumult? What had played Jabes's part in the row? Merely the branch of a fir-tree that touched my lattice, as the blast wailed by, and rattled its dry cones against the panes!

I listened doubtingly an instant, detected the disturber, then turned and dozed, and dreamt again — if possible, still more disagreeably than before.

This time I remembered I was lying in the oak closet, and I heard distinctly the gusty wind and the driving of the snow. I heard also the fir-bough repeat its teasing sound, and ascribed it to the right cause. But it annoyed me so much that I resolved to silence it, if possible; and I thought I rose and endeavoured to unhasp the casement. The hook was soldered into the staple — a circumstance observed by me when awake, but forgotten. "I must stop it, nevertheless!" I muttered, knocking my knuckles through the glass, and stretching an arm out to seize the importunate branch; instead of which, my fingers closed on the fingers of a little, ice-cold hand! The intense horror of nightmare came over me.

I tried to draw back my arm, but the hand clung to it, and a most melancholy voice sobbed, "Let me in — let me in!" "Who are you?" I asked, struggling, meanwhile, to disengage myself. "Catherine Linton," it replied shiveringly. (Why did I think of Linton? I had read Earnshaw twenty times for Linton.) "I'm come home. I'd lost my way on the moor." As it spoke, I discerned, obscurely, a child's face looking through the window. Terror made me cruel; and finding it useless to attempt shaking the creature off, I pulled its wrist on to the broken pane, and rubbed it to and fro till the blood ran down and soaked the bedclothes. Still it wailed, "Let me in!" and maintained its tenacious gripe, almost maddening me with fear. "How can I?" I said at length. "Let me go, if you want me to let you in!" The fingers relaxed; I snatched mine through the hole, hurriedly piled the books up in a pyramid against it, and stopped my ears to exclude the lamentable prayer. I seemed to keep them closed above a quarter of an hour; yet the instant I listened again, there was the doleful cry moaning on! "Begone!" I shouted; "I'll never let you in — not if you beg for twenty years."

"It is twenty years," mourned the voice — "twenty years. I've been a waif for twenty years!" Thereat began a feeble scratching outside, and the pile of books moved as if thrust forward. I tried to jump up, but could not stir a limb, and so yelled aloud in a frenzy of fright. To my confusion, I discovered the yell was not ideal. Hasty footsteps approached my chamber door; somebody pushed it open with a vigorous hand, and a light glimmered through the squares at the top of the bed. I sat shuddering yet, and wiping the perspiration from my forehead. The intruder appeared to hesitate, and muttered to himself. At last he said in a half-whisper, plainly not expecting an answer, "Is any one here?" I considered it best to confess my presence, for I knew Heathcliff's accents, and feared he might search further if I kept quiet. With this intention I turned and opened the panels. I shall not soon forget the effect my action produced.

Heathcliff stood near the entrance, in his shirt and trousers, with a candle dripping over his fingers, and his face as white as the wall behind him. The first creak of the oak startled him like an electric shock. The light leaped from his hold to a distance of some feet, and his agitation was so extreme that he could hardly pick it up. "It is only your guest, sir," I called out, desirous to spare him the humiliation of exposing his cowardice further. "I had the misfortune to scream in my sleep, owing to a frightful nightmare. I'm sorry I disturbed you." "Oh, God confound you, Mr. Lockwood! I wish you were at the — " commenced my host, setting the candle on a chair, because he found it impossible to hold it steady.

"And who showed you up into this room?" he continued, crushing his nails into his palms and grinding his teeth to subdue the maxillary convulsions. "Who was it? I've a good mind to turn them out of the house this moment."

"It was your servant Zillah," I replied, flinging myself on to the floor, and rapidly resuming my garments. "I should not care if you did, Mr. Heathcliff; she richly deserves it. I suppose that she wanted to get another proof that the place was haunted, at my expense. Well, it is — swarming with ghosts and goblins! You have reason in shutting it up, I assure you. No one will thank you for a doze in such a den!"

"What do you mean?" asked Heathcliff, "and what are you doing? Lie down and finish out the night, since you are here; but, for Heaven's sake, don't repeat that horrid noise. Nothing could excuse it, unless you were having your throat cut!" "If the little fiend had got in at the window, she probably would have strangled me!" I returned. "I'm not going to endure the persecutions of your hospitable ancestors again. Was not the Reverend Jabes Branderham akin to you on the mother's side? And that minx, Catherine Linton, or Earnshaw, or however she was called, she must have been a changeling — -wicked little soul! She told me she had been walking the earth those twenty years — a just punishment for her mortal transgressions, I've no doubt."

Scarcely were these words uttered, when I recollected the association of Heathcliff's with Catherine's name in the book, which had completely slipped from my memory, till thus awakened. I blushed at my inconsideration; but without showing further consciousness of the offence, I hastened to add, "The truth is, sir, I passed the first part of the night in — — " Here I stopped afresh. I was about to say "perusing those old volumes" — then it would have revealed my knowledge of their written as well as their printed contents; so, correcting myself, I went on, "In spelling over the name scratched on that window-ledge — a monotonous occupation, calculated to set me asleep, like counting, or — "

"What can you mean by talking in this way to me?" thundered Heathcliff, with savage vehemence. "How — how dare you, under my roof? — God, he's mad to speak so!" And he struck his forehead with rage. I did not know whether to resent this language or pursue my explanation; but he seemed so powerfully affected that I took pity and proceeded with my dreams, affirming I had never heard the appellation of "Catherine Linton" before, but reading it often over produced an impression which personified itself when I had no longer my imagination under control.

Heathcliff gradually fell back into the shelter of the bed as I spoke, finally sitting down almost concealed behind it. I guessed, however, by his irregular and intercepted breathing, that he struggled to vanquish an excess of violent emotion. Not liking to show him that I had heard the conflict, I continued my toilet rather noisily, looked at my watch, and soliloquized on the length of the night. Not three o'clock yet! I could have taken oath it had been six. Time stagnates here. We must surely have retired to rest at eight!

"Always at nine in winter, and rise at four," said my host, suppressing a groan, and, as I fancied, by the motion of his arm's shadow, dashing a tear from his eyes. "Mr. Lockwood," he added, "you may go into my room. You'll only be in the way, coming downstairs so early; and your childish outcry has sent sleep to the devil for me."

"And for me too," I replied. "I'll walk in the yard till daylight, and then I'll be off; and you need not dread a repetition of my intrusion. I'm now quite cured of seeking pleasure in society, be it country or town. A sensible man ought to find sufficient company in himself."

"Delightful company!" muttered Heathcliff. "Take the candle, and go where you please. I shall join you directly. Keep out of the yard, though — the dogs are unchained; and the house — Juno mounts sentinel there, and — -nay, you can only ramble about the steps and passages. But away with you! I'll come in two minutes!"

I obeyed, so far as to quit the chamber; when, ignorant where the narrow lobbies led, I stood still, and was witness, involuntarily, to a piece of superstition on the part of my landlord which belied oddly his apparent sense. He got on to the bed and wrenched open the lattice, bursting, as he pulled at it, into an uncontrollable passion of tears. "Come in! come in!" he sobbed. "Cathy, do come! Oh, do — once more! Oh, my heart's darling! hear me this time, Catherine, at last!" The spectre showed a spectre's ordinary caprice. It gave no sign of being; but the snow and wind whirled wildly through, even reaching my station, and blowing out the light.

There was such anguish in the gush of grief that accompanied this raving that my compassion made me overlook its folly, and I drew off, half angry to have listened at all, and vexed at having related my ridiculous nightmare, since it produced that agony; though why was beyond my comprehension. I descended cautiously to the lower regions, and landed in the back kitchen, where a gleam of fire, raked compactly together, enabled me to rekindle my candle. Nothing was stirring except a brindled, gray cat, which crept from the ashes, and saluted me with a querulous mew.

Two benches, shaped in sections of a circle, nearly enclosed the hearth. On one of these I stretched myself, and Grimalkin mounted the other. We were both of us nodding ere any one invaded our retreat, and then it was Joseph, shuffling down a wooden ladder that vanished in the roof, through a trap — the ascent to his garret, I suppose. He cast a sinister look at the little flame which I had enticed to play between the ribs, swept the cat from its elevation, and bestowing himself in the vacancy, commenced the operation of stuffing a three-inch pipe with tobacco. My presence in his sanctum was evidently esteemed a piece of impudence too shameful for remark. He silently applied the tube to his lips, folded his arms, and puffed away. I let him enjoy the luxury unannoyed; and after sucking out his last wreath, and heaving a profound sigh, he got up, and departed as solemnly as he came.

A more elastic footstep entered next; and now I opened my mouth for a "good-morning," but closed it again the salutation unachieved, for Hareton Earnshaw was performing his orisons, sotto voce, in a series of curses directed against every object he touched, while he rummaged a corner for a spade or shovel to dig through the drifts. He glanced over the back of the bench, dilating his nostrils, and thought as little of exchanging civilities with me as with my companion the cat. I guessed by his preparations that egress was allowed, and leaving my hard couch, made a movement to follow him. He noticed this, and thrust at an inner door with the end of his spade, intimating by an inarticulate sound that there was the place where I must go if I changed my locality.

It opened into the house, where the females were already astir — Zillah urging flakes of flame up the chimney with a colossal bellows; and Mrs. Heathcliff, kneeling on the hearth, reading a book by the aid of the blaze. She held her hand interposed between the furnace-heat and her eyes, and seemed absorbed in her occupation, desisting from it only to chide the servant for covering her with sparks, or to push away a dog, now and then, that snoozled its nose over-forwardly into her face. I was surprised to see Heathcliff there also. He stood by the fire, his back towards me, just finishing a stormy scene to poor Zillah, who ever and anon interrupted her labour to pluck up the corner of her apron and heave an indignant groan.

"And you, you worthless — -" he broke out as I entered, turning to his daughter-in-law, and employing an epithet as harmless as duck or sheep, but generally represented by a dash — —. "There you are at your idle tricks again! The rest of them do earn their bread; you live on my charity! Put your trash away, and find something to do. You shall pay me for the plague of having you eternally in my sight. Do you hear, damnable jade?"

"I'll put my trash away, because you can make me if I refuse," answered the young lady, closing her book and throwing it on a chair. "But I'll not do anything, though you should swear your tongue out, except what I please!"

Heathcliff lifted his hand, and the speaker sprang to a safer distance, obviously acquainted with its weight. Having no desire to be entertained by a cat-and-dog combat, I stepped forward briskly, as if eager to partake the warmth of the hearth, and innocent of any knowledge of the interrupted dispute. Each had enough decorum to suspend further hostilities.

Heathcliff placed his fists, out of temptation, in his pockets; Mrs. Heathcliff curled her lip, and walked to a seat far off, where she kept her word by playing the part of a statue during the remainder of my stay. That was not long. I declined joining their breakfast, and at the first gleam of dawn took an opportunity of escaping into the free air, now clear, and still, and cold as impalpable ice.

My landlord hallooed for me to stop ere I reached the bottom of the garden, and offered to accompany me across the moor. It was well he did, for the whole hill-back was one billowy, white ocean, the swells and falls not indicating corresponding rises and depressions in the ground. Many pits, at least, were filled to a level, and entire ranges of mounds, the refuse of the quarries, blotted from the chart which my yesterday's walk left pictured in my mind. I had remarked on one side of the road, at intervals of six or seven yards, a line of upright stones, continued through the whole length of the barren. These were erected and daubed with lime on purpose to serve as guides in the dark, and also when a fall, like the present, confounded the deep swamps on either hand with the firmer path; but, excepting a dirty dot pointing up here and there, all traces of their existence had vanished, and my companion found it necessary to warn me frequently to steer to the right or left, when I imagined I was following correctly the windings of the road.

We exchanged little conversation, and he halted at the entrance of Thrushcross Park, saying I could make no error there. Our adieus were limited to a hasty bow, and then I pushed forward, trusting to my own resources, for the porter's lodge is untenanted as yet.

The distance from the gate to the Grange is two miles; I believe I managed to make it four, what with losing myself among the trees, and sinking up to the neck in snow — a predicament which only those who have experienced it can appreciate. At any rate, whatever were my wanderings, the clock chimed twelve as I entered the house, and that gave exactly an hour for every mile of the usual way from Wuthering Heights.

My human fixture and her satellites rushed to welcome me, exclaiming tumultuously they had completely given me up. Everybody conjectured that I perished last night, and they were wondering how they must set about the search for my remains. I bid them be quiet, now that they saw me returned, and, benumbed to my very heart, I dragged upstairs; whence, after putting on dry clothes, and pacing to and fro thirty or forty minutes, to restore the animal heat, I am adjourned to my study, feeble as a kitten — almost too much so to enjoy the cheerful fire and smoking coffee which the servant has prepared for my refreshment.

Chapter

What vain weather-cocks we are ! I, who had determined to hold myself independent of all social intercourse, and thanked my stars that, at length, I had lighted on a spot where it was next to impracticable — I, weak wretch, after maintaining till dusk a struggle with low spirits and solitude, was finally compelled to strike my colours; and, under pretence of gaining information concerning the necessities of my establishment, I desired Mrs. Dean, when she brought in supper, to sit down while I ate it, hoping sincerely she would prove a regular gossip, and either rouse me to animation or lull me to sleep by her talk.

"You have lived here a considerable time," I commenced; "did you not say sixteen years ?"

"Eighteen, sir; I came, when the mistress was married, to wait on her; after she died, the master retained me for his house-keeper."

"Indeed."

l here ensued a pause. She was not a gossip, I feared, unless about her own affairs, and those could hardly interest me. However, having studied for an interval, with a fist on either knee, and a cloud of meditation over her ruddy countenance, she ejaculated —

"Ah, times are greatly changed since then!"

"Yes," I remarked; "you've seen a good many alterations, I suppose?"

"I have; and troubles too," she said.

"Oh, I'll turn the talk on my landlord's family!" I thought to myself. "A good subject to start! And that pretty girl-widow, I should like to know her history — whether she be a native of the country, or, as is more probable, an exotic that the surly indigenae will not recognize for kin." With this intention I asked Mrs. Dean why Heathcliff let

Thrushcross Grange, and preferred living in a situation and residence so much inferior. "Is he not rich enough to keep the estate in good order?" I inquired.

"Rich, sir!" she returned. "He has nobody knows what money, and every year it increases. Yes, yes; he's rich enough to live in a finer house than this. But he's very near — close-handed; and if he had meant to flit to Thrushcross Grange, as soon as he heard of a good tenant he could not have borne to miss the chance of getting a few hundreds more. It is strange people should be so greedy when they are alone in the world!"

"He had a son, it seems?"

"Yes, he had one. He is dead."

"And that young lady, Mrs. Heathcliff, is his widow?"

"Yes."

"Where did she come from originally?"

"Why, sir, she is my late master's daughter. Catherine Linton was her maiden name. I nursed her, poor thing! I did wish Mr. Heathcliff would remove here, and then we might have been together again."

"What! Catherine Linton?" I exclaimed, astonished. But a minute's reflection convinced me it was not my ghostly Catherine. "Then," I continued, "my predecessor's name was Linton?"

"It was."

"And who is that Earnshaw — Hareton Earnshaw — who lives with Mr. Heathcliff? Are they relations?"

"No; he is the late Mrs. Linton's nephew."

"The young lady's cousin, then?"

"Yes; and her husband was her cousin also — one on the mother's side, the other on the father's side. Heathcliff married Mr. Linton's sister."

"I see the house at Wuthering Heights has 'Earnshaw' carved over the front door. Are they an old family?"

"Very old, sir; and Hareton is the last of them, as our Miss Cathy is of us — I mean of the Lintons. Have you been to Wuthering Heights? I beg pardon for asking; but I should like to hear how she is."

"Mrs. Heathcliff? She looked very well, and very handsome; yet, I think, not very happy."

"Oh dear, I don't wonder! And how did you like the master?"

"A rough fellow, rather, Mrs. Dean. Is not that his character?"

"Rough as a saw-edge, and hard as whinstone. The less you meddle with him the better."

"He must have had some ups and downs in life to make him such a churl. Do you know anything of his history?"

"It's a cuckoo's, sir. I know all about it — except where he was born, and who were his parents, and how he got his money at first. And Hareton has been cast out like an unfledged dunnock! The unfortunate lad is the only one in all this parish that does not guess how he has been cheated."

"Well, Mrs. Dean, it will be a charitable deed to tell me something of my neighbours. I feel I shall not rest if I go to bed, so be good enough to sit and chat an hour."

"Oh, certainly, sir! I'll just fetch a little sewing, and then I'll sit as long as you please. But you've caught cold — I saw you shivering; and you must have some gruel to drive it out."

The worthy woman bustled off, and I crouched nearer the fire. My head felt hot, and the rest of me chill; moreover, I was excited, almost to a pitch of foolishness, through my nerves and brain. This caused me to feel, not uncomfortable, but rather fearful (as I am still) of serious effects from the incidents of to-day and yesterday. She returned presently, bringing a smoking basin and a basket of work; and having placed the former on the hob, drew in her seat, evidently pleased to find me so companionable.

Before I came to live here, she commenced — waiting no further invitation to her story — I was almost always at

Wuthering Heights, because my mother had nursed Mr. Hindley Earnshaw (that was Hareton's father), and I got used to playing with the children. I ran errands, too, and helped to make hay, and hung about the farm, ready for anything that anybody would set me to. One fine summer morning — it was the beginning of harvest, I remember — Mr. Earnshaw, the old master, came downstairs, dressed for a journey; and after he had told Joseph what was to be done during the day, he turned to Hindley, and Cathy, and me — for I sat eating my porridge with them — and he said, speaking to his son, "Now, my bonny man, I'm going to Liverpool to-day; what shall I bring you? You may choose what you like.

Only let it be little, for I shall walk there and back. Sixty miles each way — that is a long spell!" Hindley named a fiddle, and then he asked Miss Cathy. She was hardly six years old, but she could ride any horse in the stable, and she chose a whip. He did not forget me, for he had a kind heart, though he was rather severe sometimes. He promised to bring me a pocketful of apples and pears; and then he kissed his children, said good-bye, and set off.

It seemed a long while to us all — the three days of his absence — and often did little Cathy ask when he would be home. Mrs. Earnshaw expected him by supper-time on the third evening, and she put the meal off hour after hour. There were no signs of his coming, however, and at last the children got tired of running down to the gate to look. Then it grew dark. She would have had them to bed, but they begged sadly to be allowed to stay up; and just about eleven o'clock the door-latch was raised quietly, and in stepped the master. He threw himself into a chair, laughing and groaning, and bid them all stand off, for he was nearly killed. He would not have such another walk for the three kingdoms.

"And at the end of it, to be flighted to death!" he said, opening his greatcoat, which he held bundled up in his arms. "See here, wife! I was never so beaten with anything in my life; but you must e'en take it as a gift of God, though it's as dark almost as if it came from the devil."

We crowded round, and over Miss Cathy's head I had a

peep at a dirty, ragged, black-haired child, big enough both to walk and talk. Indeed, its face looked older than Catherine's; yet when it was set on its feet it only stared round, and repeated over and over again some gibberish that nobody could understand. I was frightened, and Mrs. Earnshaw was ready to fling it out of doors. She did fly up, asking how he could fashion to bring that gipsy brat into the house, when they had their own bairns to feed and fend for; what he meant to do with it, and whether he were mad.

The master tried to explain the matter; but he was really half dead with fatigue, and all that I could make out, amongst her scolding, was a tale of his seeing it starving, and houseless, and as good as dumb, in the streets of Liverpool, where he picked it up and inquired for its owner. Not a soul knew to whom it belonged, he said; and his money and time being both limited, he thought it better to take it home with him at once, than run into vain expenses there, because he was determined be would not leave it as he found it. Well, the conclusion was that my mistress grumbled herself calm; and Mr. Earnshaw told me to wash it, and give it clean things, and let it sleep with the children.

Hindley and Cathy contented themselves with looking and listening till peace was restored; then both began searching their father's pockets for the presents he had promised them. The former was a boy of fourteen, but when he drew out what had been a fiddle, crushed to morsels in the greatcoat, he blubbered aloud; and Cathy, when she learned the master had lost her whip in attending on the stranger, showed her humour by grinning and spitting at the stupid little thing, earning for her pains a sound blow from her father to teach her cleaner manners. They entirely refused to have it in bed with them, or even in their room; and I had no more sense, so I put it on the landing of the stairs, hoping it might be gone on the morrow. By chance, or else attracted by hearing his voice, it crept to Mr. Earnshaw's door, and there he found it on quitting his chamber. Inquiries were made as to how it got there. I was obliged to confess, and in recompense for my cowardice and inhumanity was sent out of the house.

This was Heathcliff's first introduction to the family. On coming back a few days afterwards (for I did not consider my banishment perpetual) I found they had christened him "Heathcliff." It was the name of a son who died in childhood, and it has served him ever since, both for Christian and surname. Miss Cathy and he were now very thick; but Hindley hated him, and, to say the truth, I did the same; and we plagued and went on with him shamefully, for I wasn't reasonable enough to feel my injustice, and the mistress never put in a word on his behalf when she saw him wronged.

He seemed a sullen, patient child, hardened, perhaps, to ill-treatment. He would stand Hindley's blows without winking or shedding a tear, and my pinches moved him only to draw in a breath and open his eyes, as if he had hurt himself by accident and nobody was to blame. This endurance made old Earnshaw furious when he discovered his son persecuting the poor, fatherless child, as he called him. He took to Heathcliff strangely, believing all he said (for that matter, he said precious little, and generally the truth), and petting him up far above Cathy, who was too mischievous and wayward for a favourite.

So from the very beginning he bred bad feeling in the house; and at Mrs. Earnshaw's death, which happened in less than two years after, the young master had learned to regard his father as an oppressor rather than a friend, and Heathcliff as a usurper of his parent's affections and his privileges, and he grew bitter with brooding over these injuries. I sympathized a while; but when the children fell ill of the measles, and I had to tend them, and take on me the cares of a woman at once, I changed my ideas. Heathcliff was dangerously sick; and while he lay at the worst he would have me constantly by his pillow. I suppose he felt I did a good deal for him, and he hadn't wit to guess that I was compelled to do it. However, I will say this — he was the quietest child that ever nurse watched over. The difference between him and the others forced me to be less partial. Cathy and her brother harassed me terribly; he was as uncomplaining as a lamb, though hardness, not gentleness, made him give little trouble.

He got through, and the doctor affirmed it was in a great measure owing to me, and praised me for my care. I was vain of his commendations, and softened towards the being by whose means I earned them; and thus Hindley lost his last ally. Still I couldn't dote on Heathcliff, and I wondered often what my master saw to admire so much in the sullen boy, who never, to my recollection, repaid his indulgence by any sign of gratitude. He was not insolent to his benefactor, he was simply insensible, though knowing perfectly the hold he had on his heart, and conscious he had only to speak and all the house would be obliged to bend to his wishes. As an instance, I remember Mr. Earnshaw once bought a couple of colts at the parish fair, and gave the lads each one. Heathcliff took the handsomest, but it soon fell lame, and when he discovered it, he said to Hindley, —

"You must exchange horses with me — I don't like mine; and if you won't, I shall tell your father of the three thrashings you've given me this week, and show him my arm, which is black to the shoulder." Hindley put out his tongue and cuffed him over the ears. "You'd better do it at once," he persisted, escaping to the porch (they were in the stable). "You will have to; and if I speak of these blows, you'll get them again with interest." "Off, dog!" cried Hindley, threatening him with an iron weight used for weighing potatoes and hay. "Throw it," he replied, standing still, "and then I'll tell how you boasted that you would turn me out of doors as soon as he died, and see whether he will not turn you out directly." Hindley threw it, hitting him on the breast, and down he fell, but staggered up immediately, breathless and white; and had I not prevented it, he would have gone just so to the master, and got full revenge by letting his condition plead for him, intimating who had caused it.

"Take my colt, gipsy, then!" said young Earnshaw. "And I pray that he may break your neck. Take him, and be damned, you beggarly interloper; and wheedle my father out of all he has. Only afterwards show him what you are, imp of Satan. And take that! I hope he'll kick out your brains!"

Heathcliff had gone to loose the beast and shift it to his

own stall. He was passing behind it, when Hindley finished his speech by knocking him under its feet, and without stopping to examine whether his hopes were fulfilled, ran away as fast as he could.

I was surprised to witness how coolly the child gathered himself up, and went on with his intention — exchanging saddles and all, and then sitting down on a bundle of hay to overcome the qualm which the violent blow occasioned, before he entered the house.

I persuaded him easily to let me lay the blame of his bruises on the horse. He minded little what tale was told, since he had what he wanted. He complained so seldom, indeed, of such stirs as these, that I really thought him not vindictive. I was deceived completely, as you will hear.

Chapter

While Miss Linton moped about the park and garden, always silent, and almost always in tears; and her brother shut himself up among books that he never opened — wearying, I guessed, with a continual vague expectation that Catherine, repenting her conduct, would come of her own accord to ask pardon, and seek a reconciliation; and she fasted pertinaciously under the idea, probably, that at every meal, Edgar was ready to choke for her absence, and pride alone held him from running to cast himself at her feet; I went about my household duties, convinced that the Grange had but one sensible soul in its walls, and that lodged in my body.

I wasted no condolences on miss, nor any expostulations on my mistress, nor did I pay attention to the sighs of my master, who yearned to hear his lady's name, since he might not hear her voice.

I determined they should come about as they pleased for me; and though it was a tiresomely slow process, I began to rejoice at length in a faint dawn of its progress, as I thought at first. Mrs. Linton, on the third day, unbarred her door; and having finished the water in her pitcher and decanter, desired a renewed supply, and a basin of gruel, for she believed she was dying. That I set down as a speech meant for Edgar's ears;

I believed no such thing, so I kept it to myself, and brought her some tea and dry toast. She ate and drank eagerly; and sank back on her pillow again, clenching her hands and groaning.

"Oh, I will die," she exclaimed, "since no one cares anything about me. I wish I had not taken that."

Then a good while after I heard her murmur,

"No, I'll not die — he'd be glad — he does not love me at all — he would never miss me!"

"Did you want anything, ma'am?" I inquired, still preserving my external composure, in spite of her ghastly countenance and strange, exaggerated manner.

"What is that apathetic being doing?" she demanded, pushing the thick entangled locks from her wasted face. "Has he fallen into a lethargy, or is he dead?"

"Neither," replied I, "if you mean Mr. Linton. He's tolerably well, I think, though his studies occupy him rather more than they ought. He is continually among his books, since he has no other society."

I should not have spoken so if I had known her true condition, but I could not get rid of the notion that she acted a part of her disorder.

"Among his books!" she cried, confounded. "And I dying — I on the brink of the grave! My God! does he know how I'm altered?" continued she, staring at her reflection in a mirror hanging against the opposite wall. "Is that Catherine Linton? He imagines me in a pet — in play, perhaps. Cannot you inform him that it is frightful earnest? Nelly, if it be not too late, as soon as I learn how he feels I'll choose between these two — either to starve at once (that would be no punishment unless he had a heart), or to recover, and leave the country. Are you speaking the truth about him now? Take care. Is he actually so utterly indifferent for my life?"

"Why, ma'am," I answered, "the master has no idea of your being deranged; and, of course, he does not fear that you will let yourself die of hunger."

"You think not? Cannot you tell him I will?" she returned. "Persuade him; speak of your own mind; say you are certain

I will!" "No, you forget, Mrs. Linton," I suggested, "that you have eaten some food with a relish this evening, and tomorrow you will perceive its good effects."

"If I were only sure it would kill him," she interrupted, "I'd kill myself directly! These three awful nights I've never closed my lids; and oh, I've been tormented! I've been haunted,

Nelly! But I begin to fancy you don't like me. How strange! I thought, though everybody hated and despised each other, they could not avoid loving me. And they have all turned to enemies in a few hours. They have, I'm positive — the people here. How dreary to meet death, surrounded by their cold faces! Isabella, terrified and repelled, afraid to enter the room; it would be so dreadful to watch Catherine go! And Edgar standing solemnly by to see it over; then offering prayers of thanks to God for restoring peace to his house, and going back to his books! What in the name of all that feels has he to do with books when I am dying?"

She could not bear the notion which I had put into her head of Mr. Linton's philosophical resignation. Tossing about, she increased her feverish bewilderment to madness, and tore the pillow with her teeth; then raising herself up, all burning, desired that I would open the window. We were in the middle of winter, the wind blew strong from the north-east, and I objected. Both the expressions flitting over her face and the changes of her moods began to alarm me terribly, and brought to my recollection her former illness, and the doctor's injunction that she should not be crossed. A minute previously she was violent; now, supported on one arm, and not noticing my refusal to obey her, she seemed to find childish diversion in pulling the feathers from the rents she had just made, and ranging them on the sheet according to their different species. Her mind had strayed to other associations.

"That's a turkey's," she murmured to herself, "and this is a wild duck's, and this is a pigeon's. Ah, they put pigeons' feathers in the pillows; no wonder I couldn't die! Let me take care to throw it on the floor when I lie down. And here is a moor-cock's; and this — I should know it among a thousand — it's a lapwing's. Bonny bird, wheeling over our heads in the middle of the moor. It wanted to get to its nest, for the clouds had touched the swells, and it felt rain coming. This feather was picked up from the heath; the bird was not shot. We saw its nest in the winter, full of little skeletons. Heathcliff set a trap over it, and the old ones dare not come. I made him promise he'd never shoot a lap-wing after that, and he didn't. Yes, here are more! Did he shoot my lapwings, Nelly? Are they red, any of them? Let me look."

"Give over with that baby-work!" I interrupted, dragging the pillow away, and turning the holes towards the mattress, for she was removing its contents by handfuls. "Lie down and shut your eyes; you're wandering. There's a mess! The down is flying about like snow."

I went here and there collecting it.

"I see in you, Nelly," she continued dreamily, "an aged woman. You have gray hair and bent shoulders. This bed is the fairy cave under Peniston Crag, and you are gathering elf-bolts to hurt our heifers, pretending, while I am near, that they are only locks of wool. That's what you'll come to fifty years hence. I know you are not so now. I'm not wandering; you're mistaken, or else I should believe you really were that withered hag, and I should think I was under Peniston Crag; and I'm conscious it's night, and there are two candles on the table making the black press shine like jet."

"The black press? Where is that?" I asked. "You are talking in your sleep!"

"It's against the wall, as it always is," she replied. "It does appear odd. I see a face in it!"

"There's no press in the room, and never was," said I, resuming my seat, and looping up the curtain, that I might watch her.

"Don't you see that face?" she inquired, gazing earnestly at the mirror.

And say what I could, I was incapable of making her comprehend it to be her own; so I rose and covered it with a shawl.

"It's behind there still!" she pursued anxiously. "And it stirred. Who is it? I hope it will not come out when you are gone! O Nelly, the room is haunted! I'm afraid of being alone!" I took her hand in mine, and bade her be composed, for a succession of shudders convulsed her frame, and she would keep straining her gaze towards the glass.

"There's nobody here!" I insisted. "It was yourself Mrs. Linton. You knew it a while since."

"Myself!" she gasped; "and the clock is striking twelve! It's true, then; that's dreadful!"

Her fingers clutched the clothes, and gathered them over her eyes. I attempted to steal to the door, with an intention of calling her husband; but I was summoned back by a piercing shriek. The shawl had dropped from the frame.

"Why, what is the matter?" cried I. "Who is coward now? Wake up! That is the glass — the mirror, Mrs. Linton; and you see yourself in it; and there am I too, by your side."

Trembling and bewildered, she held me fast, but the horror gradually passed from her countenance. Its paleness gave place to a glow of shame.

"Oh dear! I thought I was at home," she sighed — "I thought I was lying in my chamber at Wuthering Heights. Because I'm weak, my brain got confused, and I screamed unconsciously. Don't say anything, but stay with me. I dread sleeping. My dreams appall me."

"A sound sleep would do you good, ma'am," I answered; "and I hope this suffering will prevent your trying starving again." "Oh, if I were but in my own bed in the old house!" she went on bitterly, wringing her hands. "And that wind sounding in the firs by the lattice. Do let me feel it — it comes straight down the moor — do let me have one breath!"

To pacify her, I held the casement ajar a few seconds. A cold blast rushed through. I closed it, and returned to my post. She lay still now, her face bathed in tears. Exhaustion of body had entirely subdued her spirit. Our fiery Catherine was no better than a wailing child.

"How long is it since I shut myself in here?" she asked, suddenly reviving.

"It was Monday evening," I replied; "and this is Thursday night, or rather Friday morning, at present."

"What! of the same week?" she exclaimed. "Only that brief time?" "Long enough to live on nothing but cold water and ill-temper," observed I.

"Well, it seems a weary number of hours," she muttered doubtfully. "It must be more. I remember being in the parlour after they had quarrelled, and Edgar being cruelly provoking, and me running into this room desperate. As soon as ever I had barred the door, utter blackness overwhelmed me, and I fell on the floor. I couldn't explain to Edgar how certain I felt of having a fit, or going raging mad, if he persisted in teasing me. I had no command of tongue or brain, and he did not guess my agony perhaps; it barely left me sense to try to escape from him and his voice. Before I recovered sufficiently to see and hear, it began to be dawn; and, Nelly, I'll tell you what I thought, and what has kept recurring and recurring till I feared for my reason. I thought as I lay there, with my head against that table leg, and my eyes dimly discerning the gray square of the window, that I was enclosed in the oak-panelled bed at home; and my heart ached with some great grief which, just waking, I could not recollect. I pondered, and worried myself to discover what it could be; and, most strangely, the whole last seven years of my life grew a blank! I did not recall that they had been at all. I was a child; my father was just buried, and my misery arose from the separation that Hindley had ordered between me and Heathcliff. I was laid alone, for the first time; and rousing from a dismal doze, after a night of weeping, I lifted my hand to push the panels aside. It struck the table-top! I swept it along the carpet; and then memory burst in. My late anguish was swallowed in a paroxysm of despair.

I cannot say why I felt so wildly wretched. It must have been temporary derangement, for there is scarcely cause. But, supposing at twelve years old I had been wrenched from the Heights, and every early association, and my all in all, as Heathcliff was at that time, and been converted at a stroke into Mrs. Linton, the lady of Thrushcross Grange, and the wife of a stranger, an exile and outcast thenceforth from what had been my world — you may fancy a glimpse of the abyss where I grovelled! Shake your head as you will, Nelly, you have helped to unsettle me! You should have spoken to Edgar — indeed you should — and compelled him to leave me quiet! Oh, I'm burning! I wish I were out of doors! I wish I were a girl again, half savage and hardy and free, and laughing at injuries, not maddening under them! Why am I so changed? Why does my blood rush into a hell of tumult at a few words? I'm sure I should be myself were I once among the heather on those hills. Open the window again wide — fasten it open! Quick! Why don't you move?"

"Because I won't give you your death of cold," I answered.

"You won't give me a chance of life, you mean," she said sullenly. "However, I'm not helpless yet. I'll open it myself."

And sliding from the bed before I could hinder her, she crossed the room, walking very uncertainly, threw it back, and bent out, careless of the frosty air that cut about her shoulders as keen as a knife. I entreated, and finally attempted to force her to retire. But I soon found her delirious strength much surpassed mine (she was delirious, I became convinced by her subsequent actions and ravings). There was no moon, and everything beneath lay in misty darkness. Not a light gleamed from any house, far or near — all had been extinguished long ago; and those at Wuthering Heights were never visible — still she asserted she caught their shining.

"Look!" she cried eagerly; "that's my room with the candle in it, and the tree swaying before it; and the other candle is in Joseph's garret. Joseph sits up late, doesn't he? He's waiting till I come home, that he may lock the gate. Well, he'll wait a while yet. It's a rough journey, and a sad heart to travel it; and we must pass by Gimmerton Kirk to go that journey! We've braved its ghosts often together, and dared each other to stand among the graves and ask them to come. But, Heathcliff, if I dare you now, will you venture? If you do, I'll keep you. I'll not lie there by myself. They may bury me twelve feet deep, and throw the church down over me, but I won't rest till you are with me. I never will!"

She paused, and resumed with a strange smile. "He's considering; he'd rather I'd come to him! Find a way, then —

not through that kirkyard. You are slow! Be content; you always followed me!"

Perceiving it vain to argue against her insanity, I was planning how I could reach something to wrap about her, without quitting my hold of herself (for I could not trust her alone by the gaping lattice), when, to my consternation, I heard the rattle of the door-handle, and Mr. Linton entered. He had only then come from the library, and in passing through the lobby had noticed our talking, and been attracted by curiosity, or fear, to examine what it signified, at that late hour.

"O sir!" I cried, checking the exclamation risen to his lips at the sight which met him, and the bleak atmosphere of the chamber, "my poor mistress is ill, and she quite masters me. I cannot manage her at all. Pray, come and persuade her to go to bed. Forget your anger, for she's hard to guide any way but her own."

"Catherine ill?" he said, hastening to us. "Shut the window, Ellen! — Catherine! why — — "

He was silent. The haggardness of Mrs. Linton's appearance smote him speechless, and he could only glance from her to me in horrified astonishment.

"She's been fretting here," I continued, "and eating scarcely anything, and never complaining. She would admit none of us till this evening, and so we couldn't inform you of her state, as we were not aware of it ourselves; but it is nothing."

I felt I uttered my explanations awkwardly. The master frowned. "It is nothing, is it, Ellen Dean?" he said sternly. "You shall account more clearly for keeping me ignorant of this!" And he took his wife in his arms, and looked at her with anguish.

At first she gave him no glance of recognition; he was invisible to her abstracted gaze. The delirium was not fixed, however; having weaned her eyes from contemplating the outer darkness, by degrees she centred her attention on him, and discovered who it was that held her.

"Ah! you are come, are you, Edgar Linton?" she said, with angry animation. "You are one of those things that are ever found when least wanted, and when you are wanted, never! I suppose we shall have plenty of lamentations now — I see we shall; but they can't keep me from my narrow home out yonder — my resting-place, where I'm bound before spring is over! There it is — not among the Lintons, mind, under the chapel-roof, but in the open air, with a head-stone; and you may please yourself whether you go to them or come to me!"

"Catherine, what have you done?" commenced the master. "Am I nothing to you any more? Do you love that wretch Heath — — "

"Hush!" cried Mrs. Linton — "hush, this moment! You mention that name, and I end the matter instantly by a spring from the window! What you touch at present you may have; but my soul will be on that hill-top before you lay hands on me again. I don't want you, Edgar. I'm past wanting you. Return to your books. I'm glad you possess a consolation, for all you had in me is gone."

"Her mind wanders, sir," I interposed — "she has been talking nonsense the whole evening; but let her have quiet and proper attendance, and she'll rally. Hereafter we must be cautious how we vex her."

"I desire no further advice from you," answered Mr. Linton. "You knew your mistress's nature, and you encouraged me to harass her. And not to give me one hint of how she has been these three days! It was heartless! Months of sickness could not cause such a change!"

I began to defend myself, thinking it too bad to be blamed for another's wicked waywardness. "I knew Mrs. Linton's nature to be headstrong and domineering," cried I, "but I didn't know that you wished to foster her fierce temper. I didn't know that, to humour her, I should wink at Mr. Heathcliff. I performed the duty of a faithful servant in telling you, and I have got a faithful servant's wages! Well, it will teach me to be careful next time. Next time you may gather intelligence for yourself."

"The next time you bring a tale to me you shall quit my service, Ellen Dean," he replied.

"You'd rather hear nothing about it, I suppose, then, Mr.

Linton?" said I. "Heathcliff has your permission to come a-courting to miss, and to drop in at every opportunity your absence offers, on purpose to poison the mistress against you?"

Confused as Catherine was, her wits were alert at applying our conversation.

"Ah! Nelly has played traitor!" she exclaimed passionately — "Nelly is my hidden enemy! You witch! So you do seek elf-bolts to hurt us! Let me go, and I'll make her rue! I'll make her howl a recantation!"

A maniac's fury kindled under her brows. She struggled desperately to disengage herself from Linton's arms. I felt no inclination to tarry the event; and resolving to seek medical aid on my own responsibility, I quitted the chamber.

In passing the garden to reach the road, at a place where a bridle hook is driven into the wall, I saw something white moved irregularly, evidently by another agent than the wind. Notwithstanding my hurry, I stayed to examine it, lest ever after I should have the conviction impressed on my imagination that it was a creature of the other world. My surprise and perplexity were great on discovering, by touch more than vision, Miss Isabella's springer, Fanny, suspended by a handkerchief,and nearly at its last gasp. I quicklyreleased the animal, and lifted it into the garden.

I had seen it follow its mistress upstairs when she went to bed, and wondered much how it could have got out there, and what mischievous person had treated it so. While untying the knot round the hook, it seemed to me that I repeatedly caught the beat of horses' feet galloping at some distance; but there were such a number of things to occupy my reflections that I hardly gave the circumstance a thought, though it was a strange sound in that place at two o'clock in the morning.

Mr. Kenneth was fortunately just issuing from his house to see a patient in the village as I came up the street, and my account of Catherine Linton's malady induced him to accompany me back immediately. He was a plain, rough man; and he made no scruple to speak his doubts of her surviving this second attack, unless she were more submissive to his directions than she had shown herself before.

"Nelly Dean," said he, "I can't help fancying there's an extra cause for this. What has there been to do at the Grange? We've odd reports up here. A stout, hearty lass like Catherine does not fall ill for a trifle; and that sort of people should not, either. It's hard work bringing them through fevers and such things. How did it begin?"

"The master will inform you," I answered; "but you are acquainted with the Earnshaws' violent dispositions, and Mrs. Linton caps them all. I may say this; it commenced in a quarrel. She was struck during a tempest of passion with a kind of fit. That's her account, at least, for she flew off in the height of it, and locked herself up. Afterwards she refused to eat, and now she alternately raves and remains in a half dream, knowing those about her, but having her mind filled with all sorts of strange ideas and illusions."

"Mr. Linton will be sorry?" observed Kenneth interrogatively.

"Sorry? He'll break his heart should anything happen!" I replied. "Don't alarm him more than necessary."

"Well, I told him to beware," said my companion; "and he must bide the consequences of neglecting my warning. Hasn't he been intimate with Mr. Heathcliff lately?"

"Heathcliff frequently visits at the Grange," answered I, "though more on the strength of the mistress having known him when a boy than because the master likes his company. At present he's discharged from the trouble of calling, owing to some presumptuous aspirations after Miss Linton which he manifested. I hardly think he'll be taken in again."

"And does Miss Linton turn a cold shoulder on him?" was the doctor's next question.

"I'm not in her confidence," returned I, reluctant to continue the subject.

"No; she's a sly one," he remarked, shaking his head. "She keeps her own counsel. But she's a real little fool. I have it from good authority that last night (and a pretty night it was) she and Heathcliff were walking in the plantation at the back of your house above two hours; and he pressed her not to go in again, but just mount his horse and away with him. My informant said she could only put him off by pledging her word of honour to be prepared on their first meeting after that. When it was to be, he didn't hear; but you urge Mr. Linton to look sharp."

This news filled me with fresh fears. I outstripped Kenneth, and ran most of the way back. The little dog was yelping in the garden yet. I spared a minute to open the gate for it, but instead of going to the house door, it coursed up and down snuffing the grass, and would have escaped to the road had I not seized and conveyed it in with me. On ascending to Isabella's room my suspicions were confirmed. It was empty. Had I been a few hours sooner, Mrs. Linton's illness might have arrested her rash step. But what could be done now? There was a bare possibility of overtaking them if pursued instantly. I could not pursue them, however; and I dare not rouse the family, and fill the place with confusion — still less unfold the business to my master, absorbed as he was in his present calamity, and having no heart to spare for a second grief. I saw nothing for it but to hold my tongue, and suffer matters to take their course; and Kenneth being arrived, I went with a badly composed countenance to announce him. Catherine lay in a troubled sleep. Her husband had succeeded in soothing the excess of frenzy. He now hung over her pillow, watching every shade and every change of her painfully expressive features.

The doctor, on examining the case for himself, spoke hopefully to him of its having a favourable termination, if we could only preserve around her perfect and constant tranquillity. To me he signified the threatening danger was not so much death, as permanent alienation of intellect.

I did not close my eyes that night, nor did Mr. Linton — indeed, we never went to bed; and the servants were all up long before the usual hour, moving through the house with stealthy tread, and exchanging whispers as they encountered each other in their vocations. Every one was active but Miss Isabella; and they began to remark how sound she slept. Her brother, too, asked if she had risen, and seemed impatient for her presence, and hurt that she showed so little anxiety for her sister-in-law. I trembled lest he should send me to call her; but I was spared the pain of being the first proclaimant of her flight. One of the maids, a thoughtless girl, who had been on an early errand to Gimmerton, came panting upstairs, open mouthed, and dashed into the chamber, crying, —

"Oh dear, dear! What mun we have next? Master, master, our young lady — — "

"Hold your noise!" cried I hastily, enraged at her clamorous manner.

"Speak lower, Mary. What is the matter?" said Mr. Linton. "What ails your young lady?"

"She's gone, she's gone! Yon Heathcliff's run off wi' her!" gasped the girl.

"That is not true!" exclaimed Linton, rising in agitation. "It cannot be. How has the idea entered your head? — Ellen Dean, go and seek her. It is incredible. It cannot be."

As he spoke he took the servant to the door, and then repeated his demand to know her reasons for such an assertion.

"Why, I met on the road a lad that fetches milk here," she stammered, "and he asked whether we weren't in trouble at the Grange. I thought he meant for missis's sickness, so I answered yes. Then says he, 'There's somebody gone after 'em, I guess?' I stared. He saw I knew nought about it, and he told how a gentleman and lady had stopped to have a horse's shoe fastened at a blacksmith's shop, two miles out of Gimmerton, not very long after midnight; and how the blacksmith's lass had got up to spy who they were. She knew them both directly. And she noticed the man — Heathcliff it was, she felt certain; nob'dy could

mistake him, besides — put a sovereign in her father's hand for payment. The lady had a cloak about her face; but having desired a sup of water, while she drank it fell back, and she saw her very plain. Heathcliff held both bridles as they rode on, and they set their faces from the village, and went as fast as the rough roads would let them. The lass said nothing to her father, but she told it all over Gimmerton this morning."

I ran and peeped, for form's sake, into Isabella's room, confirming, when I returned, the servant's statement. Mr.

Linton had resumed his seat by the bed. On my re-entrance he raised his eyes, read the meaning of my blank aspect, and dropped them without giving an order or uttering a word.

"Are we to try any measures for overtaking and bringing her back?" I inquired. "How should we do?"

"She went of her own accord," answered the master; "she had a right to go if she pleased. Trouble me no more about her. Hereafter she is only my sister in name...not because I disown her, but because she has disowned me."

And that was all he said on the subject. He did not make a single inquiry further, or mention her in any way, except directing me to send what property she had in the house to her fresh home, wherever it was, when I knew it.

Chapter

For two months the fugitives remained absent; in those two months, Mrs. Linton encountered and conquered the worst shock of what was denominated a brain fever. No mother could have nursed an only child more devotedly than Edgar tended her. Day and night he was watching, and patiently enduring all the annoyances that irritable nerves and a shaken reason could inflict: and, though Kenneth remarked that what he saved from the grave would only recompense his care by forming the source of constant future anxiety — in fact, that his health and strength were being sacrificed to preserve a mere ruin of humanity — he knew no limits in gratitude and joy, when Catherine's life was declared out of danger; and hour after hour he would sit beside her, tracing the gradual return to bodily health, and flattering his too sanguine hopes with the illusion that her mind would settle back to its right balance also, and she would soon be entirely her former self.

The first time she left her chamber, was at the commencement of the following March. Mr. Linton had put on her pillow, in the morning, a handful of golden crocuses; her eye, long stranger to any gleam of pleasure, caught them in waking, and shone delighted as she gathered them eagerly together.

"These are the earliest flowers at the Heights!" she exclaimed. "They remind me of soft thaw winds, and warm sunshine, and nearly melted snow — Edgar, is there not a south wind, and is not the snow almost gone ?"

"The snow is quite gone down here, darling," replied her husband, "and I only see two white spots on the whole range of moors. The sky is blue, and the larks are singing, and the becks and brooks are all brim full. Catherine, last spring at this time I was longing to have you under this roof; now I wish you were a mile or two up those hills; the air blows so sweetly, I feel that it would cure you."

"I shall never be there but once more," said the invalid; "and then you'll leave me, and I shall remain for ever. Next spring you'll long again to have me under this roof, and you'll look back and think you were happy to-day."

Linton lavished on her the kindest caresses, and tried to cheer her by the fondest words; but, vaguely regarding the flowers, she let the tears collect on her lashes and stream down her cheeks unheeding. We knew she was really better, and therefore decided that long confinement to a single place produced much of this despondency, and it might be partially removed by a change of scene. The master told me to light a fire in the many-weeks-deserted parlour, and to set an easy-chair in the sunshine by the window; and then he brought her down, and she sat a long while enjoying the genial heat, and, as we expected, revived by the objects round her, which, though familiar, were free from the dreary associations investing her hated sick chamber.

By evening she seemed greatly exhausted, yet no arguments could persuade her to return to that apartment; and I had to arrange the parlour sofa for her bed, till another room could be prepared. To obviate the fatigue of mounting and descending the stairs, we fitted up this, where you lie at present, on the same floor with the parlour; and she was soon strong enough to move from one to the other, leaning on Edgar's arm. Ah, I thought myself she might recover, so waited on as she was. And there was double cause to desire it, for on her existence depended that of another; we cherished the hope that in a little while Mr. Linton's heart would be gladdened, and his lands secured from a stranger's gripe, by the birth of an heir.

I should mention that Isabella sent to her brother, some six weeks from her departure, a short note announcing her marriage with Heathcliff. It appeared dry and cold, but at the bottom was dotted in with pencil an obscure apology, and an entreaty for kind remembrance and reconciliation, if her proceeding had offended him, asserting that she could not help it then, and, being done, she had now no power to repeal it.

Linton did not reply to this, I believe; and in a fortnight more I got a long letter which I considered odd, coming from the pen of a bride just out of the honeymoon. I'll read it, for I keep it yet. Any relic of the dead is precious if they were valued living.

DEAR ELLEN, it begins, I came last night to Wuthering Heights, and heard for the first time that Catherine has been, and is yet, very ill. I must not write to her, I suppose, and my brother is either too angry or too distressed to answer what I sent him. Still, I must write to somebody, and the only choice left me is you.

Inform Edgar that I'd give the world to see his face again — that my heart returned to Thrushcross Grange in twenty-four hours after I left it, and is there at this moment, full of warm feelings for him and Catherine. I can't follow it, though (those words are underlined); they need not expect me; and they may draw what conclusions they please, taking care, however, to lay nothing at the door of my weak will or deficient affection.

The remainder of the letter is for yourself alone. I want to ask you two questions; the first is — How did you contrive to preserve the common sympathies of human nature when you resided here? I cannot recognize any sentiment which those around share with me.

The second question I have great interest in; it is this — - Is Mr. Heathcliff a man? If so, is he mad? And if not, is he a devil? I shan't tell my reasons for making this inquiry, but I beseech you to explain, if you can, what I have married — that is, when you call to see me; and you must call, Ellen, very soon. Don't write, but come, and bring me something from Edgar.

Now you shall hear how I have been received in my new home, as I am led to imagine the Heights will be. It is to amuse myself that I dwell on such subjects as the lack of external comforts; they never occupy my thoughts, except at the moment when I miss them. I should laugh and dance for joy if I found their absence was the total of my miseries, and the rest was an unnatural dream.

The sun set behind the Grange as we turned on to the moors: by that I judged it to be six o'clock; and my companion halted half an hour to inspect the park and the gardens, and probably the place itself, as well as he could; so it was dark when we dismounted in the paved yard of the farmhouse, and your old fellow-servant Joseph issued out to receive us by the light of a dip candle. He did it with a courtesy that redounded to his credit. His first act was to elevate his torch to a level with my face, squint malignantly, project his under lip, and turn away. Then he took the two horses and led them into the stables, reappearing for the purpose of locking the outer gate, as if we lived in an ancient castle.

Heathcliff stayed to speak to him, and I entered the kitchen — a dingy, untidy hole. I dare say you would not know it, it is so changed since it was in your charge. By the fire stood a ruffianly child, strong in limb and dirty in garb, with a look of Catherine in his eyes and about his mouth.

"This is Edgar's legal nephew," I reflected — "mine in a manner. I must shake hands, and — yes — I must kiss him. It is right to establish a good understanding at the beginning."

I approached, and attempting to take his chubby fist, said, "How do you do, my dear?"

He replied in a jargon I did not comprehend.

"Shall you and I be friends, Hareton?" was my next essay at conversation. An oath, and a threat to set Throttler on me if I did not "frame off," rewarded my perseverance.

"Hey, Throttler, lad!" whispered the little wretch, rousing a half-bred bull-dog from its lair in a corner. "Now, wilt thou be ganging?" he asked authoritatively.

Love for my life urged a compliance. I stepped over the threshold to wait till the others should enter. Mr. Heathcliff was nowhere visible, and Joseph, whom I followed to the stables and requested to accompany me in, after staring and muttering to himself, screwed up his nose and replied, —

"Mim! mim! mim! Did iver Christian body hear aught like it? Minching un munching! How can I tell whet ye say?"

"I say I wish you to come with me into the house!" I cried, thinking him deaf, yet highly disgusted at his rudeness.

"Nor nuh me. I getten summut else to do," he answered, and continued his work, moving his lantern jaws meanwhile, and surveying my dress and countenance (the former a great deal too fine, but the latter, I'm sure, as sad as he could desire) with sovereign contempt.

I walked round the yard and through a wicket to another door, at which I took the liberty of knocking, in hopes some more civil servant might show himself. After a short suspense it was opened by a tall, gaunt man, without neckerchief, and otherwise extremely slovenly; his features were lost in masses of shaggy hair that hung on his shoulders, and his eyes, too, were like a ghostly Catherine's with all their beauty annihilated. "What's your business here?" he demanded grimly. "Who are you?"

"My name was Isabella Linton," I replied. "You've seen me before, sir. I'm lately married to Mr. Heathcliff, and he has brought me here — I suppose by your permission."

"Is he come back, then?" asked the hermit, glaring like a hungry wolf,

"Yes, we came just now," I said; "but he left me by the kitchen door, and when I would have gone in your little boy played sentinel over the place, and frightened me off by the help of a bull-dog."

"It's well the hellish villain has kept his word!" growled my future host, searching the darkness beyond me in expectation of discovering Heathcliff; and then he indulged in a soliloquy of execrations, and threats of what he would have done had the "fiend" deceived him.

I repented having tried this second entrance, and was

almost inclined to slip away before he finished cursing; but ere I could execute that intention he ordered me in, and shut and refastened the door. There was a great fire, and that was all the light in the huge apartment, whose floor had grown a uniform gray, and the once brilliant pewter dishes, which used to attract my gaze when I was a girl, partook of a similar obscurity, created by tarnish and dust. I inquired whether I might call the maid, and be conducted to a bedroom. Mr. Earnshaw vouchsafed no answer. He walked up and down, with his hands in his pockets, apparently quite forgetting my presence; and his abstraction was evidently so deep, and his whole aspect so misanthropical, that I shrank from disturbing him again.

You'll not be surprised, Ellen, at my feeling particularly cheerless, seated in worse than solitude on that inhospitable hearth, and remembering that four miles distant lay my delightful home, containing the only people I loved on earth; and there might as well be the Atlantic to part us, instead of those four miles. I could not overpass them. I questioned with myself — Where must I turn for comfort? and (mind you don't tell Edgar or Catherine) above every sorrow beside, this rose pre-eminent — despair at finding nobody who could or would be my ally against Heathcliff. I had sought shelter at Wuthering Heights almost gladly, because I was secured by that arrangement from living alone with him; but he knew the people we were coming amongst, and he did not fear their intermeddling.

I sat and thought a doleful time. The clock struck eight, and nine, and still my companion paced to and fro, his head bent on his breast, and perfectly silent, unless a groan or a bitter ejaculation forced itself out at intervals. I listened to detect a woman's voice in the house, and filled the interim with wild regrets and dismal anticipations, which at last spoke audibly in irrepressible sighing and weeping. I was not aware how openly I grieved, till Earnshaw halted opposite, in his measured walk, and gave me a stare of newly-awakened surprise. Taking advantage of his recovered attention, I exclaimed, —

"I'm tired with my journey, and I want to go to bed! Where is the maidservant? Direct me to her, as she won't come to me." "We have none," he answered. "You must wait on yourself." "Where must I sleep, then?" I sobbed. I was beyond regarding self-respect, weighed down by fatigue and wretchedness. "Joseph will show you Heathcliff's chamber," said he. "Open that door; he's in there."

I was going to obey, but he suddenly arrested me, and added in the strangest tone, — "Be so good as to turn your lock and draw your bolt; don't omit it!" "Well!" I said; "but why, Mr. Earnshaw?" I did not relish the notion of deliberately fastening myself in with Heathcliff. "Look here!" he replied, pulling from his waistcoat a curiously constructed pistol, having a double-edged spring knife attached to the barrel. "That's a great tempter to a desperate man, is it not? I cannot resist going up with this every night and trying his door. If once I find it open, he's done for! I do it invariably, even though the minute before I have been recalling a hundred reasons that should make me refrain. It is some devil that urges me to thwart my own schemes by killing him. You fight against that devil for love as long as you may; when the time comes, not all the angels in heaven shall save him!"

I surveyed the weapon inquisitively. A hideous notion struck me. How powerful I should be, possessing such an instrument! I took it from his hand and touched the blade. He looked astonished at the expression my face assumed during a brief second; it was not horror — it was covetousness. He snatched the pistol back jealously, shut the knife, and returned it to its concealment.

"I don't care if you tell him," said he. "Put him on his guard, and watch for him. You know the terms we are on, I see. His danger does not shock you."

"What has Heathcliff done to you?" I asked. "In what has he wronged you, to warrant this appalling hatred? Wouldn't it be wiser to bid him quit the house?"

"No!" thundered Earnshaw. "Should he offer to leave me, he's a dead man. Persuade him to attempt it, and you are a murderess. Am I to lose all without a chance of retrieval? Is

Hareton to be a beggar? Oh, damnation! I will have it back, and I'll have his gold too, and then his blood, and hell shall have his soul! It will be ten times blacker with that guest than ever it was before!"

You've acquainted me, Ellen, with your old master's habits. He is clearly on the verge of madness. He was so last night at least. I shuddered to be near him, and thought on the servant's ill-bred moroseness as comparatively agreeable. He now recommenced his moody walk, and I raised the latch and escaped into the kitchen. Joseph was bending over the fire, peering into a large pan that swung above it, and a wooden bowl of oatmeal stood on the settle close by. The contents of the pan began to boil, and he turned to plunge his hand into the bowl. I conjectured that this preparation was probably for our supper, and being hungry, I resolved it should be eatable; so, crying out sharply, "I'll make the porridge!" I removed the vessel out of his reach, and proceeded to take off my hat and riding-habit.

"Mr. Earnshaw," I continued, "directs me to wait on myself. I will. I'm not going to act the lady among you, for fear I should starve."

"Gooid Lord!" he muttered, sitting down and stroking his ribbed stockings from the knee to the ankle. "If there's to be fresh ortherings, just when I getten used to two maisters, if I mun hev a mistress set o'er my heead, it's like time to be flitting. I niver did think to see t' day that I mud lave th' owld place, but I doubt it's nigh at hand!"

This lamentation drew no notice from me. I went briskly to work, sighing to remember a period when it would have been all merry fun, but compelled speedily to drive off the remembrance. It racked me to recall past happiness and the greater peril there was of conjuring up its apparition, the quicker the thible ran round, and the faster the handfuls of meal fell into the water. Joseph beheld my style of cookery with growing indignation.

"Thear!" he ejaculated. "Hareton, thou willn't sup thy porridge to-neeght; they'll be naught but lumps as big as my neive. Thear, agean! I'd fling in bowl un all, if I wer ye! There, pale t' guilp off, un then ye'll hae done wi't. Bang, bang. It's a mercy t' bothom isn't deaved out!" It was rather a rough mess, I own, when poured into the basins. Four had been provided, and a gallon pitcher of new milk was brought from the dairy, which Hareton seized and commenced drinking and spilling from the expansive lip. I expostulated, and desired that he should have his in a mug, affirming that I could not taste the liquid treated so dirtily. The old cynic chose to be vastly offended at this nicety, assuring me repeatedly that "the barn was every bit as good" as I, "and every bit as wollsome," and wondering how I could fashion to be so conceited. Meanwhile the infant ruffian continued sucking, and glowered up at me defyingly as he slavered into the jug.

"I shall have my supper in another room," I said. "Have you no place you call a parlour?"

"Parlour!" he echoed sneeringly — "parlour! Nay, we've noa parlours. If yah dunnut loike wer company, there's maister's; un if yah dunnut loike maister, there's us."

"Then I shall go upstairs," I answered. "Show me a chamber."

I put my basin on a tray, and went myself to fetch some more milk. With great grumblings the fellow rose and preceded me in my ascent. We mounted to the garrets. He opened a door now and then to look into the apartments we passed.

"Here's a rahm," he said at last, flinging back a cranky board on hinges. "It's weel eneugh to ate a few porridge in. There's a pack o' corn i' t' corner, thear, meeterly clane. If ye're feared o' muckying yer grand silk cloes, spread yer hankerchir o' to' top on't."

The "rahm" was a kind of lumber-hole smelling strong of malt

and grain, various sacks of which articles were piled around, leaving a wide, bare space in the middle.

"Why, man!" I exclaimed, facing him angrily, "this is not a place to sleep in. I wish to see my bedroom."

"Bedrume!" he repeated, in a tone of mockery. "Yah's see all t'bedrumes thear is. Yon's mine."

He pointed into the second garret, only differing from the first in being more naked about the walls, and having a large, low, curtainless bed with an indigo-coloured quilt at one end.

"What do I want with yours?" I retorted. "I suppose Mr. Heathcliff does not lodge at the top of the house, does he?"

"Oh, it's Maister Hathecliff's ye're wanting?" cried he, as if making a new discovery. "Couldn't ye ha' said soa, at onst? Un then I mud ha' telled ye, baht all this wark, that that's just one ye cannut see. He allas keeps it locked, un nob'dy iver mells on't but hisseln."

"You've a nice house, Joseph," I could not refrain from observing, "and pleasant inmates; and I think the concentrated essence of all the madness in the world took up its abode in my brain the day I linked my fate with theirs! However, that is not to the present purpose. There are other rooms. For Heaven's sake be quick, and let me settle somewhere!"

He made no reply to this adjuration, only plodding doggedly down the wooden steps, and halting before an apartment which, from that halt and the superior quality of its furniture, I conjectured to be the best one. There was a carpet — a good one — but the pattern was obliterated by dust; a fireplace hung with cut paper, dropping to pieces; a handsome oak bedstead with ample crimson curtains of rather expensive material and modern make, but they had evidently experienced rough usage — the valances hung in festoons, wrenched from their rings, and the iron rod supporting them was bent in an arc on one side, causing the drapery to trail upon the floor. The chairs were also damaged, many of them severely, and deep indentations deformed the panels of the walls. I was endeavouring to gather resolution for entering and taking possession, when my fool of a guide announced, "This here is t' maister's." My supper by this time was cold, my appetite gone, and my patience exhausted. I insisted on being provided instantly with a place of refuge and means of repose. "Whear the divil?" began the religious elder. "The Lord bless us! The Lord forgie us! Whear the hell wold ye gang, ye marred, wearisome nowt? Ye've seen all but Hareton's bit of a cham'er. There's not another hoile to lig down in i' th' hahse!"

I was so vexed, I flung my tray and its contents on the ground, and then seated myself at the stairs-head, hid my face in my hands, and cried.

"Ech! ech!" exclaimed Joseph. "Weel done, Miss Cathy! weel done, Miss Cathy! Hahsiver, t' maister sall just tum'le o'er them brocken pots, un then we's hear summut — we's hear how it's to be. Gooid-for-naught madling! ye desarve pining fro' this to Churstmas, flinging t' precious gifts o' God under fooit i' yer flaysome rages! But I'm mista'eif ye show yer sperrit lang. Will Hathecliff bide sich bonny ways, think ye? I nobbut wish he may catch ye i' that plisky. I nobbut wish he may."

And so he went on scolding to his den beneath, taking the candle with him, and I remained in the dark. The period of reflection succeeding this silly action compelled me to admit the necessity of smothering my pride and choking my wrath, and bestirring myself to remove its effects. An unexpected aid presently appeared in the shape of Throttler, whom I now recognized as a son of our old Skulker. It had spent its whelphood at the Grange, and was given by my father to Mr. Hindley. I fancy it knew me.

It pushed its nose against mine by way of salute, and then hastened to devour the porridge, while I groped from step to step, collecting the shattered earthenware, and drying the spatters of milk from the banister with my pocket-handkerchief. Our labours were scarcely over when I heard Earnshaw's tread in the passage. My assistant tucked in his tail and pressed to the wall. I stole into the nearest doorway. The dog's endeavour to avoid him was unsuccessful, as I guessed by a scutter downstairs, and a prolonged, piteous yelping. I had better luck. He passed on, entered his chamber, and shut the door. Directly after, Joseph came up with Hareton, to put him to bed. I had found shelter in Hareton's room, and the old man, on seeing me, said, —

"They's rahm for boath ye un yer pride now, I sud think, i' the hahse. It's empty; ye may hev it all to yer-seln, un Him as allas maks a third i' sich ill company!"

Gladly did I take advantage of this intimation, and the

minute I flung myself into a chair by the fire I nodded and slept. My slumber was deep and sweet, though over far too soon. Mr. Heathcliff awoke me. He had just come in, and demanded, in his loving manner, what I was doing there. I told him the cause of my staying up so late — that he had the key of our room in his pocket. The adjective our gave mortal offence. He swore it was not, nor ever should be mine, and he'd — — But I'll not repeat his language, nor describe his habitual conduct. He is ingenious and unresting in seeking to gain my abhorrence. I sometimes wonder at him with an intensity that deadens my fear; yet I assure you a tiger or a venomous serpent could not rouse terror in me equal to that which he wakens. He told me of Catherine's illness, and accused my brother of causing it, promising that I should be Edgar's proxy in suffering till he could get hold of him.

I do hate him — I am wretched — I have been a fool Beware of uttering one breath of this to any one at the Grange. I shall expect you every day. Don't disappoint me.

ISABELLA.

Chapter

As soon as I had perused this epistle, I went to the master, and informed him that his sister had arrived at the Heights, and sent me a letter expressing her sorrow for Mrs. Linton's situation, and her ardent desire to see him; with a wish that he would transmit to her, as early as possible, some token of forgiveness by me.

"Forgiveness?" said Linton. "I have nothing to forgive her, Ellen — you may call at Wuthering Heights this afternoon, if you like, and say that I am not angry, but I'm sorry to have lost her: especially as I can never think she'll be happy. It is out of the question my going to see her, however; we are eternally divided; and should she really wish to oblige me, let her persuade the villain she has married to leave the country."

"And you won't write her a little note, sir ?" I asked, imploringly.

"No," he answered. "It is needless. My communication with Heathcliff's family shall be as sparing as his with mine.

It shall not exist!" Mr. Edgar's coldness depressed me exceedingly; and all the way from the Grange I puzzled my brains how to put more heart into what he said, when I repeated it; and how to soften his refusal of even a few lines to console Isabella.

I dare say she had been on the watch for me since morning: I saw her looking through the lattice, as I came up the garden causeway, and I nodded to her; but she drew back as if afraid of being observed.

I entered without knocking. There never was such a dreary, dismal scene as the formerly cheerful house presented. I must confess that if I had been in the young lady's place I would, at least, have swept the hearth and wiped the tables with a duster. But she already partook of the pervading spirit of neglect which encompassed her. Her pretty face was wan and listless, her hair uncurled — some locks hanging lankly down, and some carelessly twisted round her head. Probably she had not touched her dress since yester evening. Hindley was not there. Mr. Heathcliff sat at a table, turning over some papers in his pocket-book; but he rose when I appeared, asked me how I did, quite friendly, and offered me a chair. He was the only thing there that seemed decent, and I thought he never looked better. So much had circumstances altered their positions that he would certainly have struck a stranger as a born and bred gentleman, and his wife as a thorough little slattern! She came forward eagerly to greet me, and held out one hand to take the expected letter. I shook my head. She wouldn't understand the hint, but followed me to a sideboard where I went to lay my bonnet, and importuned me in a whisper to give her directly what I had brought. Heathcliff guessed the meaning of her manoeuvres, and said, —

"If you have got anything for Isabella — as no doubt you have, Nelly — give it to her. You needn't make a secret of it. We have no secrets between us."

"Oh, I have nothing," I replied, thinking it best to speak the truth at once. "My master bade me tell his sister that she must not expect either a letter or a visit from him at present. He sends his love, ma'am, and his wishes for your happiness, and his pardon for the grief you have occasioned; but he thinks that after this time his household and the household here should drop intercommunication, as nothing could come of keeping it up."

Mrs. Heathcliff's lip quivered slightly, and she returned to her seat in the window. Her husband took his stand on the hearthstone near me, and began to put questions concerning Catherine. I told him as much as I thought proper of her illness, and he extorted from me, by cross-examination, most of the facts connected with its origin. I blamed her, as she deserved, for bringing it all on herself, and ended by hoping that he would follow Mr. Linton's example, and avoid future interference with his family, for good or evil.

"Mrs. Linton is now just recovering," I said. "She'll never be like she was, but her life is spared; and if you really have a regard for her, you'll shun crossing her way again — nay, you'll move out of this country entirely; and that you may not regret it, I'll inform you Catherine Linton is as different now from your old friend Catherine Earnshaw as that young lady is different from me. Her appearance is changed greatly, her character much more so; and the person who is compelled, of necessity, to be her companion will only sustain his affection hereafter by the remembrance of what she once was, by common humanity, and a sense of duty."

"That is quite possible," remarked Heathcliff, forcing himself to seem calm — "quite possible that your master should have nothing but common humanity and a sense of duty to fall back upon. But do you imagine that I shall leave Catherine to his duty and humanity? and can you compare my feelings respecting Catherine to his? Before you leave this house, I must exact a promise from you that you'll get me an interview with her. Consent or refuse, I will see her! What do you say?"

"I say, Mr. Heathcliff," I replied, "you must not. You never shall, through my means. Another encounter between you and the master would kill her altogether."

"With your aid that may be avoided," he continued; "and should there be danger of such an event — should he be the cause of adding a single trouble more to her existence — why, I think I shall be justified in going to extremes. I wish you had sincerity enough to tell me whether Catherine would suffer greatly from his loss; the fear that she would restrains me. And there you see the distinction between our feelings: had he been in my place, and I in his, though I hated him with a hatred that turned my life to gall, I never would have raised a hand against him. You may look incredulous if you please. I never would have banished him from her society as long as she desired his. The moment her regard ceased, I would have torn his heart out and drunk his blood! But till then — if you don't believe me you don't know me — till then I would have died by inches before I touched a single hair of his head!"

"And yet," I interrupted, "you have no scruples in completely ruining all hopes of her perfect restoration by thrusting yourself into her remembrance now, when she has nearly forgotten you, and involving her in a new tumult of discord and distress."

"You suppose she has nearly forgotten me?" he said. "O Nelly, you know she has not! You know as well as I do that for every thought she spends on Linton, she spends a thousand on me! At a most miserable period of my life I had a notion of the kind. It haunted me on my return to the neighbourhood last summer; but only her own assurance could make me admit the horrible idea again. And then Linton would be nothing, nor Hindley, nor all the dreams that ever I dreamt. Two words would comprehend my future — death and hell; existence, after losing her, would be hell. Yet I was a fool to fancy for a moment that she valued Edgar Linton's attachment more than mine. If he loved with all the powers of his puny being, he couldn't love as much in eighty years as I could in a day. And Catherine has a heart as deep as I have; the sea could be as readily contained in that horse-trough as her whole affection be monopolized by him! Tush! He is scarcely a degree dearer to her than her dog or her horse. It is not in him to be loved like me. How can she love in him what he has not?"

"Catherine and Edgar are as fond of each other as any two people can be," cried Isabella with sudden vivacity. "No one has a right to talk in that manner, and I won't hear my brother depreciated in silence!" "Your brother is wondrous fond of you too, isn't he?" observed Heathcliff scornfully. "He turns you adrift on the world with surprising alacrity." "He is not aware of what I suffer," she replied. "I didn't tell him that." "You have been telling him something, then. You have written, have you?"

"To say that I was married, I did write; you saw the note."

"And nothing since?"

"No."

"My young lady is looking sadly the worse for her change of condition," I remarked. "Somebody's love comes short in her case obviously. Whose, I may guess, but perhaps I shouldn't say."

"I should guess it was her own," said Heathcliff. She degenerates into a mere slut. She is tired of trying to please me uncommonly early. You'd hardly credit it, but the very morrow of our wedding she was weeping to go home. However, she'll suit this house so much the better for not being overnice, and I'll take care she does not disgrace me by rambling abroad."

"Well, sir," returned I, "I hope you'll consider that Mrs. Heathcliff is accustomed to be looked after and waited on, and that she has been brought up like an only daughter, whom every one was ready to serve. You must let her have a maid to keep things tidy about her, and you must treat her kindly. Whatever be your notion of Mr. Edgar, you cannot doubt that she has a capacity for strong attachments, or she wouldn't have abandoned the elegances, and comforts, and friends of her former home to fix contentedly in such a wilderness as this with you."

"She abandoned them under a delusion," he answered, "picturing in me a hero of romance, and expecting unlimited indulgences from my chivalrous devotion. I can hardly regard her in the light of a rational creature, so obstinately has she persisted in forming a fabulous notion of my character, and acting on the false impressions she cherished. But at last I think she begins to know me. I don't perceive the silly smiles and grimaces that provoked me at first, and the senseless incapability of discerning that I was in earnest when I gave her my opinion of her infatuation and herself.

It was a marvellous effort of perspicacity to discover that I did not love her. I believed, at one time, no lessons could teach her that. And yet it is poorly learned, for this morning she announced, as a piece of appalling intelligence, that I had actually succeeded in making her hate me – a positive labour of Hercules, I assure you! If it be achieved, I have cause to return thanks. – Can I trust your assertion, Isabella? Are you sure you hate me? If I let you alone for half a day, won't you come sighing and wheedling to me again? – I dare say she would rather I had seemed all tenderness before you; it wounds her vanity to have the truth exposed.

But I don't care who knows that the passion was wholly on one side; and I never told her a lie about it. She cannot accuse me of showing one bit of deceitful softness. The first thing she saw me do on coming out of the Grange was to hang up her little dog, and when she pleaded for it, the first words I uttered were a wish that I had the hanging of every being belonging to her, except one. Possibly she took that exception for herself. But no brutality disgusted her. I suppose she has an innate admiration of it, if only her precious person were secure from injury.

Now, was it not the depth of absurdity, of genuine idiocy, for that pitiful, slavish, mean-minded brach to dream that I could love her? Tell your master, Nelly, that I never, in all my life, met with such an abject thing as she is. She even disgraces the name of Linton; and I've sometimes relented, from pure lack of invention, in my experiments on what she could endure and still creep shamefully cringing back.

But tell him also to set his fraternal and magisterial heart at ease; that I keep strictly within the limits of the law. I have avoided, up to this period, giving her the slightest right to claim a separation; and, what's more, she'd thank nobody for dividing us. If she desired to go, she might; the nuisance of her presence outweighs the gratification to be derived from tormenting her." "Mr. Heathcliff," said I, "this is the talk of a madman. Your wife, most likely, is convinced you are mad, and for that reason she has borne with you hitherto; but now that you say she may go, she'll doubtless avail herself of the permission. — You are not so bewitched, ma'am, are you, as to remain with him of your own accord?"

"Take care, Ellen!" answered Isabella, her eyes sparkling irefully. There was no misdoubting, by their expression, the full success of her partner's endeavours to make himself detested. "Don't put faith in a single word he speaks. He's a lying fiend — a monster, and not a human being! I've been told I might leave him before, and I've made the attempt, but I dare not repeat it. Only, Ellen, promise you'll not mention a syllable of his infamous conversation to my brother or Catherine. Whatever he may pretend, he wishes to provoke Edgar to desperation. He says he has married me on purpose to obtain power over him; and he shan't obtain it. I'll die first! I just hope — I pray — that he may forget his diabolical prudence and kill me! The single pleasure I can imagine is to die or to see him dead!"

"There — that will do for the present!" said Heathcliff. — -"If you are called upon in a court of law you'll remember her language, Nelly. And take a good look at that countenance; she's near the point which would suit me — No; you're not fit to be your own guardian, Isabella, now; and I, being your legal protector, must retain you in my custody, however distasteful the obligation may be. Go upstairs; I have something to say to Ellen Dean in private. That's not the way. Upstairs, I tell you! Why, this is the road upstairs, child." He seized and thrust her from the room, and returned muttering, —

"I have no pity! I have no pity! The more the worms writhe, the more I yearn to crush out their entrails! It is a moral teething; and I grind with greater energy in proportion to the increase of pain." "Do you understand what the word pity means?" I said, hastening to resume my bonnet. "Did you ever feel a touch of it in your life?" "Put that down!" he interrupted, perceiving my intention to depart. "You are not going yet. Come here now, Nelly. I must either persuade or compel you to aid me in fulfilling my determination to see Catherine, and that without delay. I swear that I meditate no harm. I don't desire to cause any disturbance, or to exasperate or insult Mr. Linton. I only wish to hear from herself how she is, and why she has been ill, and to ask if anything that I could do would be of use to her. Last night I was in the

Grange garden six hours, and I'll return there to-night; and every night I'll haunt the place, and every day, till I find an opportunity of entering. If Edgar Linton meets me I shall not hesitate to knock him down, and give him enough to assure his quiescence while I stay. If his servants oppose me I shall threaten them off with these pistols. But wouldn't it be better to prevent my coming in contact with them or their master? And you could do it so easily. I'd warn you when I came, and then you might let me in unobserved, as soon as she was alone, and watch till I departed, your conscience quite calm. You would be hindering mischief."

I protested against playing that treacherous part in my employer's house, and, besides, I urged the cruelty and selfishness of his destroying Mrs. Linton's tranquillity for his satisfaction. "The commonest occurrence startles her painfully," I said. "She's all nerves, and she couldn't bear the surprise, I'm positive. Don't persist, sir, or else I shall be obliged to inform my master of your designs, and he'll take measures to secure his house and its inmates from any such unwarrantable intrusions!"

"In that case, I'll take measures to secure you, woman," exclaimed Heathcliff. "You shall not leave Wuthering Heights till to-morrow morning. It is a foolish story to assert that Catherine could not bear to see me; and as to surprising her, I don't desire it. You must prepare her; ask her if I may come. You say she never mentions my name, and that I am never mentioned to her.

To whom should she mention me if I am a forbidden topic in the house? She thinks you are all spies for her husband. Oh, I've no doubt she's in hell among you! I guess by her silence, as much as anything, what she feels. You say she is often restless and anxious-looking. Is that a proof of tranquillity? You talk of her mind being unsettled. How the devil could it be otherwise in her frightful isolation? And that insipid, paltry creature attending her former duty and humanity, from pity and charity! He might as well plant an oak in a flower-pot, and expect it to thrive, as imagine he can restore her to vigour in the soil of his shallow cares! Let us settle it at once. Will you stay here, and am I to fight my way to Catherine over Linton and his footman? or will you be my friend, as you have been hitherto, and do what I request? Decide, because there is no reason for my lingering another minute if you persist in your stubborn ill-nature."

Well, Mr. Lockwood, I argued and complained, and flatly refused him fifty times; but in the long run he forced me to an agreement. I engaged to carry a letter from him to my mistress; and should she consent, I promised to let him have intelligence of Linton's next absence from home, when he might come, and get in as he was able. I wouldn't be there, and my fellow-servants should be equally out of the way. Was it right or wrong? I fear it was wrong, though expedient. I thought I prevented another explosion by my compliance, and I thought, too, it might create a favourable crisis in Catherine's mental illness. And then I remembered Mr. Edgar's stern rebuke of my carrying tales, and I tried to smooth away all disquietude on the subject by affirming, with frequent iteration, that that betrayal of trust, if it merited so harsh an appellation, should be the last. Notwithstanding, my journey homeward was sadder than my journey thither, and many misgivings I had ere I could prevail on myself to put the missive into Mrs. Linton's hand.

But here is Kenneth. I'll go down and tell him how much better you are. My history is dree, as we say, and will serve to while away another morning. Dree and dreary, I reflected, as the good woman descended to receive the doctor, and not exactly of the kind which I should have chosen to amuse me. But never mind. I'll extract wholesome medicines from Mrs. Dean's bitter herbs; and firstly, let me beware the fascination that lurks in Catherine Heathcliff's brilliant eyes. I should be in a curious taking if I surrendered my heart to that young person, and the daughter turned out a second edition of the mother!

Chapter 7

Summary and Analysis

Chapter 1, Summary

In Chapter 1 the narrator, Mr. Lockwood, relates how he has just returned from a visit to his new landlord, Mr. Heathcliff. Lockwood, a self-described misanthropist, is renting Thrushcross Grange in an effort to get away from society following a failure at love. He had fallen in love with a "real goddess," but when she returned his affection he acted so coldly she "persuaded her mamma to decamp." He finds that relative to Heathcliff, however, he is extremely sociable. Heathcliff, "a dark skinned gypsy, in aspect, in dress, and manners a gentleman" treats his visitor with a minimum of friendliness, and the farm, Wuthering Heights, where he lives, is just as foreign and unfriendly.

"Wuthering" means stormy and windy in the local dialect. Dangerous-looking dogs inhabit the bare and old-fashioned rooms, and threaten to attack Lockwood: when he calls for help Heathcliff implies that Lockwood had tried to steal something. The only other inhabitants of Wuthering Heights are an old servant named Joseph and a cook. Despite his rudeness, Lockwood finds himself drawn to Heathcliff: he describes him as being intelligent, proud and morose, an unlikely farmer, and declares his intention to visit Wuthering Heights again. The visit is set in 1801.

Analysis:

This chapter introduces the reader to the frame of the story: Lockwood will gradually discover the events which led to Heathcliff - now about forty years old - living all but alone in Wuthering Heights, almost completely separated from society. The casual violence and lack of concern for manners or consideration for other people which characterizes Heathcliff here is only a hint of the atmosphere of the whole novel, in which that violence is contrasted with more genteel and civilized ways of living.

Chapter 2, Summary

Annoyed by the housework being done in the Grange, Lockwood pays a second visit to Wuthering Heights, arriving there just as snow begins to fall. The weather is cold, the ground is frozen, and his reception matches the bleak unfriendliness of the moors. After yelling at the old servant Joseph to open the door, he is finally let in by a peasant-like young man. The bare kitchen is warm, and Lockwood assumes that the young and beautiful girl there is Mrs. Heathcliff. He tries to make conversation but she is consistently scornful and inhospitable, and he only embarrasses himself. There is "a kind of desperation" in her eyes. She refuses to make him tea unless Heathcliff said he could have some. The young man and Heathcliff come in for tea.

The young man behaves boorishly and seems to suspect Lockwood of making advances to the girl. Heathcliff demands tea "savagely," and Lockwood decides he doesn't really like him. Trying to make conversation again, Lockwood gets into trouble first assuming that the girl is Heathcliff's wife, and then that she is married to the young man, who he supposes to be Heathcliff's son. He is rudely corrected, and it transpires that the girl is Heathcliff's daughter-in-law but her husband is dead, as is Heathcliff's wife.

The young man is Hareton Earnshaw. It is snowing hard and Lockwood requests a guide so he can return home safely, but he is refused: Heathcliff considers it more important that Hareton take care of the horses. Joseph, who is evidently a religious fanatic, argues with the girl, who frightens him by pretending to be a witch. The old servant doesn't like her reading. Lockwood, left stranded and ignored by all, tries to take a lantern, but Joseph offensively accuses him of stealing it, and sets dogs on him. Lockwood is humiliated and Heathcliff and Hareton laugh. The cook, Zillah, takes him in and says he can spend the night.

Analysis:

The character of the natural setting of the novel - the moors, snowstorms - begins to develop, and it becomes clear that the bleak and harsh nature of the Yorkshire hills is not merely a geographical accident. It mirrors the roughness of those who live there: Wuthering Heights is firmly planted in its location and could not exist anywhere else.

Knowing Emily Brontë's passionate fondness for her homeland, we can expect the same bleakness which Lockwood finds so disagreeable to take on a wild beauty. Its danger cannot be forgotten, though: a stranger to those parts could easily lose his way and die of exposure. Heathcliff and the wind are similar in that they have no pity for weakness. The somewhat menacing presence of the natural world can also be seen in the large number of dogs who inhabit Wuthering Heights: they are not kept for pets.

The power dynamics that Lockwood observes in the household of Wuthering Heights are extremely important. The girl is evidently frightened of Heathcliff and scornful of Hareton; Hareton behaves aggressively because he is sensitive about his status; Heathcliff does not hesitate to use his superior physical strength and impressive personality to bully other members of his household... The different ways in which different characters try to assert themselves reveal a lot about their situation. Most notably, it is evident that sheer force usually wins out over intellectual and humane pretensions. The girl is subversive and intellectual, an unwilling occupant of the house, but she can achieve little in the way of freedom or respect.

Lockwood continues to lose face: his conversational grace appears ridiculous in its new setting. Talking to Heathcliff, for example, he refers to the girl as a "beneficent fairy," which is evidently neither true nor welcome flattery. This chapter might be seen, then, as a continuation of the strict division between social ideals (grace, pleasant social interactions, Lockwood) and natural realities (storms, frost, dogs, bluntness, cruelty, Hareton, Heathcliff). If the chapter was taken by itself, out of context, the reader would see that while social ideals are ridiculed, it is clear that the cruel natural world is ugly and hardly bearable. Fortunately we are only at the beginning.

Chapter 3, Summary

Zillah quietly shows Lockwood to a chamber which, she says, Heathcliff does not like to be occupied. She doesn't know why, having only lived there for a few years. Left alone, Lockwood notices the names "Catherine Earnshaw," "Catherine Linton," and "Catherine Heathcliff" scrawled over the window ledge. He leafs through some old books stacked there, and finds that the margins are covered in handwriting - evidently the child Catherine's diary. He reads some entries which evoke a time in which Catherine and Heathcliff were playmates living together as brother and sister, and bullied by Joseph (who made them listen to sermons) and her older brother Hindley. Apparently Heathcliff was a "vagabond" taken in by Catherine's father, raised as one of the family, but when the father died Hindley made him a servant and threatened to throw him out, to Catherine's sorrow.

Lockwood then falls asleep over a religious book, and has a nightmare about a fanatical preacher leading a violent mob. Lockwood wakes up, hears that a sound in his dream had really been a branch rubbing against the window, and falls asleep again. This time he dreams that he wanted to open the window to get rid of the branch, but when he did, a "little, ice-cold hand" grabbed his arm, and a voice sobbed "let me in." He asked who it was, and was answered: "Catherine Linton. I'm come home, I'd lost my way on the moor." He saw a child's face and, afraid, drew the child's wrist back and forth on the broken glass of the window so that blood soaked the sheets. Finally he gets free, and insists that he won't let the creature in, even if it has been lost for twenty years, which it claims it has. He awakes screaming.

Heathcliff comes in, evidently disturbed and confused, unaware that Lockwood is there. Lockwood tells him what happened, mentioning the dream and Catherine Linton's name, which distresses and angers Heathcliff. Lockwood goes to the kitchen, but hears on his way Heathcliff at the window, despairingly begging "Cathy" to come in "at last." Lockwood is embarrassed by his host's obvious agony.

Morning comes: Lockwood witnesses an argument between Heathcliff and the girl, who has been reading. He bullies her, and she resists spiritedly. Heathcliff walks Lockwood most of the way home in the snow.

Analysis:

It is very important that the ghost of Catherine Linton (who is not perhaps simply a figment of Lockwood's imagination) appears as a child. Of course Lockwood thinks of her as a child, since he had just read parts of her early diary, but Heathcliff also seems to find it natural that she appeared in the form she had when they were children together. Rather than progressing from childhood on to a maturer age with its different values, Heathcliff and Catherine never really "grew up." That is to say, everything emotionally important that ever happened in their lives either took place in childhood or follows directly from commitments made then.

They never essentially outgrew their solidarity against the oppressive forces of adult authority and religion which is described in Catherine's diary. Thus the ghost of Catherine Linton (and that is her married name) tries to return to her childhood sanctuary, which Heathcliff has kept in its original state. The dominion of linear time is challenged. It might be relevant here to remember that Emily Brontë kept up the imaginary world created when she was very young well into her early twenties, and hated to leave the home of her childhood.

Chapter 4, Summary

Lockwood is bored and a little weak after his adventures, so he asks his housekeeper, Ellen Dean, to tell him about the history of Heathcliff and the old families of the area. She says he is very rich and a miser, though he has no family, since his son is dead. The girl living at Wuthering Heights was the daughter of Ellen's former employers, the Lintons, and her name was Catherine. She is the daughter of the late Mrs. Catherine Linton, was born an Earnshaw, thus Hareton's aunt. Heathcliff's wife was Mr. Linton's sister. Ellen is fond of the younger Catherine, and worries about her unhappy situation.

The narrative switches to Ellen's voice, whose language is much plainer than Lockwood's. She is a discreet narrator, rarely reminding the listener of her presence in the story, so that the events she recounts appear immediate. She says she had grown up at Wuthering Heights, and one day:

Mr. Earnshaw offered to bring his children Hindley (14 years old) and Catherine (about 6) a present each from Liverpool, where he was going. Hindley asked for a fiddle and Catherine for a whip, because she was already an excelled horsewoman. When Earnshaw returned, however, he brought with him a "dirty, ragged, black-haired child" found starving on the streets. The presents had been lost or broken.

The boy was named Heathcliff and taken into the family, though not entirely welcomed by Mrs. Earnshaw, Ellen, and Hindley. He and Catherine became very close, and Heathcliff was Earnshaw's favourite. Hindley felt that his place was usurped, and took it out on Heathcliff, who was hardened and stoical. For example, Earnshaw gave them each a colt, and Heathcliff chose the finest, which went lame. Heathcliff then claimed Hindley's, and when Hindley threw a heavy iron at him, threatened to tell Earnshaw about it if he didn't get the colt.

Analysis:

A movement to the past is made in this chapter: from now on, Lockwood will gradually lose importance as the story of Heathcliff and Catherine's childhood becomes more and more vibrant. However, we cannot entirely neglect the role Ellen Dean plays as a narrator: her personality means that the events she recounts are presented in a particular way. She is practical and, like a good housekeeper, tends to incline to the side of order. Even when she was young, she did not really participate in the private lives of the children of Wuthering Heights, and has little access to the relationship of Heathcliff and Catherine. Brontë demonstrates her versatility in using different points of view, faithfully recording her various characters' distinctive styles of speech.

Considering character development, it is interesting to know what Heathcliff and Catherine were like as children since, as we have seen in the previous chapter, their essential natures remain very much the same. Seen from Ellen's point of view. Catherine was willful and mischievous and Heathcliff was uncomplaining but vindictive.

Chapter 5, Summary

Earnshaw grew old and sick - his wife had died some years before - and with his illness he became irritable and somewhat obsessed with the idea that people disliked his favourite, Heathcliff. Heathcliff was spoiled as a result, to keep Earnshaw happy, and Hindley, who became more and more bitter about the situation, was sent away to college. Joseph, already "the wearisomest, self-righteous pharisee that ever ransacked a Bible to rake the promises to himself, and fling the curses to his neighbors," used his religious influence over Earnshaw to distance him from his children. Earnshaw thought Hindley was worthless, and didn't like Cathy's playfulness and high spirits, so in his last days he was irritable and discontented. Cathy was "much too fond" of Heathcliff, and liked to order people around. Heathcliff would do anything she asked. Her father was harsh to her and she became hardened to his reproofs.

Finally Earnshaw died one evening when Cathy had been resting her head against his knee and Heathcliff was lying on the floor with his head in her lap. When she wanted to kiss her father good night, she discovered he was dead and the two children began to cry, but that night Ellen saw that they had managed to comfort each other with "better thoughts than [she] could have hit on," imagining the old man in heaven

Analysis:

The extremely close and entirely sexless relationship between Heathcliff and Cathy already manifests itself in an opposition to the outside world of parental authority and religion. Cathy is already charming and manipulative, though her love for her father is real. The false, oppressive religion of Joseph is juxtaposed with the pure, selfless thoughts of heaven of the grieving children.

The decline and death of Earnshaw highlights the bond between the physical body and the spirit. The old man had formerly been charitable, loving, and open, but his physical weakness makes him irritable and peevish: the spirit is corrupted by the body's decline. One might remember that Emily Brontë watched her brother die wretchedly of alcohol and drug abuse, having had dreams of glory and gallantry in his youth.

Chapter 6, Summary

Hindley returns home, unexpectedly bringing his wife, a flighty woman with a strange fear of death and symptoms of consumption (although Ellen did not at first recognize them as such). Hindley also brought home new manners and rules, and informed the servants that they would have to live in inferior quarters. Most importantly, he treated Heathcliff as a servant, stopping his education and making him work in the fields like any farmboy.

Heathcliff did not mind too much at first because Cathy taught him what she learned, and worked and played with him in the fields. They stayed away from Hindley as much as possible and grew up uncivilized and free. "It was one of their chief amusements to run away to the moors in the morning and remain there all day, and after punishment grew a mere thing to laugh at."

One day they ran off after being punished, and at night Heathcliff returned. He told what had happened. He and Cathy ran to the Grange to see how people lived there, and they saw the Linton children Edgar and Isabella in a beautiful room, crying after an argument over who could hold the pet dog. Amused and scornful, Heathcliff and Cathy laughed; the Lintons head them and called for their parents. After making frightening noises, the wilder children tried to escape, but a bulldog bit Cathy's leg and refused to let go. She told Heathcliff to escape but he would not leave her, and tried to pry the animal's jaws open. They were captured and brought inside, taken for thieves. When Edgar recognized Cathy as Miss Earnshaw, the Lintons expressed their disgust at the children's wild manners and especially at Heathcliff's being allowed to keep Cathy company. They coddled Cathy and drove Heathcliff out; he left after assuring himself that Cathy was all right. When Hindley found out, he welcomed the chance to separate Cathy and Heathcliff, so Cathy was to stay for a prolonged visit with the Lintons and Heathcliff was forbidden to speak to her.

Analysis:

In this chapter we first hear Heathcliff speak for a long time, and it is worth noting how his language differs from the narrators we have heard so far. He is more expressive and emotional than the other two, and his speech is more literary than Ellen's and less artificial than Lockwood's. He tends to speak in extreme and vibrant terms: expressing his scorn for Edgar Linton's cowardice and whiny gentility, he says: "I'd not exchange, for a thousand lives, my condition here, for Edgar Linton's at Thrushcross Grange - not if I might have the privilege of flinging Joseph off the highest gable, and painting the housefront with Hindley's blood!" He admires the comparative luxury of the Grange and recognizes its beauty, but he remains entirely devoted to the freedom of his life with Cathy, and cannot understand the selfishness of the spoiled children: "When would you catch me wishing to have what Catherine wanted?" His devotion to Cathy is clear, and appears to him to be completely natural and inescapable: "she is so immeasurably superior to them - to everyone one earth; is she not, Nelly?" He admires her for her bravery, and he possesses that same kind of bravery.

The image of the two civilized children inside the beautiful room, and the two wild children outside - both boy and girl of similar ages - makes the glass of the window take on the role of a kind of mirror. However, the "mirror" shows the complete opposite rather than the true images of those who look into it.

Chapter 7, Summary

Ellen resumes the narrative. Cathy stayed at Thrushcross Grange for five weeks, until Christmas. When she returned home she had been transformed into a young lady with that role's attending restrictions: she could no longer kiss Ellen without worrying about getting flour on her dress. She hurt Heathcliff's feelings by comparing his darkness and dirtiness to Edgar and Isabella's fair complexions and clean clothes. The boy had become more and more neglected in her absence, and was cruelly put in his place by Hindley and especially by Cathy's new polish. Cathy's affection for him had not really changed, but he did not know this and ran out, refusing to come in for supper. Ellen was sorry for him.

The Linton children were invited for a Christmas party the next day. That morning Heathcliff humbly approached Ellen and asked her to "make him decent" because he was "going to be good." Ellen applauded his resolution and reassured him that Cathy still liked him and that she was grieved by his shyness. When Heathcliff said he wished he could be more like Edgar - fair, rich, and well-behaved - Ellen told him that he could be perfectly handsome without being effeminate if he smiled more and was more trustful.

However, when Heathcliff, now "clean and cheerful," tried to join the party, Hindley told him to go away because he was not fit to be there. Edgar unwisely made fun of his long hair and Heathcliff threw hot applesauce at him, and was taken away and flogged by Hindley. Cathy was angry at Edgar for mocking Heathcliff and getting him into trouble, but she didn't want to ruin her party. She kept up a good front, but didn't enjoy herself, thinking of Heathcliff alone and beaten. At her first chance - her guests gone home - she crept into the garret where he was confined.

Later Ellen gave Heathcliff dinner, since he hadn't eaten all day, but he ate little and when she asked what was wrong, he said he was thinking of how to avenge himself on Hindley.

At this point Ellen's narrative breaks off and she and Lockwood briefly discuss the merits of the active and contemplative life, with Lockwood defending his lazy habits and Ellen saying she should get things done rather than just telling Lockwood the story. He persuades her to go on.

Analysis:

This chapter marks the end of Cathy and Heathcliff's time of happiness and perfect understanding; Cathy has moved partly into a different sphere, that of the genteel Lintons, and Heathcliff cannot follow her. Although Cathy still cares for the things she did when the two of them ran wild together, she is under a lot of pressure to become a lady - and she is vain enough to enjoy the admiration and approval she gets as such from Edgar, Hindley and his wife. Cathy's desire to inhabit two worlds - the moors with Heathcliff and the parlor with Edgar - is a central driving force for the novel and eventually results in tragedy. Emily Brontë had experienced a personal inability to remain true to herself while interacting in conventional social terms, and she chose to abandon society as a result. Cathy takes a different route.

Just as the window separated the Wuthering Heights children from the Lintons in the last chapter, a material object separates Cathy from Heathcliff in this one. The fine dress she wears is a very real boundary between the old friends: it must be sacrificed (smudged, crumpled) if the two of them are to be as close as they were before. It is simultaneously valuable for economic reasons (its cost), for social ones (the respect Cathy gets on account of it), and because of its artificial beauty. These same categories will consistently come between Cathy and Heathcliff; he is right to recognize the dress and what it represents as a threat to his happiness.

Chapter 8, Summary

Hindley's wife Frances gave birth to a child, Hareton, but

did not survive long afterwards: she had consumption. Despite the doctor's warnings, Hindley persisted in believing that she would recover, and she seemed to think so too, always saying she felt better, but she died a few weeks after Hareton's birth. Ellen was happy to take care of the baby. Hindley "grew desperate; his sorrow was of a kind that will not lament, he neither wept nor prayed - he cursed and defied - execrated God and man, and gave himself up to reckless dissipation. The household more or less collapsed into violent confusion - respectable neighbors ceased to visit, except for Edgar, entranced by Catherine. Heathcliff's ill treatment and the bad example posed by Hindley made him "daily more notable for savage sullenness and ferocity." Catherine disliked having Edgar visit Wuthering Heights because she had a hard time behaving consistently when Edgar and Heathcliff met, or when they talked about each other. Edgar's presence made her feel as though she had to behave like a Linton, which was not natural for her.

One day when Hindley was away Heathcliff was offended to find Catherine putting on a "silly frock," getting ready for Edgar's visit. He asked her to turn Edgar away and spend the time with him instead but she refused. Edgar was by this time a gentle, sweet young man. He came and Heathcliff left, but Ellen stayed as a chaperone, much to Catherine's annoyance. She revealed her bad character by pinching Ellen, who was glad to have a chance to show Edgar what Catherine was like, and cried out. Catherine denied having pinched her, blushing with rage, and slapped her, then slapped Edgar for reproving her. He said he would go; she, recovering her senses, asked him to stay, and he was too weak and enchanted by her stronger will to leave. Brought closer by the quarrel, the two "confessed themselves lovers." Ellen heard Hindley come home drunk, and out of precaution unloaded his gun.

Analysis:

Hindley's dissipation and moral degradation are further evidence that only a strong character can survive defeat or bereavement without becoming distorted. His desperation is a result of his lack of firm foundations: Ellen says that he "had room in his heart for only two idols - his wife and himself - he doted on both and adored one." Evidently it is impossible to live well when only caring about one's self, as Hindley does following his wife's death. It would be interesting to compare Hindley's behaviour and Heathcliff's in the opening chapters: both survive after the deaths of their beloveds, both live in a chaotic and cheerless Wuthering Heights... Heathcliff, however, has not entirely lost contact with Cathy: their closer relationship rules out a complete separation, even with death.

Emily Brontë's obvious model for Hindley is her brother Branwell, who was sinking into dissipation when she was writing the novel. This is the first time we really see Cathy behaving badly, showing that her temper makes the gentle and repressed life led by Edgar Linton unsuitable for her. Here she blushes with rage and in a later chapter she refers to her blood being much hotter than Edgar's: heat and coolness of blood are markers of different personalities. The physical differences between Cathy and Edgar are linked to their moral differences, not only in their appearances but even in their blood and bones.

Chapter 9, Summary

Hindley came in raging drunk and swearing, and caught Ellen in the act of trying to hide Hareton in a cupboard for safety. He threatened to make Nelly swallow a carving knife, and even tried to force it between her teeth, but she bravely said she'd rather be shot, and spat it out. Then he took up Hareton and said he would crop his ears like a dog, to make him look fiercer, then held the toddler over the banister. Hearing Heathcliff walking below, Hindley accidentally dropped the child, but fortunately Heathcliff caught him. Looking up to see what had happened, he showed "the intensest anguish at having made himself the instrument of thwarting his own revenge."

In other words, he hated Hindley so much that he would have liked to have him to kill his own son by mistake. If it had been dark, Ellen said, "he would have tried to remedy the mistake by smashing Hareton's skull on the steps." Hindley was somewhat shaken, and began to drink more. Heathcliff told Nelly he wished he would drink himself to death, but he had a strong constitution.

In the kitchen Cathy came to talk to Nelly (neither of them knew Heathcliff was in the room, sitting behind the settle). Cathy said she was unhappy, that Edgar had asked her to marry him and she had accepted. She asked Nelly what she should have answered. Nelly asked her if and why she loved Edgar; she said she did for a variety of material reasons: "he will be rich, and I shall like to be the greatest woman in the neighborhood, and I shall be proud of such a husband." Nelly disapproved, and Cathy admitted that she was sure she was wrong: she had had a dream in which she went to heaven and was unhappy there because she missed Wuthering Heights.

She said: "I have no more business to marry Edgar Linton than I have to be in heaven; and if the wicked man in there had not brought Heathcliff so low, I shouldn't have thought of it. It would degrade me to marry Heathcliff, now; so he shall never know how I love him; and that, not because he's handsome, Nelly, but because he's more myself than I am. Whatever our souls are made of, his and mine are the same, and Linton's is as different as a moonbeam from lightening, or frost from fire."

(Heathcliff left after hearing that it would degrade her to marry him.) Nelly told Cathy that Heathcliff would be deserted if she married Linton, and she indignantly said that she had no intention of deserting him, but would use her influence to raise him up. Nelly said Edgar wouldn't like that, to which Cathy replied: "Every Linton on the face of the earth might melt into nothing, before I could consent to forsake Heathcliff!"

Later that night it turned out that no one knew where Heathcliff was. Cathy went out in the storm looking for him, unsuccessfully - he had run away. The next morning she was sick. After some time she went to stay with the Lintons - a healthier environment - and she got better, while Edgar and Isabella's parents caught the fever and died. She returned to

Wuthering Heights "saucier, and more passionate, and haughtier than ever." When Nelly said that Heathcliff's disappearance was her fault, Cathy stopped speaking to her. She married Edgar three years later, and Ellen unwillingly went to live with her at the Grange, leaving Hareton to live with his wretched father.

Analysis:

The atmosphere of careless violence, despair, and hatred of the first part of the chapter is almost suffocating. Heathcliff's willingness to kill an innocent child out of revenge is the first real indication of his lack of morality. It is not altogether clear whether that lack is a partly a result of his hard childhood and miserable circumstances, or whether he was always like that. Certainly he appears quite changed from the sensitive boy who wanted to look nice so Cathy wouldn't reject him for Edgar, and who relied trustfully on Ellen, but he had spoken of wanting to paint the house with Hindley's blood much earlier.

The definition of love for Cathy and Heathcliff is perhaps Emily Brontë's original creation. It is not based on appearances, material considerations, sexual attraction, or even virtue, but rather a shared being. Cathy says: "I am Heathcliff - he's always, always in my mind - not as a pleasure, any more than I am always a pleasure to myself - but as my own being." In this sense, her decision to marry Edgar is a terrible mistake: she will be abandoning the essence of herself. Apparently the sexual aspect of love is so meaningless for her that she believes marriage to Edgar will not come between her and Heathcliff: she would not consciously abandon her soul. Heathcliff thinks otherwise, since he runs away.

Chapter 10, Summary

Catherine got along surprisingly well with her husband and Isabella, mostly because they never opposed her. She had "seasons of gloom and silence" though. Edgar took these for the results of her serious illness.

When they had been married almost a year, Heathcliff came back. Nelly was outside that evening and he asked her to tell Catherine someone wanted to see her. He was quite changed: a tall and athletic man who looked as though he might have been in the army, with gentlemanly manners and educated speech - though his eyes contained a "half-civilized ferocity." Catherine was overjoyed and didn't understand why Edgar didn't share her happiness. Heathcliff stayed for tea, to Edgar's peevish irritation. It transpired that Heathcliff was staying at Wuthering Heights, paying Hindley generously, but winning his host's money at cards. Catherine wouldn't let Heathcliff actually hurt her brother.

In the following weeks, Heathcliff often visited the Grange. Isabella - a "charming young lady of eighteen" - became infatuated with him, to her brother's dismay. Isabella became angry at Catherine for keeping Heathcliff to herself, and Catherine warned her that Heathcliff was a very bad person to fall in love with and that Isabella was no match for him: "I never say to him to let this or that enemy alone, because it would be ungenerous or cruel to harm them, I say - "Let them alone, because I should hate them to be wronged"; and he'd crush you, like a sparrow's egg, Isabella, if he found you a troublesome charge."

Catherine teased Isabella by telling Heathcliff in her presence that she loved him, holding her so she couldn't run away. Isabella scratched Catherine's arm and managed to escape, and Heathcliff, alone with Catherine, expressed interest in marrying Isabella for her money and to enrage Edgar. He said he would beat Isabella if they were married because of her "mawkish, waxen face."

Analysis:

Catherine's belief that Edgar should not be jealous of her relationship with Heathcliff emphasizes the difference in her mind between their relationship and ordinary love affairs. She says that she does not envy Isabella's yellow hair, so Edgar shouldn't hate to hear her praise Heathcliff - he should be glad for her sake. The comparison with Isabella suggests that she and Heathcliff are sister and brother, which is evidently not the case - but it is a comparison that makes sense for her.

Catherine uses natural analogies: Heathcliff would crush Isabella "like a sparrow's egg," he is "an arid wilderness of furze and whinstone." Isabella uses what seems to be a natural metaphor, but is in fact a literary one: Catherine is "a dog in the manger" for keeping Heathcliff to herself. They speak and think quite differently.

There are also important differences between the ways Edgar and Catherine view class. Edgar thinks that Heathcliff, "a runaway servant," should be entertained in the kitchen, not the parlor. Catherine jokes that she will have two tables laid, one for the gentry (Edgar and Isabella) and one for the lower classes (herself and Heathcliff). She and Heathcliff both call the narrator Nelly, while Edgar coldly calls her Ellen.

Chapter 11, Summary

Nelly went to visit Wuthering Heights to see how Hindley and Hareton were doing. She saw Hareton outside; he didn't recognize his nurse, threw a rock at her and cursed. She found that his father had taught him how to curse, and that he liked Heathcliff because he wouldn't let his father curse him, and let him do what he liked. Nelly was going to go in when she saw Heathcliff there; frightened, she ran back home.

The next time Heathcliff came to visit Nelly saw him kiss Isabella in the courtyard. She told Catherine what had happened, and when Heathcliff came in the two had an argument. Heathcliff said he had a right to do as he pleased, since Catherine was married to someone else. He said: "You are welcome to torture me to death for your amusement, only, allow me to amuse myself a little in the same style."

Nelly found Edgar, who came in while Catherine was scolding Heathcliff. He scolded her for talking to "that blackguard," which made her very angry, since she had been defending the Lintons. Edgar ordered Heathcliff to leave, who scornfully ignored him. Edgar motioned for Nelly to fetch reinforcements, but Catherine angrily locked the door and threw the key into the fire when Edgar tried to get it from her. Humiliated and furious, Edgar was mocked by Catherine and Heathcliff, but he hit Heathcliff and went out by the back door to get help. Nelly told Heathcliff that he would be thrown out by the male servants if he stayed, so he chose to leave. Left with Nelly, Catherine expressed her anger at her husband and her friend: " Well, if I cannot keep Heathcliff for my friend - if Edgar will be mean and jealous, I'll try to break their hearts by breaking my own." Edgar came in and demanded to know whether she would drop Heathcliff's acquaintance, and she had a temper tantrum, ending with a faked "fit of frenzy." When Nelly revealed that the fit was faked, she ran to her room and refused to come out or to eat for several days.

Analysis:

Nelly may seem to be rather unfeeling in her unsympathetic descriptions of Catherine and Heathcliff, but her behaviour to Hareton and Hindley (who was her foster-brother) reveals her to be extremely tender-hearted and maternal at time. She is, however, independent and spirited, and doesn't like to be imposed on or bullied by Catherine, so she has no qualms about siding with Edgar when her mistress is being temperamental.

The strain imposed on the three characters, Catherine, Edgar, and Heathcliff, has finally resulted in outright violence: it is no longer possible to conceal the strength of the emotions involved. Edgar in particular is put into a difficult situation: the other two are used to violent expressions of feeling, but he is not, and hates having to adjust to their modes of communication. He is more committed to gentility of behaviour than the others, although they now appear as well-dressed and cultivated as he does.

Heathcliff and Catherine call Edgar a "lamb," a "sucking leverett," and a "milk-blooded coward." The first two insults are natural images that might easily come to mind for people who grew up on the moors; the third again uses the "blood" imagery which appears to be central to the way they think about personality.

Chapter 12, Summary

After three days in which Catherine stayed alone in her

room, Edgar sat in the library, and Isabella moped in the garden, Catherine called Nelly for some food and water because she thought she was dying. She ate some toast, and was indignant to hear that Edgar wasn't frantic about her; she said: "How strange! I thought, though everybody hated and despised each other, they could not avoid loving me - and they have all turned to enemies in a few hours." It became clear to Ellen that she was delirious, and thought she was back in her room at Wuthering Heights: she was frightened of her face in the mirror because she thought there was no mirror there. She opened the window and talked to Heathcliff (who was not there) as though they were children again. Edgar came in and was much concerned for Catherine, and angry at Ellen for not having told him what was going on.

Going to fetch a doctor, Ellen notices Isabella's little dog almost dead, hanging by a handkerchief on the gate. She released it, and found Dr. Kenneth, who told her that he had seen Isabella walking for hours in the park with Heathcliff. Ellen found that Isabella had indeed disappeared, and a little boy told her he had seen the girl riding away with Heathcliff. Ellen told Edgar, hoping he would rescue his sister from her ill-considered elopement, but he coldly refused to do so.

Analysis:

In her delirium, Catherine reveals that her true emotional identity has not altered since she was twelve, just before she stayed with the Lintons for some weeks. Everything that happened to her since then ceases to have any importance when she is irrational:

"...supposing at twelve years old, I had been wrenched from the Heights, and every early association, and my all in all, as Heathcliff was at that time, and been converted, at a stroke, into Mrs. Linton, the lady of Thrushcross Grange, and the wife of a stranger; an exile, and outcast, thenceforth, from what had been my world - You may fancy a glimpse at the abyss where I groveled!"

Time is unimportant: it has no effect on true, deep emotions in Brontë's world.

Edgar's coldness to Isabella seems to result from pique at having his sister desert him for his greatest enemy. His willingness to abandon her because of hurt pride is perhaps his greatest moral flaw. The emphasis he places on personal dignity differentiates him from the other characters, who certainly have many faults, though not that one.

Chapter 13, Summary

In the next two months Catherine "encountered and conquered the worst shock of what was denominated a brain fever," but it was realized that she would never really recover. She was pregnant. Heathcliff and Isabella returned to Wuthering Heights and Isabella wrote Edgar an apology and a plea for forgiveness, to which he gave no reply. She later sent Ellen a longer letter asking whether Heathcliff were a demon or crazy, and recounting her experiences. She found Wuthering Heights dirty, uncivilized and unwelcoming: Joseph was rude to her, Hareton was disobedient, Hindley was a half-demented mere wreck of a man, and Heathcliff treated her cruelly. He refused to let her sleep in his room, which meant she had to stay in a tiny garret. Hindley had a pistol with a blade on it, with which he dreamed of killing Heathcliff, and Isabella coveted it for the power it would have given her. She was miserable and regretted her marriage heartily.

Analysis:

Isabella's reactions to her new home reveal her character to be lacking in moral strength: although she tries at first to stand up to Joseph and Hareton, her ladylike education has in no way prepared her for her married life, so when she loses her pride she has little else to fall back on. Her envy upon seeing Hindley's pistol is a little disconcerting, and she herself is horrified by the realization of it.

It is worth noting the unfortunate position of women who depend on men: Isabella cannot escape from Heathcliff without the help of her brother, who does not want to help her. Surrounded by hatred and indifference, she can only fall back on Ellen's pity.

Chapter 14, Summary

Ellen, distressed by Edgar's refusal to console Isabella, went to visit her. She told Isabella and Heathcliff that Catherine would "never be what she was" and that Heathcliff should not bother her anymore. Heathcliff asserted that he would not leave her to Edgar's lukewarm care, and that she loved him much more than her husband. He said that if he had been in Edgar's place he would never have interfered with Catherine's friendships, although he would kill the friend the moment she no longer cared about him.

Nelly told Heathcliff to treat Isabella better, and he expressed his scorn and hatred for her (in her presence, of course). He said she knew what he was when she married him: she had seen him hanging her pet dog. Isabella told Nelly that she hated him, and Heathcliff ordered her upstairs so he could talk to Nelly. Alone with her, he told her that if she did not arrange an interview for him with Catherine, he would force his way in armed, and she agreed to give Catherine a letter from him.

Analysis:

This chapter includes a great deal of criticism for the Lintons: Edgar is called proud and unfeeling, and Heathcliff says that Isabella was actually attracted by his brutality until she herself suffered from it. Edgar's explanation of refusal to write to Isabella is extremely unconvincing: "I am not angry, but sorry to have lost her: especially as I can never think she'll be happy. It is out of the question my going to see her, however; we are eternally divided." He is angry, of course, because he hates Heathcliff: presumably he is jealous of him. Heathcliff considers Edgar's version of love to be selfish, as though Edgar thought he owned his wife, and had a right to restrict her behaviour: "Had he been in my place, and I in his, though I hated him with a hatred that turned my life to gall, I never would have raised a hand against him... I never would have banished him from her society, as long as she desired his." Correspondingly, he imagines Catherine's affection for Edgar in terms of property: "He is scarcely a degree dearer to her than her dog, or her horse - It is not in him to be loved like me." Material wealth has always been associated with the Lintons, so Heathcliff extends ideas of property and ownership to their emotions as well.

The case of Isabella is somewhat different. Heathcliff despises her because she, knowing what he is, loves him. This is an interesting point: Heathcliff is an obviously romantic figure, with his mysterious past, dark looks, and so on. But Brontë makes it very clear that although he exerts a certain amount of fascination, he should in no way be considered a "hero of romance." For doing so, Isabella is called a "pitiful, slavish, mean-minded brach." In this very romantic novel, one can never rely on conventional notions of romance: brutality should never be considered attractive. Even Catherine does not find Heathcliff attractive - she simply finds him inescapable, a part of herself.

Chapter 15, Summary

The Sunday after Ellen's visit to Wuthering Heights, while most people were at church, she gave Catherine Heathcliff's letter. Catherine was changed by her sickness: she was beautiful in an unearthly way and her eyes "appeared always to gaze beyond, and far beyond." Ellen had left the door open, so Heathcliff walked in and Catherine eagerly waited for him to find the right room. Their reunion was bitter-sweet: though passionately glad to be reunited, Catherine accused Heathcliff of having killed her, and Heathcliff warned her not to say such things when he would be tortured by them after her death - besides, she had been at fault by abandoning him. She asked him to forgive her, since she would not "be at peace" after death, and he answered:

"It is hard to forgive, and to look at those eyes, and feel those wasted hands... I love my murderer - but yours! How can I?" They held each other closely and wept until Ellen warned them that Linton was returning. Heathcliff wanted to leave, but Catherine insisted that he stay, since she was dying and would never see him again. He consented to stay, and "in the midst of the agitation, [Ellen] was sincerely glad to observe that Catherine's arms had fallen relaxed... ŒShe's fainted or dead, so much the better...'" Linton came in, Heathcliff handed him Catherine's body and told him to take care of her: "Unless you be a fiend, help her first - then you shall speak to me!" He told Nelly he would wait outside for news of Catherine's welfare, and left.

Analysis:

The passionate scene between Catherine and Heathcliff in this chapter is probably the emotional climax of the novel, though it only marks the middle of the book. It reveals how little their love relies on pleasure: they can hardly be said to be fond of one another, or to enjoy each other's company, yet they are absolutely necessary to each other. It is as though they were members of a different species from other humans, who belonged together.

Ellen says: "The two, to a cool spectator, made a strange and fearsome picture." Catherine tore Heathcliff's hair, and he left bruises on her arm. Later, he "foamed like a mad dog, and gathered her to him with greedy jealousy. [Ellen] did not feel as though [she] were in the company of a member of [her] own species." Love appears to be a form of madness. Their emotional reunion is counteracted by Ellen's cool and rather unsympathetic narration: their passionate conversation is interspersed with dry commentary on her part.

Chapter 16, Summary

Around midnight Catherine gave birth to a daughter (also named Catherine, the girl Lockwood saw at Wuthering Heights) and died two hours later without recovering consciousness. No one cared for the infant at first, and Ellen wished it had been a boy: as it was, Edgar's heir was Isabella, Heathcliff's wife. Catherine's corpse looked peaceful and beautiful, and Ellen decided that she had found heaven at last.

She went outside to tell Heathcliff and found him leaning motionless against an ash tree. He knew she was dead, and asked Ellen how it had happened, attempting to conceal his anguish. Ellen was not fooled, and told him that she had died peacefully, like a girl falling asleep. He cursed Catherine and begged her to haunt him so he would not be left in "this abyss, where I cannot find you!... I cannot live without my soul!" He dashed his head against the tree and howled "like a savage beast getting goaded to death with knives and spears." Ellen was appalled.

On Tuesday, when Catherine's body was still lying, strewn with flowers, in the Grange, Heathcliff took advantage of Edgar's short absence from the chamber of death to see her again, and to replace Edgar's hair in her locket with some of his own. Ellen noticed the change, and enclosed both locks of hair together. Catherine was buried on Friday in a green slope in a corner of the kirkyard, where, Ellen said, her husband lies now as well.

Analysis:

The question of what happens after death is important in this chapter and throughout the novel, though no firm answer is ever given. Ellen is fairly sure Catherine went to heaven, "where life is boundless in its duration, and love in its sympathy, and joy in its fullness." But Heathcliff cannot conceive of Catherine finding peace when they are still separated, or of his living without her.

In the chapter before, Catherine said: "I'm wearying to escape into that glorious world, and to be always there; not seeing it dimly through tears, and yearning for it through the walls of an aching heart, but really with it, and in it." It is as though she had in mind a heaven that was like the moors in every way but the constraints of physicality: the spirit of natural freedom.

Another interesting question that comes up in this chapter is that of the value of self-control and reserve: Heathcliff tries to conceal his weakness and grief, holding "a silent combat with his inward agony," but Ellen considers it to be worse than useless, since he only tempts God to wring his "heart and nerves." Yet we know that Emily herself was almost incredibly self-disciplined, refusing to alter her everyday life even when suffering a mortal illness.

Chapter 17, Summary

The next day, while Ellen was rocking the baby, Isabella came in laughing giddily. She was pale and her face was cut; her thin silk dress was torn by briars. She asked Ellen to call the carriage for the nearest town, Gimmerton, since she was escaping from her husband, and to have a maid get some clothes ready. Then she allowed Ellen to give her dry clothes and bind up the wound. Isabella tried to destroy her wedding-ring, and told what had happened to her in the last days:

She said that she hated Heathcliff so much that she could feel no compassion for him even when he was in agony following Catherine's death.

He hadn't eaten for days, and spent his time at Wuthering Heights in his room, "praying like a methodist; only the deity he implored was senseless dust and ashes." The evening before, Isabella sat reading while Hindley drank morosely. When they heard Heathcliff returning from his watch over Catherine's grave, Hindley told Isabella he would lock Heathcliff out, and try to kill him with his bladed pistol if he came in. Isabella would have liked Heathcliff to die, but refused to help in the scheme, so when Heathcliff knocked she refused to let him in, saying: "If I were you, I'd go stretch myself over her grave, and die like a faithful dog... The world is not worth living in now, is it?" Hindley came close to the window to kill Heathcliff, but the latter grabbed the weapon so the blade shut on Hindley's wrist; then he forced his way in. He kicked and trampled Hindley, who had fainted from the loss of blood, then roughly bound up the wound, and told Joseph and Isabella to clean up the blood.

The next morning when Isabella came down, Hindley "was sitting by the fire, deadly sick; his evil genius, almost as gaunt and ghastly, leant by the chimney." After eating breakfast by herself, she told Hindley how he had been kicked when he was down, and mocked Heathcliff for having so mistreated his beloved's brother, saying to Hindley: "everyone knows your sister would have been living now, had it not been for Mr. Heathcliff." Heathcliff was so miserable that he could hardly retaliate, so Isabella went on and said that if Catherine had married him, he would have beaten her the way he beat Hindley. Heathcliff threw a knife at her, and she fled, knocking down Hareton, "who was hanging a litter of puppies from a chairback in the doorway." She ran to the Grange.

That morning, she left, never to return to the neighborhood again. Later, in her new home, in the south, she gave birth to a son, named Linton, "an ailing, peevish creature," and died when he was about 12 years old.

Edgar grew resigned to Catherine's death, and loved his daughter, who he called Cathy, very much. Ellen points out the difference between his behaviour and Hindley's in a similar situation. Hindley died, "drunk as a lord," about six months after Catherine. He was just 27, meaning that Catherine had been 19, Heathcliff was 20, and Edgar was 21. Ellen grieved deeply for him - they had been the same age and were brought up together. She made sure he was decently buried. She wanted to take Hareton back to the Grange, but Heathcliff said he would keep him, to degrade him as much as he himself had been degraded. If Edgar insisted on taking Hareton, Heathcliff said he would claim his own son Linton, so Ellen gave the idea up.

Analysis:

Isabella's tendency toward impotent cruelty shows up again in the character of her son Linton. The question of how cruelty operates in powerful versus weak characters was evidently of great interest to Brontë and might bear further investigation. One obvious point is that weakness is not simply equated with goodness, as is often the case in the Christian tradition. Although the weak are unable to physically express their hatred, they can, like Isabella, use verbal taunts to hurt their enemies emotionally.

Ellen's particular grief for Hindley emphasizes the way characters are paired in the novel: Ellen and Hindley, Heathcliff and Catherine, Edgar and Isabella. These pairs all grew up together (Ellen's mother was Hindley's wet-nurse, so they literally shared mother's milk) under somewhat fraternal conditions. Brontë's careful structure and concern with symmetry are important presences throughout the novel, and form an interesting contrast with what might be considered the chaotic emotions that seem to prevail.

Chapter 18, Summary

In the next twelve years, Cathy Linton grew up to be "the most winning thing that ever brought sunshine into a desolate house." She was fair like a Linton, except for her mother's dark eyes. High spirited but gentle, she seemed to combine the good qualities of both the Lintons and the Earnshaws, though she was a little saucy and was used to getting her way. Her father kept her within the park of the Grange, but she dreamed of going to see some cliffs, Penistone Crags, not too far away, on the moor. When Isabella fell ill, she wrote to Edgar to come visit her, so he was gone for three weeks.

One day Cathy asked Ellen to give her some food for a ramble around the grounds - she was pretending to be an Arabian merchant going across the desert with her caravan of a pony and three dogs. She left the grounds, however, and later Ellen went after her on the road to Penistone Crags, which passed Wuthering Heights. She found Cathy safe and sound there - Heathcliff wasn't home, and the housekeeper had taken her in - chattering to Hareton, now 18 years old. She offended Hareton though by asking whether he was the master's son, and when he said he wasn't, saying he was a servant. The housekeeper told her he was her cousin, which made her cry. Hareton offered her a puppy to console her, which she refused. Ellen told her that her father didn't want her to go to Wuthering Heights, and asked her not to tell him of her negligence, to which she agreed.

Analysis

We have moved from the violent and discordant world of adulthood back to harmonious childhood. The abrupt contrast between the hellish last chapters and this relatively serene and innocent one could hardly be more clear. One might even suppose that we are witnessing a second chance: the story of the first Catherine ended in grief and bloodshed, but perhaps that of her daughter will be more serene. Indeed there are many similarities between the first Catherine and her daughter, although the mother's bad qualities are minimized in the younger Cathy.

Although Cathy appears to display more Linton characteristics than Earnshaw ones, her desire to explore the wilderness outside of the Grange's park links her strongly to the wild, Wuthering Heights clan. Her sauciness also reminds the reader of her mother, as does her aristocratic unwillingness to be related to Hareton (just as Catherine thought it would degrade her to marry Heathcliff, who was at the time very much like Hareton).

Chapter 19, Summary

Isabella died, and Edgar returned home with his half-orphaned nephew, Linton, a "pale, delicate, effeminate, boy," with a "sickly peevishness" in his appearance. Cathy was excited to see her cousin, and took to babying him when she saw that he was sickly and childish. That very evening, Joseph came and demanded the child for Heathcliff - he was after all his son. Ellen told him Edgar was asleep, but he went into his room and insisted on being given Linton. Edgar wished to keep Linton at the Grange, but could not legally claim him, so he could only put it off till the next morning.

Analysis

The contrast between Cathy and her cousin Linton is very strong: she is energetic and warm-hearted, whereas he is limp and parasitic. It is interesting to see how Brontë distributes conventionally masculine and feminine characteristics among her characters without regard for gender. Linton is pointedly described as being delicate, with fine flaxen hair even lighter than Cathy's: he is the helpless "lady" of the two, who cries when he doesn't get his way, and allows himself to be "courted" by his female cousin.

Chapter 20, Summary

The next morning, Ellen woke Linton early and took him

over to Wuthering Heights, promising dishonestly that it was only for a little while. He was surprised to hear he had a father, since Isabella had never spoken of Heathcliff. When they arrived there, Heathcliff and Joseph expressed their contempt for the delicate boy, and Heathcliff told him that his mother was a "wicked slut" not to tell him about his father. Ellen asked Heathcliff to be kind to the boy, and he said that he would indeed have him carefully tended, mostly because Linton was heir to the Grange, so he wanted him to live at least until Edgar was dead and he inherited. So when Linton refused to eat the homely oatmeal Joseph offered him, Heathcliff ordered that he be given some toast or something instead. When Ellen left, Linton cried for her not to leave him there.

Analysis

Brontë's novel is full of innocent children who are abandoned into a cold and unfriendly world: Heathcliff as an orphan in Liverpool, Hindley sent away to college, Heathcliff and Cathy again at Earnshaw's death, Hareton, Linton, Cathy Linton at her father's death... The effect of this is that each character, no matter how ruthless and cruel he or she may be, contains at their core the same wish for love and the same loneliness as their former childlike selves. We are never able to judge any character entirely objectively because we know this. Linton is a particularly interesting example of this because he is unpleasant, even as a child, yet one can only pity him for being abruptly introduced to an unloving father and a home where everyone despises him.

Chapter 21, Summary

Cathy missed her cousin when she woke up that morning, but time made her forget him. Linton grew up to be a selfish and disagreeable boy, continually complaining about his health. On Cathy's sixteenth birthday she and Ellen went out on the moors, and strayed onto Heathcliff's land, where he found them. He invited them to come to Wuthering Heights, telling Ellen that he wanted Linton and Cathy to marry so he would be doubly sure of inheriting the Grange. Cathy was glad to see her cousin, though she was somewhat taken back by his invalidish behaviour. Hareton, at Heathcliff's request, showed her around the farm, though he was shy of her and she teased him unkindly. Linton mocked his ignorance also, showing himself to be mean-spirited.

Later Cathy told her father where she had been, and asked him why he had not allowed the cousins to see each other (Heathcliff had told her that Edgar was still angry at him because he thought him too poor to marry Isabella). Edgar told her of Heathcliff's wickedness, and forbade her to return to Wuthering Heights. She was unhappy, and began a secret correspondence with Linton. By the time Ellen discovered it, they were writing love letters - affected ones on Linton's part. Ellen confronted Cathy and burned the letters, saying she would tell her father if she continued.

Analysis:

The issue of trespassing is important in this chapter, and recalls the scene in chapter 6, where Cathy Earnshaw and Heathcliff are caught on the Lintons' land. This chapter is almost an inversion of the other one, especially considering that this Cathy will marry Linton, just as the earlier Cathy married Edgar. In a static world, everyone stays on their own property and the marriages that result from trespassing would not take place. The emphasis on land and privacy might be taken for a metaphor for more emotional intimacy: in order for two people to become close, one must in some way trespass. On the other hand, the marriages that result from trespassing are unhappy, while that which results from exploration (see Cathy Linton's first meeting with Hareton in chapter 18) are happy. The essential point, of course, is that the definition of trespassing versus innocent exploration depends entirely on the attitude taken by the people whose lands are being entered.

Often in literature, land and women are identified with one another, so that trespassing could be taken for a metaphor for sex. This hardly seems to be the case in Wuthering Heights: Linton and Edgar remain passively in their places while their future wives come to see them. This is coherent with the general identification of the male Lintons with female characteristics. Isabella, both biologically female and Lintonishly feminine, meets Heathcliff when he unwelcomedly intrudes at the Grange.

Chapter 22, Summary

That fall Edgar caught a cold which confined him to the house all winter. Cathy grew sadder after the end of her little romance, and told Ellen that she was afraid of being alone when her father and Ellen were dead. Taking a walk, Cathy ended up briefly stranded outside of the wall of the park, when Heathcliff rode by. He told her that Linton was dying of a broken heart, and that she would visit him if she were kind. Ellen told her that Heathcliff was probably lying and couldn't be trusted, but the next day she was persuaded to accompany Cathy to Wuthering Heights.

Analysis:

See the analysis of chapter 20 for a discussion of children left alone in the world - Cathy Linton is not the only one to fear a parent's death, nor is her fear unjustified. In her case, she is particularly vulnerable because, as a girl, she will not inherit her father's estate: her father's nephew Linton will. This is a result not of Edgar's lack of regard for his daughter, but of legal conventions.

Emily Brontë had good reasons to be especially conscious of the position of orphaned children: although her father outlived her, her mother died when she was very young (like Cathy's) and her older sister Maria who took the place of the mother died in childhood of tuberculosis. See chapter 12 for further evidence of the importance of abandoned children: in her delirium Catherine remembers a nest of baby birds who died of starvation ("little skeletons") after Heathcliff caught their mother. She had been greatly grieved by the sight and made Heathcliff promise never to kill a mother bird again. This may actually be the key to Emily Brontë's continual emphasis on that theme: she was deeply familiar with the natural world, in which orphaned baby animals stand next to no chance of survival.

Chapter 23, Summary

Cathy and Ellen heard "a peevish voice" calling Joseph for more hot coals for the fire; they went in to see Linton, who greeted them rather ungraciously: "No - don't kiss me. It takes my breath - dear me!" He complained that writing to her had been very tiring, and that the servants didn't take care of him as they ought, and that he hated them. He said that he wished she would marry him, because wives always loved their husbands, upon which she answered that they did not always do so. Her father had told her that Isabella had not loved Heathcliff. Linton was angry and answered that Catherine's mother hadn't loved her father, but Heathcliff.

She pushed his chair and he coughed for a long time, for which she was very sorry. He took advartage of her regret and bullied her like a true hypochondriac, and made her promise to return the next day. When Cathy and Ellen were on their way home, Ellen expressed her disapproval of Linton and said he would die young - "small loss." Cathy should on no account marry him. Cathy was not so sure he would die, and was much more friendly toward him. Ellen caught a cold and was confined to her room. Cathy spent almost all her time taking care of her and Edgar, but she was free in the evenings: then, as Ellen later found out, she visited Linton.

Analysis:

In this chapter Brontë explores the intersections between love and power: to what extent does Linton want Cathy to love him freely, and to what extent does he want to have husbandly control over her? It would appear that for him, love is just another form of control: he uses Cathy's love for him to make her do whatever he likes, without any consideration for her own happiness.

Is this form of love/control essentially linked to marriage? That might well be the case: see how the relationship between the older Catherine and her husband Edgar breaks down when he tries to control her friendships. However Edgar unmistakably loved Catherine, whereas Linton seems to care for no one but himself. Marriage in Wuthering Heights is not an unqualified good: it must be accompanied by unselfish love on both sides in order to work.

Chapter 24, Summary

Three weeks later, Ellen was much better, and discovered Cathy's evening visits to Wuthering Heights. Cathy told her what had happened: She had bribed a servant with her books, to take care of saddling her pony and not telling about her escapades. On her second visit, she and Linton had had an argument about the best way of spending a summer afternoon: he wanted to lie in the heather and dream it away, and she wanted to rock in a treetop among the birds: "He wanted to lie in an ecstasy of peace; I wanted all to sparkle, and dance in a glorious jubilee."

They made up and played ball until Linton was unhappy because he always lost, but she consoled him for that. She looked forward to her next visit, but that day when she arrived she met Hareton, who showed her how he had learned to read his name. She mocked him for it. (Here Ellen rebuked Cathy for having been so rude to her cousin. Cathy was surprised, and went on.) When she was reading to Linton, Hareton came in angrily and ordered them into the kitchen. Shut out of his favourite room, Linton staged a frightening temper tantrum, wearing an expression of "frantic, powerless fury" and shrieking that he would kill Hareton.

Joseph pointed out that he was showing his father's character. Linton coughed blood and fainted; Cathy fetched Zillah. Hareton carried the boy upstairs but wouldn't let Cathy follow; she cried and he was sorry for it. She struck him with her whip and rode home. On the third day Linton refused to speak to her except to blame her for the events of the preceding day, and she left resolving not to return. She did, however, and took Linton to task for being so rude. He admitted that he was worthless, but said that she was much happier than he and should make allowances. Heathcliff hated him, and he was very unhappy. He loved her however.

Cathy was sorry Linton had such a distorted nature, and felt she had an obligation to be a friend to him. She had noticed that Heathcliff avoided her, and rebuked Linton when he did not behave well to her. Ellen told Edgar about the visits, and he forbade Cathy to return to Wuthering Heights, but wrote to Linton that he could come to the Grange if he liked.

Analysis:

The contrast between Linton and Cathy's ideas of how to spend an afternoon sums up the differences in their characters. The juxtaposition of Linton's peaceful ideal afternoon with his furious temper tantrum is somewhat disconcerting, however. Are passivity and laziness essentially related to hatred and fury in the novel? This hardly seems possible, considering Edgar's peaceful and generally loving character. However, the juxtaposition serves to remind us that weakness and goodness are not to be carelessly equated.

Chapter 25, Summary

Ellen points out to Lockwood that these events only happened the year before, and she hints that Lockwood might become interested in Cathy, who is not happy at Wuthering Heights. Then she went on with the narrative:

Edgar asked Ellen what Linton was like, and she told him that he was delicate and had little of his father in him - Cathy would probably be able to control him if they married. Edgar admitted that he was worried about what would happen to Cathy if he were to die. As spring advanced Edgar resumed his walks, but although Cathy took his flushed cheeks and bright eyes for health, Ellen was not so sure. He wrote again to Linton, asking to see him. Linton answered that his father refused to let him visit the Grange, but that he hoped to meet Edgar outside sometime. He also wrote that he would like to see Cathy again, and that his health was improved.

Edgar could not consent, because he could not walk very far, but the two began a correspondence. Linton wrote well, without complaining (since Heathcliff carefully censured his letters)and eventually Edgar agreed to Cathy's going to meet Linton on the moors, with Ellen's supervision. Edgar wished Cathy to marry Linton so she would not have to leave the

Grange when he died - but he would not have wished it if he knew that Linton was dying as fast as he was.

Analysis:

The presence of tuberculosis in such a prominent way in the novel is rather disturbing, considering that the illness was soon to be the cause of Emily's own death. Cathy fools herself into thinking that Edgar is getting better, just as Emily (and Frances, Hindley's wife) tried hard to pretend that she was not sick.

Death is a mysterious and yet unavoidable presence: you cannot simply expect people to live until they are old. A cold can turn into a fever, which can turn into consumption, ending in the grave. Life is not predictable in Wuthering Heights, just as it was not in Emily Brontë's own world.

Chapter 26, Summary

When Ellen and Cathy rode to meet Linton they had to go quite close to Wuthering Heights to find him. He was evidently very ill, though he said he was better: "his large blue eyes wandered timidly over her; the hollowness round them, transforming to haggard wildness, the languid expression they once possessed." Linton had a hard time making conversation with Cathy, and was clearly not enjoying their talk, so she said she would leave. Surprisingly Linton then looked frightenedly towards Wuthering Heights and begged her to stay longer, and to tell her father he was in "tolerable health." She half-heartedly agreed, and he soon fell into some kind of slumber. He woke suddenly and seemed to be terrified that his father might come. Soon later Cathy and Ellen returned home, perplexed by his strange behaviour.

Analysis:

This chapter reveals an extent of cruelty in Heathcliff which has not been seen before: he has no reason to hate his son beyond the fact that he is a Linton, and yet he is perfectly willing to fill his last moments with terror and despair. Linton's life is singularly hopeless, and the mere fact that Brontë invented it testifies to the real darkness of her vision. Linton is unlikable and dislikes everyone; he will die without ever achieving anything worthwhile or good, and probably without ever having been happy. A more pointless, bitter existence could hardly be imagined. Heathcliff's appears energetic and joyful by contrast.

Chapter 27, Summary

A week later they were to visit Linton again. Edgar was much sicker, and Cathy didn't want to leave him, but he encouraged her relationship with Linton, thinking to ensure his daughter's welfare thereby. Linton "received us with greater animation on this occasion; not the animation of high spirits though, nor yet of joy; it looked more like fear." Cathy was angry that she had had to leave her father, and she was disgusted by Linton's abject admissions of terror. Heathcliff came upon them, and asked Ellen how much longer Edgar had to live: he was worried that Linton would die before him. He then ordered Linton to get up and take Cathy in the house, which he did, against Cathy's will: "Linton... implored her to accompany him, with a frantic importunity that admitted no denial." Heathcliff pushed Ellen into the house as well and locked the door behind them. When Cathy protested that she must get home to her father he slapped her brutally, and made it clear that she wouldn't leave Wuthering Heights until she married Linton. Linton showed his true character: as Heathcliff said, "He'll undertake to torture any number of cats if their teeth be drawn, and their claws pared." Cathy and Heathcliff declared their mutual hatred. Ellen remained imprisoned for five days with Hareton as her jailer: he gave her food but refused to speak to her beyond what was necessary. She did not know what was happening to Cathy.

Analysis:

Further evidence of Linton's bad character. Cathy's pity and kindness are the causes of her misfortunes here: in the presence of Heathcliff's intelligent hatred, her good qualities only serve to leave her vulnerable to his plans.

Chapter 28, Summary

On the fifth afternoon of the captivity, Zillah released Ellen, and said that Heathcliff said she could go home and that Catherine would follow in time to attend her father's funeral. He was not dead yet, but soon would be. Ellen asked Linton where Catherine was, and he answered that she was shut upstairs, that they were married, and that he was glad she was being treated harshly. Apparently he was piqued that she hadn't wished to marry him. He was annoyed by her crying, and was glad when Heathcliff struck her.

Ellen rebuked him for his selfishness and unkindness, and went to the Grange to get help. Edgar was glad to hear his daughter was safe, and would be home soon: he was almost dead, at the age of 39. The men sent to Wuthering Heights to rescue Catherine returned without her, having believed Heathcliff's tale that she was too sick to travel. Very early the next morning, however, Catherine came back by herself, joyful to hear that her father was still alive. She had forced Linton to help her escape. Ellen asked her to say she would be happy with Linton, for Edgar's sake, to which she agreed. Edgar died "blissfully." Catherine was stony-eyed with grief. Heathcliff's lawyer gave all the servants but Ellen notice to quit, and hurried the funeral.

Analysis:

Part of Heathcliff's revenge fails: Catherine manages to escape in time to see her father again, and Edgar dies happy. Given the great importance attached to last words and dying moments, this is a notable victory for Catherine, and an essential one if all of Heathcliff's evil work is to be undone in the end. If Edgar had died miserably, no amount of happy endings could ever have undone that tragedy.

Chapter 29, Summary

Heathcliff came to the Grange to fetch Catherine to Wuthering Heights to take care of Linton, who was dying in terror of his father, and because he wanted to get a tenant for the Grange (Mr. Lockwood, as it turned out). Catherine agreed to go, because Linton was all she had to love, and left the room. Heathcliff, in a strange mood, told Ellen what he had done the night before. He had bribed the sexton who was digging Edgar's grave to uncover his Catherine's coffin, so he could see her face again - he said it was hers yet.

The sexton told him that the face would change if air blew on it, so he tore himself away from contemplating it, and struck one side of the coffin loose and bribed the sexton to put his body in with Catherine's when he was dead. Ellen was shocked, and scolded him for disturbing the dead, at which he replied that on the contrary she had haunted him night and day for eighteen years, and - "yesternight, I was tranquil. I dreamt I was sleeping my last sleep, by that sleeper, with my heart stopped, and my cheek frozen against hers."

Then Heathcliff told Ellen what he had done the night after Catherine's burial (the night he beat up Hindley). He had gone to the kirkyard and dug up the coffin "to have her in his arms again," but while he was wrenching at the screws he suddenly felt sure of her living presence. He was consoled, but tortured as well: from that night for 18 years he constantly felt as though he could almost see her, but not quite. He tried sleeping in her room, but constantly opened his eyes to see if she were there, he felt so sure she was. Heathcliff finished his narrative, and Catherine sadly bade farewell to Ellen.

Analysis:

Heathcliff's continued love for Catherine's dead body after 18 years emphasizes the physical, yet non-physical nature of their relationship. It would appear to physical in a way that transcends conventional ideas about sexuality: Heathcliff was pleased to see that Catherine still looked like herself after 18 years, but claimed that if she had been "dissolved into earth, or worse," he would have been no less comforted by the proximity to her body. His idea of heaven is to be utterly and completely unified with Catherine in body, as in spirit - and this could just as well mean to disintegrate into dust together as to be joined in the act of love. The difference between these two forms of union is that while people are joined during sexual intercourse, their separate bodies and identities remain clear. But in Heathcliff and Catherine's corporeal and spiritual unity, as envisaged by him, an observer would not be able to tell "which is which." This is like Catherine's statement in chapter 9 that she was Heathcliff.

Chapter 30, Summary

Ellen has now more or less reached the present time in her narrative, and tells Lockwood what Zillah told her about Catherine's reception at Wuthering Heights. She spent all her time in Linton's room, and when she came out she asked Heathcliff to call a doctor, because Linton was very sick. Heathcliff replied: "We know that! But his life is not worth a farthing." Catherine was thus left to care for her dying cousin all by herself (Zillah, Hareton and Joseph would not help her) and became haggard and bewildered from lack of sleep. Finally Linton died, and when Heathcliff asked Catherine how she felt, she said: "He's safe and I'm free. I should feel very well - but you have left me so long to struggle against death, alone, that I feel and see only death! I feel like death!" Hareton was sorry for her. Catherine was ill for the next two weeks. Heathcliff informed her that Linton had left all of his and his wife's property to himself. One day when Heathcliff was out, Catherine came downstairs.

Hareton made shy, friendly advances, which she angrily rejected. He asked Zillah to ask her to read for them (he was illiterate, but wished to learn) but she refused on the grounds that she had been forsaken during Linton's illness, and had no reason to care for Hareton or Zillah. Hareton said that he had in fact asked Heathcliff to be allowed to relieve her of some of her duties, but was denied.

She was in no mood to forgive, however, and thus became the unfriendly Catherine Lockwood had seen at Wuthering Heights. According to Zillah: "She'll snap at the master himself, and as good dares him to thrash her; and the more hurt she gets, the more venomous she grows." Ellen wanted to get a cottage and live there with Catherine, but Heathcliff would not permit it.

Analysis:

See the analysis of the next chapter for a discussion of the roles of education and books in the relationship of Catherine and Hareton.

It is generally considered that difficult and painful experiences are also, in a way, valuable as "growing experiences." If this is the case, Catherine's short marriage to Linton should have caused her to grow a great deal from the happy and innocent girl she had formerly been. Instead, it appears to make her venomous and permanently angry. However, one might make the argument that the humbling she undergoes is necessary because, without it, she never would have bothered to see the good in Hareton. Is the time Catherine spends caring for Linton a complete loss, or does she learn anything valuable from it? This is related to the question of whether Wuthering Heights is a Christian novel: in Christian theology, suffering is usually considered ennobling.

Chapter 31, Summary

Lockwood went to Wuthering Heights to see Heathcliff and tell him he didn't want to stay at the Grange any longer. He noticed that Hareton was "as handsome a rustic as need be seen." He gave Catherine a note from Ellen; she thought it was from him at first and when he made it clear that it wasn't, Hareton snatched it away, saying that Heathcliff should look at it first (he wasn't home yet). Catherine tried to hide her tears, but Hareton noticed and let the letter drop beside her seat. She read it and expressed her longing for freedom, telling Lockwood that she couldn't even write Ellen back because Heathcliff had destroyed her books.

Hareton had all the other books in the house: he had been trying to read. Catherine mocked him for his clumsy attempts at self-education: "Those books, both prose and verse, were consecrated to me by other associations, and I hate to hear them debased and profaned in his mouth!" Poor Hareton fetched the books and threw them into her lap, saying he didn't want to think about them any longer. She persisted in her mockery, reading aloud in "the drawling tone of a beginner," following which he slapped her and threw the books into the fire. Lockwood "read in his countenance what anguish it was to offer that sacrifice to spleen."

Heathcliff came in and Hareton left, "to enjoy his grief and anger in solitude." Heathcliff moodily confided to Lockwood that Hareton reminded him much more of Catherine, than of Hindley. He also told Lockwood that he would still have to pay his full rent even if he left the Grange, to which Lockwood, insulted, agreed. Heathcliff invited Lockwood to dinner, and informed Catherine that she could eat with Joseph in the kitchen. Lockwood ate the cheerless meal and left, contemplating the possibility of his courting Catherine and going together "into the stirring atmosphere of the town."

Analysis:

Books take on an important role in the relationship between Hareton and Catherine: Hareton's illiteracy is the most glaring result of Heathcliff's treatment of him, designed to reduce him to rustic ignorance. Hareton never rebels against Heathcliff, but his contact with Catherine, who was carefully educated by her father, makes him extremely conscious of his shortcomings. One might wonder how great the value of book-learning is, in the novel: Linton, who can read, is obviously inferior to his more vigorous cousin Hareton, which might lead one to think that Brontë is championing native energy over imposed refinement. However, for Catherine and Hareton to become close it is absolutely necessary for Hareton to wish to educate himself, and in the last chapter their love will be symbolized in the joint reading of a book. Similarly, Heathcliff's youthful degradation really takes place when he ceases to follow Catherine's lessons. It appears that book-learning is not enough to make a person good, but that the lack of it is enough to make someone ridiculous. It is, in short, an essential quality.

Chapter 32, Summary

In the fall of 1802, later that year, Lockwood returned to

the Grange because he was passing through the area on a hunting trip. He found the Grange more or less empty: Ellen was at Wuthering Heights, and an old woman had replaced her. Lockwood visited Wuthering Heights to see what had changed. He noticed flowers growing around the old farm house, and overheard a pleasant lesson from indoors. Catherine, sounding "sweet as a silver bell," was teaching Hareton, now respectably dressed. The lesson was interspersed with kisses and very kind words. Lockwood was loth to disturb them, and went around to the kitchen to find Nelly singing and Joseph complaining as usual. She was glad to see Lockwood and told them that he would have to settle the rent with her, since she was acting for Catherine. Heathcliff had been dead for three months. She told him what had happened.

A fortnight after Lockwood left the Grange the previous spring, Nelly was summoned to Wuthering Heights, where she gladly went - her job was to keep Catherine out of Heathcliff's way. She was pleased to see Catherine, but sorry at the way she had changed.

One day when they and Hareton were sitting in the kitchen, Catherine grew tired of the animosity between herself and the young man, and offered him a book, which he refused. She left it close to him, but he never touched it. Hareton was injured in a shooting accident in March, and since Heathcliff didn't like to see him, he spent a lot of time sitting in the kitchen, where Catherine found many reasons to go. Finally her efforts at reconciliation succeeded, and they became loving friends, much to Joseph's indignation.

Analysis:

The union of Hareton and Catherine should not surprise the reader, who has been following the symmetrical unfolding of the novel. At the beginning of the story, Hindley and Catherine inhabited Wuthering Heights and Edgar and Isabella inhabited the Grange. The obvious symmetrical plot would have been: Hindley married Isabella producing "Hareton," while Catherine married Edgar, producing Cathy. Then Cathy and "Hareton" would marry, unifying the two houses completely, and Cathy Linton would become Catherine Earnshaw, taking on her mother's maiden name. The harmony of this plot was disrupted by the introduction of Heathcliff, an alien figure who destroyed the potential marital balance. By the end of the novel, however, Heathcliff and his issue will be eliminated, and the unifying marriage between the families of Linton and Earnshaw will take place after all, as though Heathcliff had never existed. Hindley, sent away to college because of the outsider, Heathcliff, married an outsider, Frances, producing Hareton Earnshaw. Catherine Earnshaw married Edgar Linton, producing Cathy Linton, and Isabella Linton married Heathcliff, producing Linton Heathcliff. The union between Isabella and Heathcliff should not have taken place, so naturally Linton Heathcliff was a mistake, an unlikable and weakly being. Cathy Linton's marriage to Linton Heathcliff was likewise a mistake, forced by Heathcliff, and in order to preserve the integrity of the pattern, their marriage was childless. No descendants of Heathcliff must remain by the end of the novel, for harmony to be reinstated. Linton's death eliminated a character who should never have existed, and freed Catherine to marry again. In fact, the nature of their marriage made it particularly easy to forget: it seems unthinkable that the marriage could have been consummated. When Cathy Heathcliff marries Hareton, thus becoming Cathy Earnshaw, she will be a virgin. With the death of Heathcliff and his offspring, and the unifying marriage of the Linton and Earnshaw heirs, it is almost as though Heathcliff had never existed.

In this analysis we looked at one alternate plot - that in which Heathcliff never entered the novel. It is not, however, the only possible alternate plot. The other obvious one would involve the elimination (in terms of offspring) of Edgar Linton, or of both Edgar and Hindley. Then Heathcliff would marry Catherine, and Isabella could marry Hindley or an outsider or not at all, and Edgar could marry an outsider or not at all. It is evidently less elegant than the other alternate plot, involving more outsiders and no unification of the two houses - but emotional integrity would have been preserved in the unification of Catherine and Heathcliff. As it is, that unification is finally attained when Heathcliff's body merges with Catherine's as they disintegrate into dust, and their spirits roam the moors together.

Another beauty of Brontë's plot is that the three names that Lockwood reads when he stays at Wuthering Heights in chapter 3 - Catherine Earnshaw, Catherine Heathcliff, and Catherine Linton - are all taken on at one point or another by the two Catherines. The first Catherine is named Earnshaw, then Linton when she marries Edgar, then perhaps Heathcliff when she and Heathcliff are finally united in the grave. Her daughter is first Catherine Linton, then Heathcliff, then Earnshaw.

Chapter 33, Summary

The next morning Ellen found Catherine with Hareton in the garden, planning a flower garden in the middle of Joseph's cherished currant bushes. She warned them that they would be punished, but Hareton said he would take the blame. At tea, Catherine was careful not to talk to Hareton too much, but she put flowers into his porridge, which made him laugh, which made Heathcliff angry. He assumed Catherine had laughed, but Hareton quietly admitted his fault. Joseph came in and incoherently bewailed the fate of his bushes. Hareton said he was uprooted some, but would plant them again, and Catherine said it had been at her instigation. Heathcliff called her an "insolent slut," and she accused him of having stolen her land and Hareton's.

Heathcliff commanded Hareton to throw her out - the poor boy was torn between his two loyalties and tried to persuade Catherine to leave. Heathcliff seemed "ready to tear Catherine to pieces" when he suddenly calmed down and told everyone to leave. Later Hareton asked Catherine not to accuse Heathcliff in front of him, and she understood his position and refrained from insulting her oppressor from then on. Ellen was glad to see her two "children" happy together; Hareton quickly shook off his ignorance and boorishness and Catherine became sweet again.

When Heathcliff saw them together he was struck by their resemblances to his Catherine, and told Ellen that he had lost his motivation for destruction. He no longer took any interest in everyday life; Catherine and Hareton didn't appear to him to be distinct characters of their own, but sources of past associations to his beloved. He also felt Hareton to be very much like himself as a youth. But most importantly, his Catherine haunted him completely: "The most ordinary faces of men, and women - my own features mock me with a resemblance. The entire world is a dreadful collection of memoranda that she did exist, and that I have lost her!" He told Nelly that he felt a change coming - that he could no longer exist in the living world when he felt so close to that of the dead, or the immortal. Nelly wondered whether he was ill, but decided that he was in fine health and mind, except for his unworldly obsession.

Analysis:

We are given an extraordinary window into Heathcliff's mind in the chapter. Whenever he looks at something, he sees Catherine in it - he hears her voice in every sound. This is Brontë's conception of true haunting, which seems to bear far more resemblance to madness than to scary noises in the dark. It is mainly an interior phenomenon: if the ghost of Catherine is at work, she has found her home in Heathcliff's mind and her vocation in distorting his perception and his ability to communicate with the outside world.

Chapter 34, Summary

In the next few days Heathcliff all but stopped eating, and spent the nights walking outside. Catherine, happily working on her garden, came across him and was surprised to see him looking "very much excited, and wild, and glad." Ellen told him he should eat, and indeed at dinner he took a heaped plate, but abruptly lost interest in food, seemed to be watching something by the window, and went outside. Hareton followed to ask him what was wrong, and Heathcliff told him to go back to Catherine and not bother him.

He came back an hour or two later, with the same "unnatural appearance of joy," shivering the way a "tight-stretched cord vibrates - a strong thrilling, rather than trembling." Ellen asked him what was going on, and he answered that he was within sight of his heaven, hardly three feet away. Later that evening, Ellen found him sitting in the dark with the windows all open. She was frightened by the pallor of his face and his black eyes. Ellen half-wondered if he were a vampire, but told herself that she was foolish, since she had watched him grow up. The next day he was even more restless and could hardly speak coherently, and stared fascinatedly at nothing with an "anguished, yet raptured expression." Early the next morning - having spent the night outside or pacing in his room, he declared he wanted to settle things with his lawyer. Ellen said he should eat, and get some sleep, but he replied that he could do neither: "My soul's bliss kills my body, but does not satisfy itself." Ellen told him to repent his sins, and he thanked her for the reminder and asked her to make sure he was buried next to Catherine: "I have nearly attained my heaven; and that of others is altogether unvalued, and uncoveted by me." He behaved more and more strangely, talking openly of his Catherine. Ellen called the doctor, but Heathcliff wouldn't see him.

The next morning she found him dead in his room, by the open window, wet from the rain and cut by the broken window-pane, with his eyes fiercely open and wearing a savage smile. Hareton mourned deeply for him. The doctor wondered what could have killed him. He was buried as he had asked. People said that his ghost roamed the moors with Catherine: Ellen once came across a little boy crying amid his panicked lambs, and he said that Heathcliff was "yonder" with a woman and that he didn't dare pass them.

Catherine and Hareton were to be married, and they would move to the Grange, leaving Wuthering Heights to Joseph and the ghosts. Lockwood noticed on his walk home that the kirk was falling apart from neglect, and he found the three headstones, Catherine's, Edgar's, and Heathcliff's, covered by varying degrees of heather. He "wondered how anyone could ever imagine unquiet slumbers, for sleepers in that quiet earth."

Analysis:

An essential question for thinking about this novel is: does it end happily or not, and why? Is the novel on the side of the Grange and civilization, since Catherine and Hareton move there after Heathcliff dies? Or should we miss the intensity of the passion in Wuthering Heights? Who wins? It seems at first that the Grange wins, and yet we should remember that Heathcliff achieves his version of heaven as well. Several film versions of Wuthering Heights prefer to delete the whole second half of the novel, ending dramatically with Catherine's death - they find that the restabilizing second half detracts from the romance and the power of the first part. Is this the case? Did Emily add the second half because society would not have accepted the first half alone?

The answer to the last question must be negative: the symmetrical structure of the novel is too carefully designed and too deeply imbedded to be the product of outside social pressures. This might lead to the conclusion that civilization really does win, since the marriage of Catherine and Hareton is the final and necessary conclusion to two generations of unrest, and all traces of Heathcliff disappear, at least in genetic terms. In another sense, however, Catherine and Hareton resemble the earlier Catherine and Heathcliff, purified of their wilder and more antisocial elements: so one might assume that their marriage is an echo of the marriage that never took place between Catherine and Heathcliff. This is supported by the fact that the story begins and ends with a Catherine Earnshaw, and that the name Hareton is very similar to Heathcliff.

In another reading, one might remember that the first Catherine and Heathcliff belonged above all to the natural and immaterial world, whereas the Lintons belonged to a material society. Then the reunion in death of the two lovers constitutes their achievement of complete freedom - and it hardly matters what happens on earth.

One might also conclude that Emily Brontë was really

more drawn to her wild characters - Catherine and Heathcliff - but realized that they posed a great threat to the existence of peaceful life on earth. Perhaps she eliminated them because she was unwilling to sacrifice the rest of the world for such a wild ideal - but with Heathcliff's death the novel ultimately had to end because it no longer captured her interest. In this case the ambiguous conclusion of the novel represents an inner conflict in the author herself.

Chapter 8

The Bronte Family

When Mrs. Gaskell published The Life of Charlotte Brontë, she was forty-seven, and had already written Mary Barton; Cranford and Ruth. In six years, there were to follow Sylvia's Lovers and that story in which is embalmed the charm of all things fading—Cousin Phillis. The biography was worthy of its author. Here was presented, not less truthfully than exquisitely, all that it was essential to know of the sad story of Charlotte Brontë's life, and, interwoven in its texture, and consummately in place, the beautiful piece of prose in which Ellen Nussey told of Anne Brontë's death.

It was surprising that this masterpiece, at its first appearance, should have been marred by indiscretions of revelation, relating, in part, to the father of the sisters, to whose paternal care the book paid tribute, and who was still alive, an octogenarian. The explanation was, partly, that Mrs. Gaskell was a novelist whose first obligation was truth to character, and who was interested in the subordinate personages of her narrative mainly in so far as they illustrated the figure of its heroine; and, also, partly, that the task she had set herself—to tell soon and fully Charlotte Brontë's life-story—was not one that could possibly have been executed without giving some temporary offence. Yet, the main lines of the story were seized and held with the unerring hand of genius, and, in the amended version, we now possess a book that, both in its candour and in its restraint, remains the true record for posterity.

Of the substantial accuracy of its picture of the Brontë household, there is no longer any question. Some of the original domestic details now banished from the volume may not have been correct; but such stories as attached themselves to Patrick Brontë do not gather round a man of an exacting character. His custom of dining alone in a house with two sittingrooms is sufficiently significant. "No one," writes Mary Taylor to Ellen Nussey, a year after Charlotte's death, "ever gave up more than she did and with full consciousness of what she sacrificed." Family affection for his offspring, on the one side, of course, there was, and, on the other, deep filial piety and that cherishing fondness which springs from piety; but it is a main element in Charlotte Brontë's later history that talk in the lonely house must often have been "but a tinkling cymbal."

Patrick Brunty or Brontë, as, at Haworth, he came finally to write the name, was, so far as we know, a pure Irishman. He was born in Emdale, county Down, in 1777, and, in 1802, presumably with the aid of some slender savings, he entered St. John's College, Cambridge. After taking his degree, he held various curacies, settling down finally, in 1820, in the incumbency of Haworth. But the troubles of life were not over; for, in less than two years, his always delicate wife, Maria Branwell, whom he had married in 1812, had died, leaving him the care of six children, Maria, Elizabeth, Charlotte, Patrick Branwell, Emily Jane and Anne, of whom the eldest was eight and the youngest not yet two years of age. In this difficulty, his wife's sister Elizabeth Branwell took up her residence with him at Haworth, remaining there as mistress of his house till her death. Thus was the household constituted till Charlotte Brontë was twenty-six.

For so large a family, the house in the graveyard was a confined habitation: it stood at the top of the steep and drab village, its front windows looking on the church and the graves, and its back on the wide-stretching moors over which the tiny girls loved constantly to ramble. Their father was not a learned man; but he knew enough to teach infants, and it was a mistake that, in order to provide them with more systematic instruction, he should have sent four of them to a clergy daughters' boarding school. This was an absurdly cheap subsidised institution, for no other was within his means; and the disastrous experiment, afterwards forming the basis of the account of Lowood in Jane Eyre, came to an end within a year. Charlotte Brontë believed that the precarious health of her two elder sisters had suffered from the experience. In any case, the first tragedies of her home were the early deaths of the much-loved Maria and Elizabeth.

The household, thus reduced in numbers, remained at Haworth for the next six years, occupied with reading, rambling, household management and, above all, with literary invention; and it was not till 1831, when Charlotte was nearly fifteen, that she was again sent to a boarding school, this time to Miss Wooler's at Roe Head, where she made the acquaintance of Ellen Nussey and Mary Taylor, who became her lifelong friends. Miss Wooler was kind and competent, and eighteen fairly happy months of pupilage resulted, three years later, in Charlotte's returning as an instructress, while Emily and Anne also became pupils in the same school. But Charlotte was not born to be a teacher of young girls, and, after another interval of three years, she returned to Haworth, fretted in mind and spirit.

Yet, something had to be done to replenish the family exchequer on which the one, and thoroughly unsatisfactory, brother was beginning to make a series of claims. Emily had attempted and failed to live the life of an assistant schoolmistress under peculiarly exacting conditions, and there was nothing left for Charlotte and Anne except to become governesses in private families. But, though the gentle Anne was, apparently, a good governess, retaining one post for four years, the experiences of neither of the pair met their wishes, and it occurred to Charlotte and Emily that they should qualify for the three setting up school by themselves. For this, some knowledge of foreign languages was indispensable, and, in February, 1842, the two sisters, aged, respectively, twentyfive and twenty-three, had found their way as pupils into a foreign school, the pensionnat Héger, rue d'Isabelle, Brussels. The short year spent there was made especially interesting on account of the lectures of the professor of literature, Constantin

Héger, a man of thirty-three who, obviously, added to some of the usual Napoleonisms of the professeur des jeunes filles (Napoleonisms to which Charlotte Brontë was not blind) a genuine force of character, something of the genius of exposition and a touch of that ironic or semi-humorous malice which is the salt of personality. But this brightening episode was not to last, and, in eight months, the sisters were hurrying home too late to attend the deathbed of their aunt Branwell.

The home was reorganised, Emily being left to keep house. Branwell, who had failed in several occupations, found a post as tutor in the same family where Anne was governess, and Charlotte Brontë allowed herself to be tempted to return to Brussels, in January, 1843, as instructress in English. She was now verging on twenty-seven, and at Brussels were the surroundings that had broken the dull monotony of her life. Hitherto, this monotony had been endurable; henceforth, it was no longer so.

As she taught in the school of the Hégers, at times instructing Constantin Héger and his brother-in-law in English, and hearing from him constantly of the high things in literature and life, there was set up that rapport of intelligence, and, more than this, that interplay where soul responds to soul, of which, hitherto, she had known nothing. In a year, she was back in the lonely house, herself now twice lonely "for remembering happier things." All had not gone well in her absence: the brother was hastening down a career that ended in an early grave; the plan of a school had come tc nothing; the tone of the communications she sent to her adored professor, too exalté led to the ending of all communication; and in the letters she wrote to Brussels in these barren years we can hear the cry of a stifled heart. In March, 1845, she writes to Ellen Nussey:

I can hardly tell you how time gets on at Haworth. There is no event whatever to mark its progress. One day resembles another: and all have heavy lifeless physiognomies... There was a time when Haworth was a very pleasant place to me: it is not so now. I feel as if we were all buried here... Write very soon dear Ellen.

There was one way of escape and one only—for "the imagination is not a state," as Blake tells us, "it is the human existence itself."

Emily Bronte's Wuthering Heights and Poems.

Emily Brontë left only one book and some verses. As to her novel, critical judgment is still in suspense. It is not desirable to read; to take Wuthering Heights from the shelf is to prepare for oneself no pleasure. The song of love and of morning that makes Jane Eyre an imperishable possession is not sung here. On the contrary, in this strange tale of outland natures on outland moors all is thunder-clad—darkness, and the light more awful that breaks the storm, passions that, in their tempestuous strength at once terrify us for human nature and enlarge our conception of its dignity. It bears the same relation to Jane Eyre that Webster bears to Shakespeare, if one could imagine Webster greater than Shakespeare.

This, indeed, is its defect, and in seeking to estimate the proportional value of this defect judgment is at a loss. It is a tale of diablerie, not of life. What happened in Jane Eyre might have happened, part of it did actually happen, but all of it, leaving out of account a little melodrama, here and there, which is not essential, might have happened. These are beings agitated by our desires, and we are reading about ourselves. In Wuthering Heights, it is not so; we see Heathcliff from the outside, and observe this triumph of imagination. When we have admitted that this is not a tale of our own life, the door is closed upon detraction.

In every other respect and of its kind, the work done here is absolute. In these chapters, echoing with apprehension, chapters that Bring the unreal world too strangely near and in which the disaster that one would often think has culminated goes on culminating to the close, everything is found in place, and, though it is a wild consistency, as Dobell was the first to say, consonant. Perfectly "in keeping" with the nature of Heathcliff, as perfectly as the abduction of Isabella or the forced marriage of the shivering Linton, are the hanging of the Springer—a demoniac revelation—and the attack upon the younger Catherine, those stunning and unceasing slaps on the young girl's face that madden the reader as if he had been present. Undeviatingly, almost without thinking, from Lockwood's nightmare at the beginning to the last scene in Joseph's kitchen, when Heathcliff's glazing eyes are tense with love's vision, the imagination pursues its course because the authoress never for a moment dreams of questioning the imagination.

In reading such a work, we are oppressed by an intensity of personal feeling. There is no friendly author between us and what is seen. The fury of the events is by no means harmonised or softened by human comment explanatory or apologetic. The hideous drama merely comes before us, and is there; and yet we do not absolutely hate Heathcliff. The scene in the death-chamber with Catherine entitles him to speak of his affection as an "immortal love," a feeling which "shackles accidents and bolts up change," and testifies to the infinity of humanity.

In those few pages, where the stormy villain and his dying beloved override time and snatch a moment from eternity, we learn, as in Othello, something of passion's transfiguring power. And this passion is not physical. No doubt, a writer older and with more experience than Emily Brontë must, of necessity, have known that the attraction exercised by such a man, or by any man the least like Heathcliff, could only be of that kind. She did not know, and in her ignorance she gave to the transcendent a new setting, a setting far stranger than that in Jane Eyre, but, also, more arresting. It is the main mark of the Brontë's books and the inner reason why they are cherished that, out of the innocence of the heart, the mouth speaketh.

Emily Brontë's poems.

Of Emily Brontë's poems, it may be said that they are on the edge of greatness. So much cannot be pretended for those of her sisters. Charlotte's have a strong autobiographical reference, and, when they are most autobiographical, the truthful tenderness of her emotion sometimes finds expression; but, in the main, they are not poetry. Charlotte Brontë, though she did not care for three volumes, achieves her results, as a prose authoress, by a series of effects, not by single blows. Such a method is unsuited to short poems, where poetry loses everything if it loses the quintessential. The verse-writing of the gentle Anne, like all her work, has something winning in its appeal, or, it would be more correct to say, in its absence of appeal. It compasses more only when it is religious; but the religious poems are distinguished rather by a few rare verses than as complete or satisfying wholes. At their best, they have more sincerity and less sentimentalism than most hymns. 19

Since the poems of Emily challenge a much graver attention, it should be noted at once that, judged from a higher standpoint, the chief defect of Anne's is, also, very observable here. Except where the poems are very short—such as The Old Stoic, Remembrance, or Stanzas—they seldom hold attention to the end, and the poetical experience is not coextensive with the poem. It is there often—at the beginnings or episodically—but it is seldom continuous. Besides this, even the best of them are too frequently dependent upon scaffolding. They have a set theme, or they work through a set pronouncement. They have, generally, something definite to say, as prose has. The poetry does not express itself for its own sake or mould its own setting. Yet, they have been greatly prized by many fine critics. Their independence of the ordinary aids to comfort, their habit of resting on an accepted despondency, predisposes the modern reader in their favour. Especially their pagan feeling for nature, and their deeply melancholy but unrepining sentiment, appeal to minds that have been already influenced by Meredith. Moreover, Emily's verse has—what is scarcely to be traced at all in that of her sisters—metrical music: For if your former words were true

How useless would such sorrow be;
As wise, to mourn the seed which grew
Unnoticed on its parent tree,

and, sometimes, a very original feeling in the metre: Silent is the house, all are laid asleep, where the hesitancy of the verse, together with the stumbling treatment of the allegory, expresses perfectly the quiver of the girl as she withdraws into the world of dream. Occasionally, there is a tenderness for which one would hardly have looked in the author of Wuthering Heights—the real Emily that lived, one would think, and to whom that vision came: To-day, I will seek not the shadowy region;

Its unsustaining vastness waxes drear.

In one farewell verse only, the great wind blows:

Though earth and man were gone,
And suns and universes ceased to be,
And Thou wert left alone,
Every existence would exist in Thee; for, in poetry, what was elemental in her was not to find expression. The graves and the moors are in these poems as they are in Wuthering Heights, and it is the same Emily who is walking by them, but how differently—without the delirium of strength. Here, we are in contact with the actual human being, and find ourselves listening to the low tones natural to the girl who, all her life, and except when she was writing Wuthering Heights, controlled the utterances of the heart: So I knew that he was dying,

Stooped and raised his languid head,
Felt no breath and heard no sighing,
So I knew that he was dead.

The feeling beneath those poems, perhaps just because it is a controlled feeling, does not always find full expression. One likes them the better on rereading, one has to come again and taste, for the atmosphere of the poet's thought is not quite communicated: they are not poems that compel one to feel with the poet. To be complimentary, it might be said that they "speak in silences." They do speak, but to an attentive ear, with something of soundlessness, something estranged, at least something very far away from the sounding sureness of the prose. The lyric medium did not supply her with sufficient imaginative material, and this, perhaps, may suffice to explain why there is not more to praise; for, in her verse, though she communes freely with her spirit of imagination, that spirit is not freely exercised. Perhaps it also explains why their constant readers love these poems; for, in them, in the absence of her strange imaginings, what is chiefly disclosed is her individualism, the author of Wuthering Heights in her loneliness. A word may be added as to the novels of Anne Brontë. Agnes Grey has interest, a record of her governess experiences, treated, so far as one can judge, not very freely, and, for this reason, affording, in its mild way, something of the pleasure of discovery. The eager interest in everything connected with the biography of the Brontës aroused by Mrs.

Gaskell's Life has given to those faint pages an attraction beyond their own. Yet, what her sister once wrote to Mr. Williams, in reply to a letter full of family references, is not without appositeness: "I think details of character always have a charm, even when they relate to people we have never seen, nor expect to see." The Tenant of Wildfell Hall is as interesting a novel as was ever written without any element of greatness. It is pleasant to read of all sorts of intrigue and bad doings just as if they were a fairy tale and altogether outside the atmosphere of badness. There is one drawback—the tale is told by a man meant by the authoress to be quite "nice," but, in fact, less likeable than Crimsworth in The Professor. The Brontës had observed men not unclosely; but they were not able to see things through the eyes of men.

Chapter 9

Comparison of Heroines in Wuthering Heights and the Great Gatsby

Comparison of the presentation of the heroines in F. Scott Fitzgerald's 'TheGreat Gatsby' and Emily Bronte's 'Wuthering Heights'

Introduction to 'The Great Gatsby'

F. Scott Fitzgerald wrote 'The Great Gatsby'. He presents us with many characters, one of which is quite complex, Daisy Buchanan. She is stuck in a love triangle, with the affairs brings tension and envy to an unexpected ending to the novel

Introduction to 'Wuthering Heights'

Emily Bronte wrote 'Wuthering Heights'. It tells a story of a young woman's love for two men, Heathcliff and Edgar Linton. Through their love of such truth, imagination and emotional intensity leads us to the heroine's tragedy.

How the heroines are first introduced

Nick's (the narrator) 'second cousin once removed' this shows that Nick's has a closely-knit family so Daisy is seen as a distant relative. Nick tells us that he 'drove over to East Egg to see two old friends whom I scarcely knew at all' In 'The Great Gatsby' the houses are symbolic of the people that live there as we see with the Buchanan's house. We can tell a lot about Daisy's character through her house in which she lives in with her husband Tom Buchanan. Their house is described in very great detail 'a red-and-white Georgian colonial mansion' this shows that they are old money, old fashioned people it had Italian gardens with sundials and bright vines. The house had French windows 'now with reflected gold' the fact that Fitzgerald has chosen this colour gold gives Daisy a sense of wealth about her as well as her lavish setting.

Emily Bronte first introduces 'Wuthering Heights' heroine, Catherine, in the same way as Daisy, we hear about these women before we see them. We are first introduced to Catherine when there is a blizzard becomes worse when Lockwood was visiting his landlord, Heathcliff, and he has to stay the night at Wuthering Heights and with out knowing it he stays in a secret room of the house. This used to be Catherine's room; Lockwood notices the name Catherine with many surnames attached: Catherine Earnshaw, Catherine Linton and Catherine Heathcliff. Here Bronte presenting the heroine as a young woman who is trying to choose between these men of whom she should marry. This is also a parallel to 'The Great Gatsby' between Daisy, Tom and and Gatsby but only Daisy is married to Tom but feel for materialistic reasons that she wants to be with Gatsby. We do not yet know if this Catherine is still alive, still a child or a grown woman. In Chapter 5, Nelly Dean gives us a description of what Catherine was like as a child 'A wild, wick slip she was - but she had the bonniest eye, and the sweetest smile, and the lightest foot in the parish' this illustrates the fact that Catherine was beautiful and full of life from she was a young age.

Like the 'The Great Gatsby' Wuthering Heights and Thrushcross Grange both represent the characters that are staying there. From its descriptions, 'Above the chimney Wuthering Heights appears to be a cold, dark and stormy place. When Catherine has to leave Wuthering Heights because she is sick, she goes to Thrushcross Grange, this place is depicted to be much calmer, lighter, and warmer than the cold exposed house on the moors. Nelly tells us that when she came back from her short stay at Thrushcross Grange, that she was a transformed lady. This shows the influence that these different houses have on the characters. Also Wuthering Heights had an effective change on Lockwood when he stayed there by the dreams and hallucinations.

Descriptions

Personal appearance - Fitzgerald gives us a description of Daisy 'her face was sad and lovely with bright things in it'. This show that she is obviously attractive, and is confirmed when Jordan tells us that she was 'most popular of all the young girls'. Catherine is also beautiful even when she has died and was buried a few years later Heathcliff went back to see her, but dug up her grave. You would expect to find a decomposed body but instead she is still as she was the minute she was buried.

Throughout 'The Great Gatsby' Daisy is always described as wearing white, 'They were both in white, and their dresses were rippling and fluttering' apart from one occasion when she is wearing a lavender hat. The characterisation of this colour in particular portrays her in a sweet and innocent light. It also is a colour of purity but later on in the novel she is we are told that she is smoking which contrasts with her pure, innocent character. There are other times when she is wearing different colours when she goes to meets with Gatsby she is described as wearing a metallic colours 'she wore a suit going to Gatsby's house with brass buttons' this again shows her wealth and is also emphasised when Gatsby says 'her voice is full of money' and another time she is described as wearing a lavender hat.

Emily Bronte gives us in chapter three what seems to be a ghost of a child, this section gets allot of critical attention whether or not this actually happened, if it was a hallucination or a dream. Lockwood could not sleep because of what he thought was a branch tapping at the window, he could not get the window open and so smashed the window when he put his hand out his 'fingers closed on the fingers of a little, ice-cold hand' the child tells us that her name is Catherine Linton and that she wants back in because she has been lost in the moors and she wishes to return after 20 years. But why is she introduced as Catherine Linton when there were more markings of Catherine Heathcliff? Emily Bronte is making us think of the past life of Catherine, did she get married to Linton? Why does she want back to the place where Heathcliff is? In comparison to "The Great Gatsby' the parallel to the way that Daisy used to have Gatsby and then she left him and now she wants him back again just like Catherine wants back in to Wuthering Heights again after all these years.

The way in which Bronte has written this part makes it seem as though it is really happening to him, but it couldn't possibly be because Lockwood smashed the window because he could not get it open but when Heathcliff came in the window was not smashed and Heathcliff opened it with ease. There is a time that we hear of a description of Catherine's appearance when she is lying on her bed dying and she is wearing a white dress, like Daisy. These two women seem alike here because Catherine is on her death bed and is practically lifeless and needs to be looked after whereas Daisy, although not at death's door, is helpless and needs looking after, maybe not needs but wants to be looked after, they both become dependant on their loved ones at this time.

Behaviour - in our first meeting with Daisy she is described as sitting as though tied to a balloon. This floating metaphor suggests that Daisy has no direction in life, like a balloon, whatever wind goes the balloon goes along with it. This is reflected in Daisy's character by her disorganisation. She even says 'what'll we plan, how do people plan"' and the floating in and out of conversations, from candles to the longest day of the year in a matter of seconds.

She and Tom living in France for a year, not to fight in the war but to follow the sport of polo, also mirrors this floating along whatever way life goes image. Daisy and Tom go to places where people are rich together. Compared to Catherine in Wuthering Heights she appears to be more of a grounded character she knows how things should be, for example, that she wants her and Heathcliff to be together not only on earth but in heaven to. Even as a child she is the same, wants a whip for her horse, shows she has control unlike Daisy who wants everything done for her.

Fitzgerald also presents Daisy as a non-maternal mother to her daughter. We never hear that she has a child we are not shown her nor told her name. All the information we get is about the birth and it was all about Daisy 'I wake up', 'I turned', and there is no emotional attachment to the child. She refers to the child as 'the baby' and later on we find that the child is 3 years old 'And I hope she'll be a fool - that's the best thing a girl in this world today, a beautiful little fool' but here she is talking about herself showing again that she is self-absorbed. Catherine of 'Wuthering Heights' also has a daughter but Catherine never gets to be a mother to her as she died when her daughter called Catherine was born.

Although Daisy has a husband she enjoys the attention from other men. In doing so she does not talk, she whispers. She does this to have men attentive in listening to her. When she talks to men she can be very flirtatious like when she said to Nick 'you remind me a rose, an absolute rose' she does this to make her husband, Tom, jealous and to make him appreciate her more. We don't see Catherine doing this, she knows that she has two men that love her dearly and she is able to pick and choose because the both of them will always want her.

Daisy is a weak and fragile character in comparison to Tom's mistress, Myrtle. When Tom accidentally bruises Daisy's little finger, she made a big commotion about it, whereas Tom breaks Myrtles nose in an argument over Daisy and she is worried about covering the sofa with a newspaper so the blood wont stain it. This again shows Daisy wanting attention all the time.

Unlike Daisy, Catherine was always mischievous and badly behaved 'wild and wick(-ed) she was full of life and even though she was infuriating she was greatly loved. As Nelly states 'she was much too fond of Heathcliff' this not only describes Nelly's jealousy but also shows that Catherine does have feelings for Heathcliff. But Daisy's feelings for Gatsby were materialistic and do not have the love that Catherine and Heathcliff have, a love beyond the grave. This is proven by Daisy remaining with Tom at the end of the novel and not grieving over Gatsby.

How the heroine is presented in the love story

Fitzgerald presents Daisy in a love triangle situation with her husband, Tom and an ex-lover Gatsby. She marries Tom for materialistic reasons; he came from the same type of background as her and has lots of money. She once loved Gatsby before he went to war. Gatsby had told her that he had inherited millions to make her fall in love with him, which she did. Daisy promised to wait for him until he came back from the war but she didn't it was too long and she met a man called Tom whom she felt could give the same as Gatsby. This shows how materialistic Daisy so she went on to marry Tom.

There seems to be a similar attitude to that of Catherine in 'Wuthering Heights' she tells Nelly that Edgar asked him to marry her, but she does not tell her that she actually loves him, says she loves him 'as everybody loves' because he is handsome and rich. She becomes materialistic and self absorbed like Daisy, 'And I will be rich, and I shall like to be the greatest woman of the neighbourhood, and I shall be proud of having such a husband' Nelly tries to tell her how this is so wrong and how things can change but the important thing is that Catherine knows that in her heart its wrong. This shows that how strong her love for Heathcliff is and it doesn't matter about the money or youth or looks she knows that her and Heathcliff's souls should be together. She is trapped, her body wants to be with Linton for comfort and a good future but her soul wants to be with Heathcliff.

Gatsby talks about his want for Daisy as 'following a grail' he feels married to her but feels that if she were to find out the truth about how he became wealthy she would not feel the same way. He feels he has to protect and stand up for Daisy and is willing to take the blame for her knocking over Myrtle. He sees himself as a medieval knight type figure and he feels his relationship with Daisy is something more, like a religion on which he bases his whole persona.

Nick characterises Daisy and Tom as 'careless people who breaks things and then retreat into their wealth and let other people clean up their messes.' An example of this is when George Wilson kills Gatsby and then shoots himself Daisy and

Tom run away together and don't attend to Gatsby's funeral. At the end of the showdown in New York everyone thinks that Daisy is in her room but she not she is in the kitchen with Tom eating cold chicken and drinking ale, reminding themselves of their intimate times together it is as though at heart everything else doesn't get, through everything they are just ordinary people who will always come back to each other. This love story ending is very different from that of 'Wuthering Heights'. Catherine and Heathcliff's physical love has to end due to the death of Catherine but Heathcliff's emotional love for Catherine clearly lives on until he dies. Eighteen years after Catherine's death when her grave is being dug up for Linton to be buried in, Heathcliff asks the sexton can he open Catherine's coffin to see her for one last time and request for his and Catherine's coffins to lye side by side and to no have no walls of their coffin between them and so he kicked out the side of her coffin. Eighteen years after her death she has remained the same. It is although she is waiting for Heathcliff to come to her so she can rest properly, as she wanted him in heaven with her.

'Wuthering Heights' shows us a different love than in 'The Great Gatsby'. Catherine and Heathcliff take solace in comforting each other when they were children. When they are older they talk of their expectations of heaven but later on in a dream when she is dying she realises that it is not a place that she would want to be with out Heathcliff. Here Bronte is presenting us with a love with a spiritual dimension to it, that their souls will be together beyond the grave. This contrasts very much so with the "material love" in 'The Great Gatsby'. Catherine and Heathcliff share the same experiences and are on the same level on which the two of them can understand each other. She even tells Nelly that her and Heathcliff's soul must be made of the same thing. Emily Bronte presents Catherine and Heathcliff as one unit but when Hindley (Catherine's brother) splits them up but is unsuccessful. When Linton comes his offering of luxury is more appealing to Catherine and so goes with him. But she still loves Heathcliff, this becomes the "love triangle" situation that appears in 'The

Great Gatsby' and so now begins the divide of her love between Linton and Heathcliff. She declared her love to Nelly very strongly 'I am Heathcliff - he's always in my mind'.

At the same time she informs Nelly how she knows Edgar and her are not right together 'Linton's is as different as a moonbeam from lightning, or frost from fire'. Her burst out expression of her true love for Heathcliff and her realisation of her superficial love for Edgar Linton is expressed in one proclamation 'my love for Linton is like the foliage in the wood. Time will change it.......My love for Heathcliff resembles the eternal rocks beneath-a source of visible delight, but necessary'. Even though she decides to marry Edgar she tells Nelly that she love every thing around Edgar but does not love him, 'what ever place the sole lives in my soul and in my heart is what's right.' Emily Bronte presents us with a very emotional attachment to Catherine, he quotes 'I struggled for you' this runs a parallel to 'The Great Gatsby' because Heathcliff changed and made himself be someone he wasn't, just like Gatsby.

Narrator's attitude / other characters

Nick, the narrator, is Daisy's second cousin. Initially we feel they are close in their passing comments to each other such as Nick's comment to Daisy that she 'opens up in a flower-like way', although this contrasts with the manufactured environment she lives in with telephone and cars. Nick's observation seems to link with natural occurrences such as her name and the characterisation of white on Daisy. Nick and Daisy know very little about each other this is shown through Daisy asking Nick why was he not at her wedding; he was not there because he was fighting in the war. I think Fitzgerald is trying to present Daisy as one of these people who once they get married no longer associate with their family.

Gatsby, he is an ex-lover of Daisy and they both still have feelings for each other and Daisy becomes torn between her husband, Tom and Gatsby. It is his dream to get Daisy back again and she is the motivation for him in getting millions in illegal deals to win her over on Tom. He tries to impress her with his mansion and the amazing shirts in every colour of the rainbow, this is when Daisy breaks down and cries because she realises what she has been missing out on because her materialistic character she knows that Gatsby can give her everything she wants. Gatsby held parties in which people came who he didn't know, the reason for having these parties was in hope that Daisy would one day turn up at one, in which she did with the help of Nick. Fitzgerald presents a character with a strong love for Daisy like in the way Bronte does this with Heathcliff.

Fitzgerald gives us two women characters to compare Daisy to, Jordan and Myrtle. Fitzgerald presents Daisy and Myrtle at the same time when they are sitting in the living room and both described as wearing white. They are also similar in the way that they are both upper class but at the same time they are two very different women. Jordan has a purpose in life, she plays golf, is 'in training', contrast to Daisy who has no direction or purpose in life. In comparing looks there is a big difference here; Jordan is a woman who holds her self like a 'cadet' this reflects her confidence and a strong character. Fitzgerald describes her actions as 'deft movements', and also being small-breasted shows she is not feminine.

Daisy is described as prettier and more popular with men. Daisy is the weakest of the three women this is shown through the pathetic hurt little finger scene. Fitzgerald presents a strong contrast between Daisy and Myrtle, Daisy is languid, beautiful, waiflike, appealing face wants men to protect her, whereas Myrtle is sensuous, in her mid thirties, faintly stout no gleam of beauty, she walks through her husband, a soft coarse voice. In our first meeting with Myrtle she is wearing a spotted blue dress this gives the impression of being dirty and another time she is wearing cream, here she is trying to be like Daisy isn't quite. Daisy has a quite passive nature whereas Myrtle is full of vitality, which is what makes her attractive to Tom.

How she is presented as part of society

During the time that The Great Gatsby was written women began to become more independent and wanted equal rights, became more masculine in their look and started to look for jobs. Daisy does not go along with these changes she stays the old fashioned way she does not wear the new short dresses or cut her hair short she wanted to keep the traditional values that she had been brought up with. The new age women "flappers" went to every party and got drunk, near the end of 'The Great Gatsby' there is a description of a woman that is being carried home because she is drunk. This shows that women were beginning to loose their traditional status and behaviour but still want to be carried. They are reliant on men yet still demand freedom and rebel towards traditional standards (the woman's white dress shows this) this is why Daisy does not wish to turn out like this.

Imagery idol / grail, name, colours, driving cars

Fitzgerald uses allot of imagery in portraying the character of Daisy. He has started with her name; her name is very closely linked to her character. At first thought daisies are pretty little flowers, which is like Daisy. But daisies are weeds that are annoying, unwanted and very common which suggests some of Daisy's characteristics that resemble that she is popular with men and I have found her to be an annoying character. A daisy's petals are white and around the outside of the flower which alike to Daisy as she is described most of the time as wearing white this is her image on the outside which makes her seem innocent and sweet but the centre of a daisy is a gold colour which could mean that Daisy's heart is after money and shows materialistic she is. The stem of a Daisy is green; this colour is indirectly linked to Daisy.

It is linked to Gatsby, this colour is constantly related to Gatsby, for example when he looks out across the bay and sees 'a single green light, minute and far away, that might have been the end of the dock' the green represents Gatsby's envy towards Tom because he wants Daisy and Tom has her, but this colour is also associated with the word 'go' this colour gives him drive to get Daisy back "I'm going to fix everything the it was before." We later find out that the green light came from Daisy's dock. Green signifies serenity and the sense of perfection, which is what Gatsby wants his life to be, but it won't happen unless Daisy is with him. Daisy destroys this by choosing Tom over him.

More imagery used by Fitzgerald is through the cars. We hear of Daisy having a little white roadster before she met Tom and when she was going out with Gatsby, this shows her independence and freedom all the other times we are told that she gets driven by someone else now that is with Tom. But when Tom allows Gatsby to drive Daisy home she wants to drive because it would steady her nerves which also shows that when she is with Gatsby that she is more relaxed then with Tom when she has to put on a "trophy wife" act.

Like Fitzgerald, Emily Bronte uses imagery to portray the characters of 'Wuthering Heights' in particular, Catherine. We are told that Catherine's father, Mr. Earnshaw, goes to Liverpool and Hindley asks for a fiddle, but Catherine asks for a whip for when she is horse riding. The fact that Catherine is only a young child having the horse shows freedom, a form of escape but also cruelty, dominance and torture. They never got the presents; they got lost or broken on the journey, instead they got a child Heathcliff this is symbolic because of the reality that Heathcliff breaks things and deprives Catherine of her freedom as a child by her not having a whip and when she is older when she cannot live with out him.

Through Nelly's descriptions Bronte portrays the heroine as coming from a warm and loving family and this is presented through their house this is an example of what Wuthering Heights was like when Catherine's family ran it 'it sounded wild and stormy yet it was not cold' this shows a strong parallel to 'The Great Gatsby' of how the homes reflect their owners.

Emily Bronte uses symbolism of nature to compare Catherine's feelings towards the two men she is torn between. Catherine describes Linton as 'foliage in the woods' meaning that it will go away and return through the seasons, but for Heathcliff she describes her love more solidly, 'My love for Heathcliff resembles the eternal rocks beneath' rocks can be dangerous but also solid strong and reliable.

At Wuthering Heights the weather reflects on the mood, in one case the storm shows the rage of Heathcliff as he fleas from Wuthering heights after hearing Catherine saying that if she were to marry him it would degrade her, but he didn't stay to hear the rest of the conversation about their souls. In 'Wuthering Heights' the same element appears that love is being used like a religion. Edgar describes Catherine as being an'idol'. These two heroines are being worshipped by their lovers.

To get to Wuthering Heights, you have to travel through a grave yard, this symbolizes the idea that the only way that Catherine can be happy, like she was as a child with her father and in the moors with Heathcliff, is if she dies. Her soul will become free and ready for Heathcliff as she believes that their souls should be together. Also the fir trees around Wuthering Heights are twisted this suggests that the characters that experience Wuthering Heights become affected and change.

Heathcliff's Obsessions

Throughout Wuthering Heights, Heathcliff's personality could be defined as dark, menacing, and brooding. He is a dangerous character, with rapidly changing moods, capable of deep-seeded hatred, and incapable, it seems, of any kind of forgiveness or compromise. In the first 33 chapters, the text clearly establishes Heathcliff as an untamed, volatile, wild man and establishes his great love of Catherine and her usage of him as the source of his ill humour and resentment towards many other characters. However, there are certain tensions, contradictions, and ambiguities present in Chapter 34 that establish the true intensity Heathcliff's feelings towards Catherine; feelings so intense that they border on a jealous obsession.

Chapter 34 begins with a tension in regard to Heathcliff's disposition. Since Heathcliff's countenance has seldom expressed anything but a sullen disposition, certainly nothing even remotely resembling joy, it comes as somewhat of a surprise when in the last chapter, young Cathy, upon seeing Heathcliff, reports that he looks, "almost bright and cheerful — No, almost nothing — very much excited, and wild and glad !" This is entirely unlike the Heathcliff that has been established up until this point. Even Nelly, who is well-accustomed to Heathcliff's personality and dark moods is taken aback by the sudden change, so uncharacteristic of his usual temper —"...anxious to ascertain the truth of her statement, for to see the master looking glad would not be an everyday spectacle, I framed an excuse to go in." Since Catherine has previously almost always been the cause of such wild mood fluctuations, it stands to reason that she has somehow inspired this wild and frightening joy in him as well.

During the final days of his life, Heathcliff's curious behaviour continues. He refuses to eat, absents himself from the company of Cathy, Hareton, or Nelly, disappears inexplicably for long intervals of time and refuses to explain his absences. Most disturbing, his strange excitement continues, causing discomfort to all those around him, especially Nelly. When Nelly asks him where he was the night before his he began to exhibit this odd elation, he tells her, "Last night, I was on the threshold of hell. To-day I am within sight of my heaven — I have my eyes on it — hardly three feet to sever me !" His statement is ambiguous—it does little to explain his sudden change of humour and little to satisfy Nelly's curiosity and wonder at his state. Joy in most characters in Wuthering Heights is an uplifting state associated with happiness and delighted exhilaration. However in Heathcliff, as Nelly observes, it is a horrible, frightening thing. In Heathcliff, the mood arouses wariness and fear in others and indicates some inner change so dramatic that its cause is almost unthinkable.

Heathcliff offers no coherent explanation for his sudden change of state and the text offers no concrete solution as to what could have caused his dark exhilaration. Thus, the question of his condition is left largely unanswered as Heathcliff continues to exhibit such uncharacteristic behaviour, inspiring all the more uneasiness in Nelly, especially. He frightens her greatly several times with his agitated state. Once, upon encountering him in his room, Nelly tells Mr. Lockwood, "I cannot express what a terrible start I got, by the momentary view! Those deep black eyes! That smile, and ghastly paleness! It appeared to me, not Mr. Heathcliff, but a goblin; and, in my terror, I let the candle bend towards the wall, and it left me in darkness ". Even Nelly, who has never before, even after many, many years of acquaintance to Heathcliff, shown any intimidation or fear of him despite his blatant displays of brutality, is shaken and haunted by his strange appearance and his agitated condition. So shocking is his countenance that she even asks herself if he is a ghoul or a vampire. Since he is not willing to divulge entirely what it is that is causing him such excitement, Nelly, and all of Bronte's audience, are left to ponder for themselves what could effect such a change.

Of course, the only thing previously that has caused Heathcliff to fluctuate so wildly in his moods and to hover between such dramatically varying temperaments is Catherine. Nelly, having been witness to Heathcliff's fits of passion and rages in regard to Catherine before is shrewd enough to credit his appearance and strange condition to her former mistress, even though she has been dead for many years. Heathcliff has previously professed the misery Catherine's death has caused him and stated his desire to be close to her — his anticipation to meet her when he dies.

When Nelly attempts to serve Heathcliff food in the last chapter she finds Heathcliff watching some invisible apparition with rapt attention. Though Nelly admonishes him for his refusal to eat and his poor condition, he never moves his eyes from whatever it is he sees — one may assume it is vision of Catherine, since his expression is a conflicting one of "both pleasure and pain, in exquisite extremes...". Little else could arouse such extreme emotion in Heathcliff, and nothing else, it seems, could make them apparent on his face. Apparently Heathcliff, seeing himself near death, and despite their present separation, feels himself as near to Catherine as he can possibly be given the fact that he is still alive. And given this relative proximity, his mood has been heightened to a delirious agitation at the prospect of seeing her again.

With this anticipation, the text introduces another contradiction. Heathcliff assumes that he will be united again with Catherine in eternal bliss when he dies. Given this belief, Heathcliff apparently believes that Catherine is in heaven. He has admitted to Nelly numerous times that he is an evil man, merciless, and bent on revenge towards his enemies, even if it means hurting those who have never wronged him—young Edgar Linton, and young Cathy, in particular. Heathcliff realizes that he is filled with hate and vengeance and makes no excuse for his behaviour. Yet, since he imagines himself being reunited with Catherine after his death, he apparently feels that he will go to heaven when he dies. This is a curious contradiction coming from a man who recognizes his evil and makes no attempt to reform himself. Maybe Heathcliff holds no beliefs concerning heaven or hell, but in the last chapter, he tells Nelly how close his soul is to bliss, which seems to indicate that he does believe in something following death.

When Heathcliff does finally die, the cause of his death is never really ascertained. His countenance in death is almost a smile, at the same time a sneer, according to Nelly—a look of life-like exultation. His countenance doesn't suggest which end he met—the sneer he wears in death is close to his normal expression in life. It must be assumed that his obsession with Catherine, his desperate yearning to be with her, and his longing for death was what ultimately killed him.

That such a longing could actually kill Heathcliff suggests that perhaps what he was experiencing was more than love. It seems unlikely that love would inspire in Heathcliff such rage and anger as consumed his life for the many years following Catherine's death. That love alone could cause his physical decline and death seems unlikely as well. Heathcliff's condition indicates that what he felt towards Catherine was more than love—it was more like a violent obsession, fueled by a mad jealousy and hatred of anyone who dared to stand between himself and her.

The text in the last chapter introduces several contradictions and tensions, but also resolves them, in a subtle way. Heathcliff's strange behaviour and mysterious death, according to the text, seems ultimately to be the result of his mad obsession with Catherine, and his inability to function rationally without her. The text implicates Heathcliff as nearly a madman—seeing apparitions, rambling almost incoherently about his approaching death, shunning food or anything else that might keep him alive. Heathcliff went beyond what was reasonable and rational in his love for Catherine—his behaviour, as illustrated in the last chapter was erratic, and his death disturbing—all indications that Heathcliff was wildly obsessed with Catherine, a premise which does much to resolve many of the complexities in Chapter 34. Bronte does an excellent job of introducing complexities and tensions within the text and then resolving them subtlety and exquisitely through Nelly's narration and observations and through Heathcliff's wild moods and unpredictable actions.

The Narrative Structure

Although Lockwood and Nelly serve as the obvious narrators, others are interspersed throughout the novel—Heathcliff, Isabella, Cathy, even Zillah—who narrate a chapter or two, providing insight into both character and plot development. Catherine does not speak directly to the readers (except in quoted dialogue), but through her diary, she narrates important aspects of the childhood she and Heathcliff shared on the moors and the treatment they received at the hands of Joseph and Hindley. All of the voices weave together to provide a choral narrative. Initially, they speak to Lockwood, answering his inquiries, but they speak to readers, also, providing multiple views of the tangled lives of the inhabitants of Thrushcross Grange and Wuthering Heights.

Brontë appears to present objective observers, in an attempt to allow the story to speak for itself. Objective observations by outsiders would presumably not be tainted by having a direct involvement; unfortunately, a closer examination of these two seemingly objective narrators reveals their bias.

For example, Lockwood's narrative enables readers to begin the story when most of the action is already completed. Although the main story is being told in flashback, having Lockwood interact with Heathcliff and the others at Wuthering Heights immediately displaces his objectivity. What he records in his diary is not just what he is being told by Nelly but his memories and interpretation of Nelly's tale. Likewise, Nelly's narrative directly involves the reader and engages them in the action. While reporting the past, she is able to foreshadow future events, which builds suspense, thereby engaging readers even more. But her involvement is problematic because she is hypocritical in her actions: sometimes choosing Edgar over Heathcliff (and vice versa), and at times working with Cathy while at other times betraying Cathy's confidence. Nonetheless, she is quite an engaging storyteller, so readers readily forgive her shortcomings.

Ultimately, both Lockwood and Nelly are merely facilitators, enabling readers to enter the world of Wuthering Heights. All readers know more than any one narrator, and therefore are empowered as they read.

Chapter 10

Later Critical Response to Wuthering Heights

Initially Jane Eyre was regarded as the best of the Brontë sisters' novels, a judgment which continued nearly to the end of the century. By the 1880s critics began to place Emily's achievement above Charlotte's; a major factor in this shift was Mary Robinson's book-length biography of Emily (1883). In 1926, Charles Percy Sanger worked out the chronology of Wuthering Heights by closely examining the text; though other critics have since worked out alternate chronologies, his work affirmed Emily's literary craft and meticulous planning of the novel and disproved Charlotte's presentation of her sister as an unconscious artist who "did not know what she had done." Critics are still arguing about the structure of Wuthering Heights: for Mark Schorer it is one of the most carefully constructed novels in English, but for Albert J. Guerard it is a splendid, imperfect novel which Brontë loses control over occasionally.

Despite the increasing critical admiration for Wuthering Heights, Lord David Cecil could write, in 1935, that Emily Brontë was not properly appreciated; even her admirers saw her as an "unequal genius." He countered this view by identifying the operation of cosmic forces as the central impetus and controlling force in the novel. He was not the first critic to perceive cosmic forces in the novel; Virginia Woolf, for one, had earlier written of Emily Brontë and her novel that

She looked out upon a world cleft into gigantic disorder and felt within her the power to unite it in a book. That gigantic ambition is to be felt throughout the novel–a struggle, half thwarted but of superb conviction, to say something through the mouths of her characters which is not merely "I love" or "I hate," but "we, the whole human race" and "you, the eternal powers..." the sentence remains unfinished.

Nevertheless, Cecil's theory that a principle of calm and storm informed the novel was a critical milestone because it provided a comprehensive interpretation which presented the novel as a unified whole. He introduced a reading which later critics have generally responded to, whether to build on or to reject. Cecil premised that, because Emily was concerned with what life means, she focused on her characters' place in the cosmos, in which everything–alive or not, intellectual or physical–was animated by one of two spiritual principles: the principle of the storm, which was harsh, ruthless, wild, dynamic and wild, and the principle of calm, which was gentle, merciful, passive, and tame. The usual distinction between human being and nature did not exist for her, for they were alive in the same way; an angry man and an angry sky both literally manifesting the same spiritual principle of storm. Cecil cautioned that

> in spite of their apparent opposition these principles are not conflicting. Either–Emily Brontë does not make clear which she thinks–each is the expression of a different aspect of a single pervading spirit; or they are the component parts of a harmony. They may not seem so to us. The world of our experience is, on the face of it, full of discord. But that is only because in the cramped condition of their earthly incarnation these principles are diverted from following the course that their nature dictates, and get in each other's way. They are changed from positive into negative forces; the calm becomes a source of weakness, not of harmony, in the natural scheme, the storm a source not of fruitful vigour, but of disturbance. But when they are free from fleshly bonds they flow unimpeded and unconflicting; and even in this world their discords are transitory. The single principle that ultimately directs them sooner or later imposes an equilibrium....

Because these principles were neither good nor evil but

just were, the novel was not concerned with moral issues and judgments; rather, it presented, in Cecil's view, a pre-moral world. Just as Brontë resolved the usual conflict between the principles of storm and calm into equilibrium, so she resolved the traditional opposition between life and death by allowing for the immorality of the soul in life as well as in the afterlife. Cecil extrapolated, "The spiritual principle of which the soul is a manifestation is active in this life: therefore, the disembodied soul continues to be active in this life. Its ruling preoccupations remain the same after death as before." In other words, the individual's nature and passions did not end with death; rather death allowed their free expression and fulfillment and so held the promise of peace. This was why Catherine's spirit haunted Wutheirng Heights after her death.

Cecil's theory is one of the twentieth century outpourings of interpretations trying to prove the novel had a unified structure. Surveying these myriad efforts, J. Hillis Miller challenged the assumption that the novel presents a unified, coherent, single meaning: "The secret truth about Wuthering Heights, rather, is that there is no secret truth which criticism might formulate in this way... It leaves something important still unaccounted for... The text is over-rich." He suggests that readers and critics should push their reading of or theory about the novel as far as they can, until they can face the fact that their interpretation fails to account for all the elements in the novel, that the novel is not amenable to logical interpretation or to one interpretation which accounts for the entire novel.

Perhaps F.R. Leavis penned the most quoted modern interpretation of Wuthering Heights when he excluded it from the great tradition of the English novel because it was a "sport," i.e., had no meaningful connection to fiction which preceded it or influence on fiction which followed it.

Class Structure

In the Victorian Era, social class was not solely dependent upon the amount of money a person had; rather, the source of income, birth, and family connections played a major role in determining one's position in society. And, significantly, most people accepted their place in the hierarchy. In addition to money, manners, speech, clothing, education, and values revealed a person's class. The three main classes were the elite class, the middle class, and the working class. Further divisions existed within these three class distinctions.

The characters in Wuthering Heights demonstrate the nature of this class-structured society. The Lintons were the most elite family in the novel, and Thrushcross Grange was a superior property to Wuthering Heights, yet they were not members of the uppercrust of society; rather, they were the professional middle class.

Although Wuthering Heights was a farmhouse, the Earnshaws were not members of the working class because they were landowners who had servants. Their station in society was below the Lintons but not significantly below. Nelly, a servant of the Earnshaws, represents the lower middle class—those who worked non-manual labour. Servants were superior to manual laborers, which explains the problems created by Heathcliff.

Heathcliff is an orphan; therefore, his station is below everyone else in Wuthering Heights. It was unheard of to raise someone from the working class as a member of the middle-to-upper middle class. Even Nelly, who was raised with the Earnshaw children, understood her place below her childhood friends. When Mr. Earnshaw elevates the status of Heathcliff, eventually favoring him to his own son, this goes against societal norms.

This combination of elevation and usurpation is why Hindley returns Heathcliff to his previous low station after the death of Mr. Earnshaw, and that is why Heathcliff relishes in the fact that Hindley's son Hareton is reduced to the level of a common, uneducated laborer. And social class must be the reason Catherine marries Edgar; she is attracted to the social comforts he can supply her. No other plausible explanation exists. Catherine naively thinks she can marry Edgar and then use her position and his money to assist Heathcliff, but that would never happen.

When Heathcliff returns, having money is not enough for

Edgar to consider him a part of acceptable society. Heathcliff uses his role as the outcast to encourage Isabella's infatuation. The feelings that both Catherine and Isabella have for Heathcliff, the common laborer, cause them to lose favour with their brothers. Hindley and Edgar cannot accept the choices their sisters make and therefore, withdraw their love. When a woman betrays her class, she is betraying her family and her class—both unacceptable actions.

Major Themes

Of the major themes in Wuthering Heights, the nature of love—both romantic and brotherly but, oddly enough, not erotic—applies to the principal characters as well as the minor ones. Every relationship in the text is strained at one point or another. Brontë's exploration of love is best discussed in the context of good versus evil (which is another way of saying love versus hate). Although the polarities between good and evil are easily understood, the differences are not that easily applied to the characters and their actions.

The most important relationship is the one between Heathcliff and Catherine. The nature of their love seems to go beyond the kind of love most people know. In fact, it is as if their love is beyond this world, belonging on a spiritual plane that supercedes anything available to everyone else on Earth. Their love seems to be born out of their rebellion and not merely a sexual desire. They both, however, do not fully understand the nature of their love, for they betray one another: Each of them marry a person whom they know they do not love as much as they love each other.

Contrasting the capacity for love is the ability to hate. And Heathcliff hates with a vengeance. Heathcliff initially focuses his hate toward Hindley, then to Edgar, and then to a certain extent, to Catherine. Because of his hate, Heathcliff resorts to what is another major theme in Wuthering Heights—revenge. Hate and revenge intertwine with selfishness to reveal the conflicting emotions that drive people to do things that are not particularly nice or rationale. Some choices are regretted while others are relished.

These emotions make the majority of the characters in Wuthering Heights well rounded and more than just traditional stereotypes. Instead of symbolizing a particular emotion, characters symbolize real people with real, oftentimes not-so-nice emotions. Every character has at least one redeeming trait or action with which the reader can empathize. This empathy is a result of the complex nature of the characters and results in a depiction of life in the Victorian Era, a time when people behaved very similarly to the way they do today.

Analysis of Wuthering Heights

"Wuthering Heights is a strange, inartistic story". "Wuthering Heights is a strange sort of book". "This is a strange book". "His work [Wuthering Heights] is strangely original". These brief quotes show that early critics of Emily Bronte's first edition of Wuthering Heights, found the novel baffling in its meaning - they each agreed separately, that no moral existed within the story therefore it was deemed to have no real literary value.

The original critical reviews had very little in the way of praise for the unknown author or the novel. The critics begrudgingly acknowledged elements of Wuthering Heights that could be considered strengths – such as, "rugged power" and "unconscious strength", "purposeless power", "evidences of considerable power", "power and originality". Strange and Powerful are two recurring critical interpretations of the novel. The critics did not attempt to provide in depth analysis of the work, simply because they felt that the meaning or moral of the story was either entirely absent or seriously confused.

The authorship of Wuthering Heights was an element of much discussion by critics. They believed the work to be the efforts of an inexperienced and unpracticed writer. The critical reviews, in my opinion, would have expressed even harsher judgments had it been commonly known that the author was in fact a young woman. "In Wuthering Heights, the reader is shocked, disgusted, almost sickened by details of cruelty, inhumanity, and the most diabolical hate and vengeance...". Had this particular critic been aware of the author's true identity, his barely concealed dislike for the work would have had no constraint. Charlotte Bronte assumed the role of intermediary between her late sister and the perplexed and hostile readers of Wuthering Heights. Charlotte attempted to provide Emily's readers with a more complete perspective of her sister and her works. She selectively included biographical information and critical commentary into the revised 1850 edition of Wuthering Heights, which gave the reader a fuller appreciation of the works of Emily Bronte.

Charlotte championed the efforts of her younger sister and believed that Emily's inexperience and unpracticed hand were her only shortcomings. Charlotte explains much of Emily's character to the readers through the disclosure of biographical information. Through Charlotte, we come to know Emily as a reclusive and unrestrained lover of nature.

Emily's only absence from her home amongst the hills of Yorkshire and Lancashire, occurred in her sixteenth year, when she attended a distant school – the duration of which was cut short due to the extreme homesickness that Emily was experiencing. Emily went on to experience the isolation and drudgery of earning her living as a governess. Emily's experiences, related to us by Charlotte, transform our perspective of the author and give an understanding of the source of Emily's inspiration.

Chapter 11

The Magnanimity of Wuthering Heights

Once upon a time, it seems, an English clergyman born Brunty or Branty, self-baptized the more romantic Brontë, brought home to his four children a box of twelve wooden soldiers. The children lived in isolation in a parsonage high on the Yorkshire moors, which is to say, at the edge of the world; each was possessed of an extraordinarily fecund imagination; the wooden soldiers soon acquired life and identities (among them the Duke of Wellington and Bonaparte).

The way by which a masterpiece as unanticipated as Wuthering Heights comes to be written, involving, as it did, the gradual evolution from such early childish games to more complex games of written language (serial stories transcribed by the children in minute italic handwriting meant to resemble print; secret plays, or "bed plays," written at bedtime; the transcribing of the ambitious Gondal and Angria sagas, which were to be viable for nearly fifteen years) is so compelling a tale, so irresistible a legend, one is tempted to see in it a miniature history of the imagination's triumph, in the most socially restricted of environments. No poet or novelist would wish to reduce his mature works to the status of mere games, or even to acknowledge an explicit kinship with the prodigies of the child's dreaming mind; but it is clear that the play of the imagination has much to do with childish origins, and may, in truth, be inseparable from it.

As Henry James has observed, in a somewhat peevish

aside regarding the "romantic tradition" and the "public ecstasies" surrounding the Brontë sisters, "Literature is an objective, a projected result; it is life that is the unconscious, the agitated, the struggling, floundering cause." Certainly this is true, but its dogma is too blunt, too assured, to inspire absolute confidence. The unconscious energies feed the objective project; life fuels art, in disguised forms, though art is, of course, a highly conscious activity. Literature is far more than a game of words, a game ingeniously constructed of words, but the imagination is expansive enough to accommodate both the child's fantasies and the stratagems of the adult. Out of that long-lost box of wooden soldiers, or its forgotten equivalent, we have all sprung.

It is not simply in contrast to its origins that Wuthering Heights strikes us as so unique, so unanticipated. This great novel, though not inordinately long, and, contrary to general assumption, not inordinately complicated, manages to be a number of things: a romance that brilliantly challenges the basic presumptions of the "romantic"; a "gothic" that evolves—with an absolutely inevitable grace—into its temperamental opposite; a parable of innocence and loss, and childhood's necessary defeat; and a work of consummate skill on its primary level, that is, the level of language. Above all, it is a history. its first statement is the date 1801; and one of its final statements involves New Year's Day (of 1803).

It seeks both to dramatize and to explain how the ancient stock of the Earnshaws are restored to their rights (the somber house of Wuthering Heights, built in 1500), and, at the same time, how and why the last of the Earnshaws, Hareton, will be leaving the Heights to live, with his cousin-bride, at Thrushcross Grange. One generation has given way to the next: the primitive energies of childhood have given way to the intelligent compromises of adulthood. The history of the Earnshaws and the Lintons begins to seem a history, writ small, albeit with exquisite detail, of civilization itself.

As a historical novel, published in 1847, "narrated" by Lockwood in 1801-1802, and encompassing an interior story that begins in the late summer of 1771, Wuthering Heights is expansive enough to present two overlapping and starkly contrasting tales: the first, and more famous, a somewhat lurid tragedy of betrayal erected upon a fantasy of childhood (or incestuous) romance"; the second, a story of education, maturing, and accommodation to the exigencies of time. Both stories partake of the slightly fabulous, especially the first (in which, with fairy-tale inevitability, a "gypsy" foundling, named for a dead son, usurps a father's love); both seem to progress less as a consequence of individual and personal desire than of the abstract (and predetermined) evolution of "Nature" into "Society."

The great theme of Wuthering Heights, perversely overlooked by many of its admiring critics, as well as by its detractors, is precisely this inevitability: how present-day harmony, in September of 1802, has come about. Far from being a rhapsodical ode to primitive dark energies, populated by savages (whether noble or otherwise), the novel is, in fact, as its elaborate structure makes clear, an assured demonstration of the finite and tragically self-consuming nature of "passion." Romantic and gothic elements cannot survive in the sunlit world of sanity (as Lockwood jealously observes, the second Catherine and her fiancee Hareton look as if, together, "they would brave Satan and all his legions"); the new generation will settle in the more commodious Thrushcross Grange, opening, as it does, in symbolic and literal terms, onto the rest of the world.

The curious spell or curse has lifted from the principals of the drama, and will continue to hold sway—so local rumor will have it, doubtless for centuries—only on the moors, where the redoubtable Heathcliff and a woman yet walk, on every rainy night. ("Idle tales," says Mrs. Dean, "and so say I." The citybred Lockwood concurs, and we are invited, however ambiguously, to concur, in the history's closing remark, as Lockwood wonders how any one could ever imagine unquiet slumbers for the sleepers in that quiet earth.")

A novel's strategy reveals itself in structure and process, not in isolated passages or speeches, however striking. Any complex work that aspires to a statement about something larger than the experiences it depicts must be understood as a proposition on two levels: that of the immediate, or present time (the shared fiction of the "immediate" as it is evidently experienced by both participant and reader, simultaneously), and that of the historical (in which the fiction of the simultaneous experience of participant and reader is dissolved, and the reader emerges, ideally, at least, with a god's-eye view of the novelist's design).

The playful braiding of narrators and magisterial creator that is so pronounced a characteristic of Nabokov's novels is perhaps more willfully ingenious than the "Chinese box" narration of Emily Brontë (which, one should hasten to say, she chose to employ, as a felicitous convention, and did not invent), but scarcely more effective. As much as any Modernist work, Wuthering Heights demands to be reread: the first three chapters (charting the disingenuous Lockwood's introduction to the surly enigmatic inhabitants of Wuthering Heights, both living and dead) yield the author's intention only upon a second reading. And this has not only to do with the time-honored device of withheld information, but with the reader's literal interpretation of Lockwood's experience: for Lockwood is himself a "reader," albeit a most confused one, in these initial chapters.

It is on the level of visceral immediacy, as a fictional "world" is evoked through the employment of language, that a novel lives or dies, or struggles along in a sort of twilit sleep; it is on this higher level, where structure and design are grasped, and all novels make claim to be "histories" (the eager demands of how and why, as well as what, accommodated), that it acquires a more cultural or generalized value. Emily Brontë's sense of the parable residing beneath her melodramatic tale guides us throughout: for we are allowed to know, despite the passionate and painfully convincing nostalgia for the Heights, the moors, and childhood, evinced by Catherine and Heathcliff, that their values, and hence their world (the Heights) are doomed.

We acquiesce rather to the lyricism of the text, than to its actual claims: the triumph of the second Catherine and Hareton (the "second" Heathcliff), not only in their union but in their proposed move away from the ancient home of the Earnshaws, is a triumph that quite refutes traditional readings of the novel that dwell upon its dark, brooding, unconscious, and even savage energies. Meaning in literature cannot of course reside solely in the apprehension of design, for one might argue that "meaning" is present in every paragraph, every sentence, every word; but for the novelist such elements as scenes of a dramatic nature, description, historical background, summary of action, etc., are subordinate to the larger, grander, more spacious structure. If Wuthering Heights is the title of this phase of "our" collective history, ending on New Year's Day of 1803, Thrushcross Grange will be the title of the next.

Who will inherit the earth's riches? Who will inherit a stable, rather than a self-consuming, love? What endures, for mankind's sake, is not the violent and narcissistic love of Catherine and Heathcliff (who identify with each other, as fatal twins, rather than individuals), but the easier, more friendly, and altogether more plausible love of the second Catherine and Hareton Earnshaw.

How ironic, then, that Brontë's brilliantly imagined dialectic, arguing for the inevitable exorcism of the old demons of childhood, and professing an attitude toward time and change that might even be called optimistic, should have been, and continues to be, misread. That professional critics identify subject matter in process with an ambitious novel's design is one of the curiosities of literary history, and bears an uncomfortable resemblance to the myopic activities of the self-appointed censor, who judges a book by a certain word, on page 58 or 339, and has no need to trouble himself with the rest. Wuthering Heights is no less orderly and ritualistic a work than a representative Greek tragedy, or a novel of Jane Austen's, though its author's concerns are with disorderly and even chaotic elements.

One of the wonders of the novel is its astonishing magnanimity, for all the cliches of Emily Brontë's "narrowness." Where else might we find a tough-minded lyricism evoking the mystical value of Nature, contiguous with a vision of the possibilities of erotic experience very like that of the Decadents, or of Sade himself? Where else might we find passionate soliloquies and self-lacerations, of a Dostoyevskian quality, housed in utterly homely, and fastidiously rendered, surroundings? Both Brontë and Melville draw upon Shakespeare for the speeches of certain of their principals (Heathcliff being, in the remarkable concluding pages of the novel, as succinctly eloquent as Edmund, Iago, Macbeth), but it is Brontë's novel that avoids the unnatural strain of allegory, and gives a local habitation to outsized passions.

Wuthering Heights is erected upon not only the accumulated tensions and part-formed characters of adolescent fantasy (adumbrated in the Gondal sagas) but upon the very theme of adolescent, or even childish, or infantile, fantasy. In the famous and unfailingly moving early scene in which Catherine Earnshaw tries to get into Lockwood's chamber (more specifically her old oak-paneled bed, in which, nearly a quarter of a century earlier, she and the child Heathcliff customarily slept together), it is significant that she identifies herself as Catherine Linton though she is in fact a child; and that she informs Lockwood that she had lost her way on the moor, for twenty years.

As Catherine Linton, married, and even pregnant, she has never been anything other than a child: this is the pathos of her situation, and not the fact that she wrongly, or even rightly, chose to marry Edgar Linton over Heathcliff. Brontë's emotions are clearly caught up with these child's predilections, as the evidence of her poetry reveals, but the greatness of her genius as a novelist allows her a magnanimity, an imaginative elasticity, that challenges the very premises (which aspire to philosophical detachment) of the Romantic exaltation of the child and childhood's innocence.

The highly passionate relationship between Catherine and Heathcliff, forged in their embittered and savage childhood, has been variously interpreted: it is a doomed "gothic" romance, whose depth of feeling makes the inane Lockwood and his narrative-mate Mrs. Dean appear all the more shallow;

it is curiously chaste, for all its emotional outpourings, and as finally "innocent" as any love between sister and brother; then again, it is rude, lurid, unwholesome, intensely erotic, and suggestive of an incestuous bond—indeed. Heathcliff is named for a dead brother of Catherine's, and he, Hindley, and Catherine have slept together as children. (The reasons for Mr. Earnshaw's adoption of the gypsy waif, the goblin, the parentless demon, the dark-skinned "cuckoo," are never made plausible within the story; but it is perhaps instructive to learn that Emily Brontë's great-great-grandfather Hugh Brunty had adopted a blackhaired foundling from Liverpool—who in turn adopted their own grandfather, the younger Hugh. So the vertiginous interrelations and mirror-selves of the novel's central household have, for all their fairy-tale implausibility, an ancestral authenticity.)

So famous are certain speeches in Wuthering Heights proclaiming Catherine's bond with Heathcliff ("Nelly, I am Heathcliff—he's always, always in my mind"),1 and Heathcliff's with Catherine (Oh, God! it is unutterable! I cannot live without my life! I cannot live without my soul!") that they scarcely require reference, at any length: the peculiarity in the lovers' feeling for each other being their intense and unshakable identification, which is an identification with the moors, and with Nature itself, that seems to preclude any human, let alone sexual" bond.

They do not behave like adulterous lovers, but speak freely of their relationship before Catherine's husband, Edgar; and they embrace, desperately and fatally, in the presence of the ubiquitous and somewhat voyeuristic Mrs. Dean. (Mrs. Dean is even present, in a sense, when, many years later, Heathcliff bribes the sexton to unearth Catherine's coffin, so that he can embrace her mummified corpse, and dream of dissolving with her, and being more happy still.) So intense an identification between lover and beloved has nothing to do with the dramatic relationship of opposites, who yearn to come together in order to be complete: it is the at-one-ness of the mystic with his God, the peaceful solitude of the unborn babe in the womb.

That Heathcliff's prolonged love for the dead Catherine shades by degrees into actual madness is signaled by his breakdown at the novel's conclusion, when the "monomania" for his idol becomes a monomania for death. She, the beloved, implored to return to haunt him, has returned in a terrifying and malevolent way, and will not give him peace. "... For what is not connected with her to me? and what does not recall her? I cannot look down to this floor, but her features are shaped in the flags! In every cloud, in every tree-filling the air at night, and caught by glimpses in every object by day—I am surrounded with her image! The most ordinary faces of men and women—my own features—mock me with a resemblance." So Heathcliff tries to explain the frightening "change" that is upon him, when he sees that he and Catherine have been duplicated, in a sense, and supplanted, by the second Catherine and young Hareton.

The old energies of the child's untrammeled life have passed over into the ghoulish energies of death, to which Heathcliff succumbs by degrees. "I have to remind myself to breathe—almost to remind my heart to beat!" Heathcliff, that most physical of beings, declares. "And it is like bending back a stiff spring; it is by compulsion that I do the slightest act not prompted by one thought, and by compulsion, that I notice anything alive, or dead, which is not associated with one universal idea.... I am swallowed up in the anticipation of its fulfillment."4

So far as the romantic plot is concerned, it is Catherine's decision to enter into a misguided engagement with Edgar Linton that precipitates the tragedy: more specifically, a melodramatic accident by which Heathcliff overhears part of Catherine's declaration to Mrs. Dean, but creeps away in shame before he can hear her avowal of abiding love for him. In truth, however, the "tragedy" has very little to do with Catherine's conscious will, but seems to have sprung from a phenomenon so impersonal as the passage of time itself. How exquisite, because irremediable, the anguish of "growing up"! Brontë's first-generation lovers would share a kingdom on the moors as timeless, and as phantasmal, as any imagined by Poe.

In place of Poe's androgynous male lovers we have the immature Heathcliff (only twenty years old when Catherine dies); in place of the vampire Ligeia, or the amenorrheic Lady Madeleine, is the tomboyish Catherine, whose life has become a terrifying "blank" since the onset of puberty.

No more poignant words have been written on the baffled anguish of the child-self, propelled into an unwanted maturity, and accursed by a centripetal force as pitiless as the north wind that blows upon the Heights. Catherine, though pregnant, and soon to give birth, has absolutely no consciousness of the life in her womb, which belongs to the unimagined future and will become, in fact, the "second" Catherine: she is all self, only self, so arrested in childhood that she cannot recognize her own altered face in the mirror. Brontë's genius consists in giving an unforgettable voice to this seductive and deathly centripetal force we all carry within us:

> I thought... that I was enclosed in the oak-panelled bed at home; and my heart ached with some great grief which, just waking, I could not recollect. I pondered, and worried myself to discover what it could be, and, most strangely, the whole past seven years of my life grew a blank! I did not recall that they had been at all. I was a child; my father was just buried, and my misery arose from the separation that Hindley had ordered between me and Heathcliff. I was laid alone, for the first time, and, rousing from a dismal doze after a night of weeping, I lifted my hand to push the panels aside.... I cannot say why I felt so wildly wretched... I wish I were a girl again, half savage, and hardy, and free; and laughing at injuries, not maddening under them! Why am I so changed? Why does my blood rush into a hell of tumult at a few words? I'm sure I should be myself were I once among the heather on those hills.5

Why the presumably robust Catherine Earnshaw's life should end, in a sense, at the age of twelve; why, as a married woman of nineteen, she should know herself irrevocably "changed"—the novel does not presume to explain. This is the substance of tragedy, the hell of tumult that is character and fate combined. Her passion for Heathcliff notwithstanding,

Catherine's identification is with the frozen and peopleless void of an irrecoverable past, and not with anything human. The feathers she pulls out of her pillow are of course the feathers of dead, wild birds, moorcocks and lapwings: they compel her to think not of the exuberance of childhood, but of death, and even premature death, which is associated with her companion Heathcliff. (Since Heathcliff had set a trap over the lapwing's nest, the mother dared not return, and "we saw its nest in the winter, full of little skeletons.")

This bleak, somber, deathly wisdom is as memorably expressed by Sylvia Plath in her poem "Wuthering Heights," with its characteristic images of a dissolving landscape opening upon the void. Plath, like the fictitious Catherine, suffered a stubborn and irrevocable loss in childhood, and her recognition of the precise nature of this loss is expressed in a depersonalized vocabulary. How seductive, how chill, how terrifying Brontë's beloved moor!

There is no life higher than the grasstops
Or the hearts of sheep, and the wind
Pours by like destiny, bending
Everything in one direction.
I can feel it trying
To funnel my heat away.
If I pay the roots of the heather
Too close attention, they will invite me
To whiten my bones among them.6

It is to the roots of the heather that Catherine has paid her fiercest attention.

The novel's second movement, less dramatically focused, but no less rich in observed and often witty detail, transcribes the gradual metamorphosis of the "gothic romance" into its approximate opposite. The abandoned and brutish child Hareton, once discovered in the act of hanging puppies from a chair-back, matures into a goodhearted youth who aids the second Catherine in planting flowers in a forbidden "garden"—and becomes her protector at the Heights. Where all marriages were blighted, and two most perversely (the marriages between Heathcliff and Isabella, and the second

Catherine and Heathcliff's son Linton), a marriage of emblematic significance will be celebrated. Everyone will leave the Heights, save the comically embittered old Joseph, the very spirit of sour, gnarled, uncharitable Christianity, who presumably cannot die.

How this miraculous transformation comes about, why it must be grasped as inevitable, has to do with the novelist's grasp of a cyclical timelessness beneath the melodramatic action. The rhythm of the narrative is systaltic, by which I mean not only the strophe and antistrophe of the sudden cuts back to Lockwood in Mrs. Dean's presence, and alone (musing in his diary) but also the subtle counterpoint between the poetic and theatrical speeches of the principal characters, and the life of the Heights with its harvests and apple-pickings and hearths that must be swept clean, its tenant farmers, its vividly observed and felt reality.

The canny physicality of Wuthering Heights distinguishes it at once from the "gothic," and from Shakespeare's tragedies as well, where we are presented with an exorcism of evil and an implied (but often ritualistic) survival of good, but never really convinced that this survival is a genuine and not merely a thematic possibility.

Heathcliff, who is said never to read books, comments scornfully on the fact that his young bride Isabella had pictured in him a hero of romance. So wildly deluded was this sheltered daughter of Thrushcross Grange, she expected chivalrous devotion to her, and "unlimited indulgences." Heathcliff's mockery makes us aware of our own bookish expectations of him, for he is defiantly not a hero, and we are warned to avoid Isabella's error in "forming a fabulous notion of my character." Brontë's wit in this passage is supreme, for she allows her "hero" to define himself in opposition to a gothic-romantic stereotype she suspects her readers (well into the twentieth century) cherish; and she allows him, by way of ridiculing poor masochistic Isabella, to ridicule such readers as well.

Are you sure you hate me? If I let you alone for half a day, won't you come sighing and wheedling to me again?... The first thing she saw me do, on coming out of the Grange, was to hang up her little dog; and when she pleaded for it the first words I uttered were a wish that I had the hanging of every being belonging to her, except one: possibly she took that exception for herself. But no brutality disgusted her: I suppose she has an innate admiration of it, if only her precious person were secure from injury! Now, was it not the depth of absurdity—of genuine idiocy—for that pitiful, slavish, mean-minded brach to dream that I could love her?... I never, in all my life, met with such an abject thing as she is. She even disgraces the name of Linton; and I've sometimes relented, from pure lack of invention, in my experiments on what she could endure, and still creep shamefully cringing back!

This, in Isabella's presence; and naturally Isabella is pregnant. But then Heathcliff observes, in an aside, that he, too, is caught up in this relentless "moral teething," and seems incapable of feeling pity for his victims or for himself. "The more the worms writhe, the more I yearn to crush out their entrails!" he says. "And I grind with greater energy, in proportion to the increase of pain."8 He observes elsewhere that the mere sight of cowering, weak, fearful persons awakens the desire in him to hurt; and an evening's "slow vivisection" of his own son and his child-bride Catherine would amuse him. Even the elder Catherine, who recognizes her kinship with him, calls him a cruel, wolfish man; and she, of all the persons who know him, understands that he is beyond redemption—precisely because he is not a character in a romantic novel, or, indeed, answerable to any "fabulous notions" at all. (If he weakens at the novel's end, it is only physically. His forthright judgment on his actions is: "... As to repenting of my injustices, I've done no injustice, and I repent of nothing—I'm too happy, and yet I'm not happy enough.")

Heathcliff's enduring appeal is approximately that of Edmund, Iago, Richard III, the intermittent Macbeth: the villain who impresses by way of his energy, his cleverness, his peculiar sort of courage; and by his asides, inviting, as they do, the audience's or reader's collaboration in wickedness. Brontë is perfectly accurate in having her villain tell us, by way of Mrs. Dean and Lockwood, that brutality does not always disgust; and that there are those persons— often of weak, cringing, undeveloped character—who "innately admire" it, provided they themselves are not injured. (Though, in Isabella's case, it would seem that she has enjoyed, and even provoked, her husband's "experimental" sadism.) Heathcliff presides over a veritable cornucopia of darksome episodes: he beats and kicks the fallen Hindley, he throws a knife at Isabella, he savagely slaps young Catherine, he doesn't trouble to summon a doctor for his dying son, as he no longer has any use for him.

Unfailingly cruel, yet sly enough to appear exasperated with his victims' testing of his cruelty, Heathcliff arouses the reader to this peculiar collaborative bond by the sheer force of his language, and his wit: for is he not, with his beloved gone, the lifeforce gone wild? He has no opposition worthy of him; he has no natural mate remaining; he is characterless and depersonalized will—a masklike grimace that can never relax into a smile. (Significantly, Heathcliff is grinning as a corpse—"grinning at death" as old Joseph notes.)

Very few readers of Wuthering Heights have cared to observe that there is no necessary or even probable connection between the devoted lover of Catherine, and the devoted hater of all the remaining world (including—and this most improbably—Catherine's own daughter Catherine, who resembles her): for certain stereotypes persist so stubbornly they may very well be archetypes, evoking, as they do, an involuntary identification with energy, evil, will, action.

The mass murderer who is really tenderhearted, the rapist whose victims provoke him, the Fuhrer who is a vegetarian and in any case loves dogs.... Our anxieties, which may well spring from childhood experiences, have much to do with denying the actual physicality of the outrages, whether those of Heathcliff or any villain, literary or historic, and supplanting for them, however magically, however pitiably, "spiritual" values.

If Heathcliff grinds his victims beneath his feet like worms, is it not natural to imagine that they are worms, and deserve their suffering, is it not natural to imagine that they are not us? We feel only contempt for the potential sadist Linton, who sucks on sugar candy, and whose relationship with his child-wife parodies a normal love relationship (he asks her not to kiss him, because it makes him breathless). Consequently our temptation is to align ourselves with Heathcliff, as Brontë shrewdly understands. Heathcliff pricks the reader's Linton-like imagination in such passages:

I was embarrassed how to punish him, when I discovered his part in the business—he's such a cobweb, a pinch would annihilate him, but you'll see by his look that he has received his due! I brought him down one evening... and just set him in a chair, and never touched him afterwards. I sent Hareton out, and we had the room to ourselves. In two hours, I called Joseph to carry him up again; and, since then, my presence is as potent on his nerves as a ghost; and I fancy he sees me often, though I am not near. Hareton says he wakes and shrieks in the night by the hour together....

Yet the novel is saturated with gothic episodes and images, as many critics have noted, and the tone of motiveless cruelty that prevails, in the opening chapters, clearly has nothing to do with the mature Heathcliff's "plan for revenge." The presumably goodhearted and maternal Mrs. Dean tells Heathcliff that since he is taller than Edgar Linton, and twice as broad across the shoulders, he could "knock him down in a twinkling"—whereupon the boy's face brightens for a moment. The presumably genteel Lintons of Thrushcross Grange are not upset that their bulldog Skulker has caught a little girl by the ankle, and that she is bleeding badly; they evince alarmed surprise only when they learn that the child is Miss Earnshaw, of Wuthering Heights. (As for the child Heathcliff: "... The villain scowls so plainly in his face: would it not be a kindness to the country to hang him at once, before he shows his nature in acts, as well as features?")10 One of the most puzzling revelations in the early section is that, after Mr. Earnshaw has gone to the trouble of bringing the foundling home, his own wife's wish is to "fling it out of doors"; and Mrs. Dean places "it" on the landing with the hope that "it might be gone on the morrow"—though where the luckless creature might go in this wild landscape, one would be hard pressed to say. Clearly we are in a gothic world contiguous with Lear's, where daughters turn their fathers out into the storm, and blinded men are invited to sniff their way to safety.

This combative atmosphere is the natural and unspoiled Eden for which the dying Catherine yearns, however inhuman it is. For, like Heathcliff, she is an "exile" and "outcast" elsewhere: only the primitive and amoral child's world can accommodate her stunted character, until she is reborn and transmogrified in a Catherine part Earnshaw and part-Linton.

As for Heathcliff, with his diabolical brow and basilisk eyes, his cannibal teeth, his desperate passion for revenge, is he not a "romantic" incarnation of Iago or Vendice (of The Revenger's Tragedy), another Edmund fired to destroy an Edgar, a revenge-motive imposed upon a fairy tale of love and betrayal? He does not require Hindley to flog and beat him, in order to turn stoically wicked, since he has possessed an implacable will from the very first, having demonstrated no affection or gratitude for the elder Mr. Earnshaw, who had not only saved his life in Liverpool but (for reasons not at all clear in realistic terms) had loved him above his own children. Near the end of the novel Mrs. Dean wonders aloud if her master might be a ghoul or a vampire, since he has begun to prowl the moor at night, and she has read of "such hideous, incarnate demons."

Her characteristic common sense wavers; she sinks into sleep, taxing herself with the rhetorical question: "But where did he come from, the little dark thing, harboured by a good man to his bane?"—a question that is presumably ours as well. From where does "evil" spring, after all, if not from "good"? And is it sired by "good"? And "harboured" by it? This particular demon is Heathcliff only: Heathcliff Heathcliff, possessing no other name: sired, it would seem, by himself, and never legally adopted by Mr. Earnshaw. (His headstone reads only "Heathcliff" and the date of his death: no one can think of an appropriate inscription for his monument.)

Yet if Heathcliff must enact the depersonalized role of a damned spirit, the "romantic" motif of the novel necessitates his having been a victim himself—not of Hindley or of the "ruling classes," but of his soul-mate Catherine. He is unkillable but may die from within, willing his own extinction, as his "soul's bliss kills his body, but does not satisfy itself." Just as the narcissistic self-laceration of the childlovers cannot yield to so social and communal a ritual as marriage, so, too, does the "romantic-gothic" mode consume itself, and retreat into history: for the fiction of Wuthering Heights must be that we have had Lockwood's diary put into our hands, many years after his transcription of events belonging to another century. We read his "reading" of Mrs. Dean's tale, parts of which seem remote and even legendary. Ghosts are by popular tradition trapped on an earthly plane, cursed by the need, which any compulsive-obsessive neurotic might understand, to cross and recross the same unyielding terrain, never advancing, never progressing, never attaining the freedom of adulthood. Even Edgar, the wronged husband, the master of Thrushcross Grange, soliloquizes:

I've prayed often... for the approach of what is coming: and now I begin to shrink, and fear it. I thought the memory of the hour I came down that glen a bridegroom would be less sweet than the anticipation that I was soon, in a few months, or, possibly, weeks, to be carried up, and laid in its lonely hollow! Ellen, I've been very happy with my little Cathy.... But I've been as happy musing by myself among those stones, under that old church, lying, through the long June evenings, on the green mound of her mother's grave, and wishing—yearning for the time when I might lie beneath it.11

Considering his late wife's vehement rejection of him, this is an extraordinary statement, and Edgar goes on to say that, to prevent Heathcliff's victimization of his daughter, he would "rather resign her to God, and lay her in the earth before me." Nothing is learned in the older generation; the ease of death is preferred to the combat of life. The wonder is that so strong-willed a personality as young Catherine can have sprung from such debilitated soil.

So with the perpetual childhood of myths, fairy tales, legends, and gothic romances, which, occupying a timeless "present," relate to no time at all. Being outsized and exemplary of passions, their characters cannot be human: they are frozen in a single attitude, they are an attitude, and can never develop. Only young Catherine undergoes a change of personality, and, in willfully altering her own fate, transforms the Heights itself. She alone resists Heathcliff; she nurses her invalid husband in his final sickness, and nearly succumbs to death herself. When Heathcliff somewhat uncharacteristically asks her how she feels, after Linton has died, she says: "He's safe, and I'm free.... I should feel well—but... you have left me so long to struggle against death alone, that I feel and see only death! I feel like death!"12—a speech that allows us to see how very far Catherine has come, within a remarkably brief span of time.

In another sort of novel Heathcliff would assuredly have been drawn to his widowed daughter-in-law, if only for sexual, or exploitative purposes: but Wuthering Heights is fiercely chaste, and none of its characters gives any impression of being violated by a sexual idea. (The fact that Catherine is pregnant, and that her pregnancy is advanced, during the final tempestuous love scene between her and Heathcliff, is never commented upon by anyone: not even by the unequivocal Mrs. Dean, whose domain is the physical world and whose eye is presumably undimmed by romance.

One must be forgiven for wondering if the pregnancy—the incontestably huge belly of Catherine Linton—is not acknowledged because it is so blatant a fact of physical life, so absolute a fact of her wifehood, which excludes Heathcliff; or because, given the Victorian strictures governing author as well as characters, it cannot be acknowledged. Perhaps there is simply no vocabulary to enclose it.)

Young Catherine, however, has not inherited her mother's predilection for the grave. She soon exhibits an altogether welcome instinct for self-knowledge and compromise—for the subtle stratagems of adult life—that have been, all along, absent in her elders. Where Heathcliff by his nature remains fixed and two-dimensional, a character in a bygone drama, until his final "change" draws him so unresistingly to death,

Catherine's nature is bound up with, and enforced by, the cyclical motion of the seasons: her triumph over him is therefore inevitable. Once or twice she lapses to the self-absorbed manner of the elder Catherine, in seeking (futilely) to provoke two men into fighting over her; but she is too clever to persist.

That she learns to accommodate Hareton's filial affection for his monstrous "father" indicates the scope and range of her new maturity—an attribute, it must be said, that genuinely surprises the reader. For suddenly it becomes possible at Wuthering Heights, as if for the first time in human history, that one generation will not be doomed to repeat the tragic errors of its parents. Suddenly, childhood is past; it retreats to a darkly romantic and altogether poignant legend, a "fiction" of surpassing beauty but belonging to a remote time.

As the stylized gothic romance yields to something approaching "realism," the artfully fractured chronology begins to sort itself out, as if we are waking rapidly from a dream, and the present time of September 1802 is the authentic present, for both the diarist Lockwood and the inhabitants of Wuthering Heights. Mysteries are gradually dispelled; we have gained a more certain footing; as Lockwood makes his way to the Heights, he notes that "all that remained of day was a beamless, amber light along the west; but I could see every pebble on the path, and every blade of grass by that splendid moon."

The shift from the gothic sensibility has been prepared from the very first, by Brontë's systematically detailed settings, which are rendered in careful prose by the narrators Lockwood and Mrs. Dean—the only characters we might reasonably expect to see the Heights, the Grange, and the moors. The romantic lovers consume themselves in feeling; they feel deeply enough but their feeling relates only to themselves, and excludes the rest of the world. But the narrators, and, through them, the reader, are privileged to see. (It is significant that the ghost-lovers of the older generation walk the moors on rainy nights, and that the lovers of the new generation walk by moonlight.)

For all that she has been demeaned as ordinary, unimaginative, and incapable of comprehending a "grand passion" of the operatic scale of Catherine's and Heathcliff's, the novel's central narrator, Ellen Dean, in her solitary fashion, remains unshakably faithful to the actual world in which romance burns itself out: the workaday world of "splendidly reflected" light and heat, and smooth white paving stone, and high-backed chairs, and immense pewter vessels and tankards, and kitchens cheerful with great fires.

Never has the physical world been rendered with more precision, and more obvious sympathy, whether it is the primitive outer world of the moors, or the interiors of the houses; that curious and endlessly fascinating oak paneled bed, with "squares cut out near the top, resembling coach windows"; Miss Catherine Earnshaw's silken costume, when she returns from five weeks at the Grange; the pipes old Joseph smokes, with evident pleasure. "I smelt the rich scent of the heating spices," Mrs. Dean reports, "and admired the shining kitchen utensils, the polished clock, decked in holly, the silver mugs ranged on a tray ready to be filled with mule ale for supper; and, above all, the speckless purity of my particular care—the scoured and well-swept floor. I gave due inward applause to every object...."

It is this fidelity to the observed physical world, and Brontë's own inward applause, that makes the metamorphosis of the dark tale into its opposite so plausible, as well as so ceremonially appropriate. Though the grave is misjudged by certain persons as a place of fulfillment, the world is not after all phantasmal: it is by daylight that love survives.

Long misread as a poetic and metaphysical work given a sort of sickly, fevered radiance by way of the "narrowness" of Emily Brontë's imagination, Wuthering Heights can be more accurately be seen as a work of mature and astonishing magnitude. The poetic and the "prosaic" are in exquisite harmony; the metaphysical is balanced by the physical. An anomaly, a sport, a freak in its own time, it can be seen by us, in ours, as brilliantly of that time—and contemporaneous with our own.

The Vampire Archetype in Wuthering Heights and Jane Eyre

The academic industry that feeds on the Brontë sisters is enormous. Especially tasty are Emily Brontë's Wuthering Heights (1847) and Charlotte Brontë's Jane Eyre (1847), which until the rise of feminist criticism in the last fifteen to twenty years has in this century taken second place to Emily's one powerful novel.

(In the nineteenth century, the situation was generally reversed.)1 My purpose here is not to survey the myriad fruits the Brontë industry has produced, although since my approach is Jungian, a word about the psychological treatment of these two Brontë novels seems appropriate.2 Recently, Linda H. Peterson has summarized the psychoanalytic treatments of Wuthering Heights:

Modern psychoanalytic critics have applied multiple theories to Brontë's novel—finding everything from Freudian "phallic" symbols, to Jungian archetypes, to traits of vampirism and even lycanthropy (werewolfism). Peterson naturally finds the essay she includes in her edition of the novel and critical approaches to it, Philip Wion's "The Absent Mother in Wuthering Heights," a "less extreme (and more convincing) approach". Yet Wion's article betrays a fault too often found in so-called psychoanalytical approaches; that is, he uses Emily Brontë's life to analyse her novel, thus risking what Jung himself warned against: reducing the "artist's creativity" to "a mere symptom" ("Psychology and Literature" 86). Another Freudian critic, Thomas Moser, maintains that

Emily Brontë dramatized what Freud subsequently called the id. She discovered and symbolized in Heathcliff and, to a lesser extent, in Cathy that part of us we know so little about, the secret wellspring of vitality, the child that lurks within everyone, even within so ordinary a person as Nelly Dean or one so weak as Lockwood.

Heathcliff, Moser believes, is "the embodiment of sexual energy". Interestingly, Wion sees "the relationship between Catherine and Heathcliff as a displaced version of the symbiotic relationship between mother and child". There is some truth to the claims of both critics, though Wion weakens his claim by linking his interpretation to the author's personal life. Unfortunately, the late eminent Jungian analyst, Barbara Hannah, who should have known better, does the same kind of analysis of Emily Brontë (and her family) as does Wion. In Striving for Wholeness, Hannah writes:

I venture the hypothesis that the entrance of Heathcliff into the Earnshaw family depicts or is an analogy of the entrance of a symbol of the process of individuation into the whole Brontë family. The individual characteristics of Heathcliff and the further developments of the story show the individual way that Emily dealt with it, or rather the way it dealt with her, what her soul suffered itself and which she here records in a unique document.

Some investigation of an author's life is useful and even necessary, but as Jung warned, if the novel can be explained solely in terms of the author's biography, it is "psychological," not "visionary." To be visionary a work must stem from the collective unconscious and thus have universal (mythic) application—its meaning can never be fully explained for, like archetypal symbols, it reflects as in a mirror the infinite facets of the collective psyche as it is exposed to the work. Each generation will find new (or perhaps similar) responses. Joan Carson, another Jungian critic, is more on the mark when she analyzes the "regression to childhood and the primal situation" Catherine and Heathcliff symbolize, as well as "the archetypal experience of the night sea journey". Stevie Davies compares Wuthering Heights to the Psyche and Cupid myth and maintains the elder Catherine's story

is an original myth of loss, exile, rebirth and return. It has the self-contained and opaque quality of all myth. It imagines the human soul as being female, seeking a lost male counterpart. sexual union is not the subject of the story, rather it is the metaphor for a search which is metaphysical and "human" in the largest sense.

Virginia Woolf, as perceptive a critic as she was a genius in writing fiction, understood the mythic power of Wuthering Heights, the "struggle," as she calls it, "to say something through the mouths of her [Emily Brontë's] characters which is not merely 'I love' or 'I hate,' but 'we, the whole human race' and 'you, the eternal powers...' the sentence remains unfinished" (164), which implies that a visionary work can never be fully explained. Feminist critics such as Sandra M. Gilbert and Susan Gubar also recognize the "myth-making" aspect of Emily's masterpiece "created by a woman in the misogynistic context of Western literary culture".

Although Jane Eyre is only recently, with studies such as that by Gilbert and Gubar in The Madwoman in the Attic, receiving the same kind of serious attention as has been received by Wuthering Heights, it too is a mythic work, one which, unlike Wuthering Heights, depicts a woman's individuation process. Here I differ with Hannah, who writes, Wuthering Heights undoubtedly represents the crown of what Emily found in the unconscious, for in it we can see an image of the process of individuation, carried as far, I think, as possible in its projected form. Gilbert and Gubar see Charlotte Brontë as "Borrowing the mythic quest-plot—but not the devout substance—of Bunyan's male Pilgrim's Progress ".

As may be expected because of the greater esteem held for Wuthering Heights, there are virtually no Jungian studies of Jane Eyre, albeit Hannah includes a chapter on Charlotte Brontë in Striving Towards Wholeness. Helene Moglen, in her perceptive study, Charlotte Brontë: The Self Conceived, does use Jung indirectly by quoting Northrop Frye on the romance versus the novel: "The romancer does not attempt to create 'real people' so much as stylized figures which expand into psychological archetypes. It is in the romance that we find Jung's Libido, Anima, and Shadow reflected in a hero, heroine and villain respectively". To Moglen, Jane Eyre is a combination of novel and romance, a "benign alternative to the Byronic myth" indeed, the novel is, as the title of her chapter on Jane Eyre declares, "The Creation of a Feminist Myth".

Jane Eyre was by far the most well received and popular of the three Brontë novels published in 1847. Although written later than Wuthering Heights and Anne Brontë's Agnes Grey (which appeared together), Jane Eyre was published on 16 October 1847, some two months before the other novels came out (Fraser 277 and 286). An unsigned review of Wuthering Heights in the Examiner (January 1848) declares: "This is a strange book. It is not without evidences of considerable power Heathcliff is an incarnation of evil qualities; implacable hate, ingratitude, cruelty, falsehood, selfishness, and revenge". The anonymous reviewer for Britannia (15 January 1848) believes Wuthering Heights is "strangely original" but feels the novel "would have been a far better romance if Heathcliff alone had been a being of stormy passions, instead of all the other characters being nearly as violent and destructive as himself". Another unsigned review in Douglas Jerrold's Weekly Newspaper (15 January 1848) remarks:

Wuthering Heights is a strange sort of book,—baffling all regular criticism; yet, it is impossible to begin and not finish it; and quite impossible to lay it aside afterwards and say nothing about it. the reader is shocked, disgusted, almost sickened by details of cruelty, inhumanity, and the most diabolical hate and vengeance, and anon come passages of powerful testimony to the supreme power of love—even over demons in the human form. The women in the book are of a strange fiendish-angelic nature, tantalizing, and terrible, and the men are indescribable out of the book itself.

The initial critics seem to agree on the strangeness and power of Wuthering Heights, not to mention the outrageous evil depicted in it, especially in the character of Heathcliff. Such strong reaction suggests the book struck an archetypal chord, as it continues to do so today.

Critics also recognized power in Charlotte's novel. The anonymous critic for the Atlas (23 October 1847) writes of Jane Eyre: "It is one of the most powerful domestic romances which have been published for many years". As with Wuthering Heights, some readers could hardly put it down once they began reading it. W. M. Thackeray, the novelist Charlotte so much admired, wrote to W. S. Williams, her publisher's reader, on 23 October 1847: "I wish you had not sent me Jane Eyre. It interested me so much that I have lost (or won if you like) a whole day in reading it at the busiest period ". The anonymous reviewer for the Critic (30 October 1847) writes: Jane Eyre "is a story of surpassing interest, riveting the attention from the very first chapter".

Not all the reviews were positive. The anonymous reviewer for the Christian Remembrancer (April 1848), an organ of the High Church Party, speculates that the author is a woman (the book was published under the pseudonym Currer Bell, just as Emily and Anne used the names Ellis and Acton Bell), yet ironically a book more unfeminine, both in its excellences and defects, it would be hard to find in the annals of female authorship. Throughout there is masculine power, breadth and shrewdness, combined with masculine hardness, coarseness, and freedom of expression. Slang is not rare.

The humour is frequently produced by a use of Scripture, at which one is rather sorry to have smiled. The love-scenes glow with a fire as fierce as that of Sappho, and somewhat more fuliginous. There is an intimate acquaintance with the worst parts of human nature, a practised sagacity in discovering the latent ulcer, and a ruthless rigour in exposing it, which must commend our admiration, but are most startling in one of the softer sex.

The reviewer, whose sexist comments suggest why the Brontës chose to publish under ambiguous pseudonyms, further comments: "The plot is most extravagantly improbable, verging all along upon the supernatural, and at last running fairly into it. All the power is shown and all the interest lies in the characters ". The strong sexual undercurrents in both Wuthering Heights and Jane Eyre and the supernatural elements are both in part aspects of the vampire archetype Charlotte and Emily Brontë use. As visionary literature in the sense Jung uses the term, both novels thus compensate for contemporary collective psychic imbalance—specifically for Victorian prudery, prejudice, and hyperrationalism, a legacy from the eighteenth century which the Brontës' hero, Lord Byron (2), as well as the other Romantics, also compensated for. James B. Twitchell has already done a more than adequate job of discussing the vampiric elements in these novels in his book, The Living Dead: A Study of the Vampire in Romantic Literature. However, no one as far as I know has examined the archetypal implications of the Brontës' use of vampiric elements.4 I intend to examine these implications here.

Before investigating the vampire archetype, I want briefly to discuss Charlotte Brontë's oft-repeated comments in her Editor's Preface to the New Edition of Wuthering Heights (1850). Her comments about the creative act apply to Emily as well as to herself and to Anne, for in the Biographical Notice of Ellis and Acton Bell (1850) published with the Editor's Preface to Wuthering Heights, she writes of her sisters: "they always wrote from the impulse of nature, the dictates of intuition ". In the Editor's Preface Charlotte further declares:

Whether it is right or advisable to create beings like Heathcliff, I do not know: I scarcely think it is. But this I know; the writer who possesses the creative gift owns something of which he is not always master—something that at times strangely wills and works for itself. it sets to work on statue-hewing, and you have a Pluto or a Jove, a Tisiphone or a Psyche, a Mermaid or a Madonna, as Fate or Inspiration direct. Be the work grim or glorious, dread or divine, you have little choice left but quiescent adoption. As for you—the nominal artist—your share in it has been to work passively under dictates you neither delivered nor could question—that would not be uttered at your prayer, nor suppressed nor changed at your caprice. If the result be attractive, the World will praise you, who little deserve praise; if it be repulsive, the same World will blame you, who almost as little deserve blame.

This romantic view of the artistic process corresponds almost exactly to Jung's neoPlatonic ideas. For example, in "On The Relation of Analytical Psychology to Poetry," Jung writes: "Analysis of artists consistently shows not only the strength of the creative impulse arising from the unconscious, but also its capricious and wilful character. The unborn work in the psyche of the artist is a force of nature that achieves its end either with tyrannical might or with the subtle cunning of nature herself We would do well, therefore, to think of the creative process as a living thing implanted in the human psyche". In "Psychology and Literature," Jung further comments: "The artist is not a person endowed with free will who seeks his own ends, but one who allows art to realise its purposes through him". Jung is referring especially to artists who create what he calls visionary art, art that compensates for collective psychic imbalance. "In itself," Jung writes, an archetype is neither good nor evil. It is morally neutral, like the gods of antiquity, and becomes good or evil only by contact with the conscious mind, or else a paradoxical mixture of both. There are many such archetypal images, but they do not appear in the dreams of individuals or in works of art unless they are activated by a deviation from the middle way.

Whenever conscious life becomes one-sided or adopts a false attitude, these images "instinctively" rise to the surface in dreams and in the visions of artists and seers to restore the psychic balance, whether of the individual or of the epoch. (104) This is precisely what happened with the creation of Wuthering Heights and Jane Eyre—they both compensate for contemporary prudery, hyperrationalism, and, particularly in the case of Jane Eyre,sexism. These novels are visionary art, contemporary myths that apply to our era as much as they applied to the mid-nineteenth century.

By examining the vampire archetype in Wuthering Heights and Jane Eyreit goes without saying I am not attempting to give the definitive reading of these complex novels. I am not even attempting to give the definitive Jungian reading, as if such a thing were possible. Rather, I want simply to add another layer of meaning, as it were, to the novels, to make a contribution to our understanding of them as visionary literature.

Not much has been written by Jung and Jungians on the vampire.5 If you consult the General Index to Jung's Collected Works, you will find exactly one reference to the word "vampire." It appears in paragraph 370 of volume seven, Two Essays on Analytical Psychology—a seminal volume to be sure. Jung is discussing the anima and the animus. When a patient fails to consciously accommodate these contrasexual archetypes, Jung says, they give rise to a negative activity and personification, i.e., to the autonomy of animus and anima. Psychic abnormalities then develop, states of possession ranging in degree from ordinary moods and "ideas" to psychoses. All these states are characterized by one and the same fact that an unknown "something" has taken possession of asmaller or greater portion of the psyche and asserts its hateful and harmful existence undeterred by all our insight, reason, and energy, thereby proclaiming the power of the unconscious over the conscious mind, the sovereign power of possession. In this state the possessed part of the psyche generally develops an animus or anima psychology. The woman's incubus consists of a host of masculine demons; the man's succubus is a vampire.

There is also a single reference to a vampire in Jung's oral biography as recorded by Aniela Jaffé, Memories, Dreams, Reflections.Here Jung discusses the case of a "young catatonic patient" whose fantasy (revealed after Jung was able to get her to talk) was that she had lived on the moon. The moon, it seemed, was inhabited, but at first she had seen only men. They had at once taken her with them and deposited her in a sublunar dwelling where their children and wives were kept. For on the high mountains of the moon there lived a vampire who kidnaped and killed the women and children, so that the moon people were threatened with extinction. That was the reason for the sublunar existence of the feminine half of the population.

Jung's patient decides to kill the vampire, and to this end she waits "on the platform of a tower... erected for this purpose." She waits for a few nights until the vampire appears, "winging his way toward her like a great black bird." Hiding her "sacrificial knife," she waits for him to stand in front of her, as he does, covered by "several pairs of wings. Wonder-struck, she was seized by curiosity to find out what he really looked like. She approached, hand on the knife. Suddenly the wings opened and a man of unearthly beauty stood before her." The power of the archetype is demonstrated by the fact that she is so "spellbound" by the beauty of the vampire she can not kill him. He flies off with her. Jung concludes his discussion of this case, which I will not detail here, by noting the following: "By telling me her story she had in a sense betrayed the demon and attached herself to an earthly human being. Hence she was able to return to life and even to marry".

Interestingly, the vampire here lives not under ground, as is usual for vampires (during the day at least), but "on the high mountains of the moon." Although the unconscious is probably most often symbolized by images of depth and enclosure—the ocean, caves, cellars, anything beneath the feet—here the "demon" is above, just as Bertha Mason Rochester lives on the third floor of Thornfield, her husband's mansion. Perhaps for these women, Jung's patient and Jane Eyre, because they are women and hence more closely tied than most men to the earth, the terror of the vampire, an unconscious symbol realized consciously, comes from above, from the realm, not of the Earth Mother but of the Father, for in Western, patriarchal culture, the masculine is more often associated with the sky and the feminine with the earth

To say that a vampire is a creature who returns to the realm of the living after having died and lives by sucking blood is to define merely one manifestation, for there are "psychic or astral vampires or those peculiar species that are nonhuman". The Brontës don't portray the undead so much as they portray psychic vampires; Twitchell's phrase, the "living dead," might be an apt term.

Barbara Holt's description of the psychic vampire as a "predatory" individual with "charisma" certainly applies to Heathcliff, Bertha (albeit the charisma applies mainly to her younger persona), and Rochester. The first two of these characters become the "heartless as well as soulless" people Hort describes. Rochester becomes such after his failed marriage with Bertha. Unlike the other two, Rochester, as we shall see, is able to change for the better.

Jung obviously was not very interested in elucidating the symbolism of the vampire, though he recognized its existence as a malignant image from the collective unconscious. In the quotation from Two Essays on Analytical Psychology, Jung identifies a negative image of the anima as a vampire, perhaps a kind of lamia. If the vampire can be an image of the anima, it can also symbolize the animus (for the vampire is, or can be, a kind of demon). It also symbolizes the shadow, as Jungian psychologist Anthony Stevens recognizes in a discussion of fear of possession by "the powers of darkness".

Furthermore, the vampire is a trickster, able to change into many shapes, among them bats, wolves, spiders, butterflies, fog, or even a bit of straw. Both Wuthering Heights and Jane Eyre are rife with vicious animals and animal imagery that are images of the trickster. Lockwood is attacked by a female dog, part of a "hive" of "four-footed fiends" upon his first visit to Wuthering Heights. He mistakes a "heap of dead rabbits" for an "obscure cushion full of something like cats". Catherine is injured by, significantly, a male bulldog named Skulker). This injury disrupts forever her childish union with Heathcliff. Heathcliff is more than once called a dog. Jane Eyre's first encounter with Rochester is filled with trickster imagery:

> The din was on the causeway; a horse was coming; the windings of the lane yet hid it, but it approached. I remembered certain of Bessie's tales, wherein figured a North-of-England spirit, called a "Gytrash," which, in the form of horse, mule, or large dog, haunted solitary ways, and sometimes came upon belated travellers, as this horse was now coming upon me.

Now, along with the "tramp, tramp" of the horse, Jane hears "a rush under the hedge, and close down by the hazel stems glided a great dog, whose black and white colour made him a distinct object against the trees. It was exactly one mask of Bessie's Gytrash,—a lion-like creature with long hair and a huge head [... and] pretercanine eyes". Soon the horse comes with a man on it, and Jane realizes this is no Gytrash, for "it was always alone". Then man and horse slip on some ice and Rochester takes his famous fall, not the last of which he will have to take before he and Jane can truly be one. Jane dreams prophetically "that Thornfield Hall was a dreary ruin, the retreat of bats and owls". Significantly, these are night creatures, one of which, the bat, is especially associated with the vampire. The child, the "scared infant" Jane carries in her dream through the house symbolizes her growing consciousness. The fact it and she fall suggests, like the split chestnut tree, that she and Rochester are not ready psychically to be united. Finally, Jane calls Bertha a "clothed hyena", and Rochester says Bertha made of her room on the third floor of Thornfield a "wild beast's den—a goblin's cell".

Twitchell describes well the operation of the literary (as opposed to the folkloric) vampire, a combination of the contrasexual/shadow/trickster archetypes:

The actual "attack" is almost always the same: it is nighttime, probably midnight, the bewitching hour. The moon should be full, for the vampire is not only revived by moonlight, he is energized by it. Assuming that the vampire is male, the female victim is preparing to sleep, in that dim world between sleeping and waking. She sees her recently deceased lover (often her late husband) standing before her, perhaps outside the window. Now the victim must make some inviting move; she must unhasp the window, open the door, do anything that shows she is acceding, even slightly.... the vampire cannot cross a threshold without this invitation; he is bound to wait pathetically like a schoolboy until invited in. Once inside, however, his powers gradually increase.

The vampire must then "entrance her with his hypnotic stare This trance, if successful, will put the victim under his power, and she will have no memory of their encounters". The encounter, of course, involves the vampire's taking of blood, usually, since Bram Stoker's Dracula (1897), from the neck, although in folklore the bite can be almost anywhere on the body. Bertha, in Jane Eyre, has no need of an invitation to attack her brother or her husband. Her problem is the threshold guardian, Grace Poole, who can be circumvented when she drinks too much. Also, in regard to both Wuthering Heights and Jane Eyre, it is significant that a vampire's victims are "those whom he loved most when alive. The initial victims are friends and family who, of course, recognize the vampire as one who was loved and trusted".

Another archetype the vampire symbolizes, one that

figures in both Wuthering Heights and Jane Eyre, is the scapegoat. Paul Barber, in his fine study, Vampires, Burial, and Death, points out that in folklore one could become a vampire after death simply "by being a difficult and troublesome person people who are different, unpopular, or great sinners are apt to return from the dead". Suicides especially are likely to become vampires, as are sorcerers and alcoholics: "lists of potential revenants [a term that can be applied to vampires] tend to contain people who are distinguished primarily by being different from the people who make the lists". Furthermore, "Although vampires are far more often male than female, the exceptions to the rule are commonly mothers who have died in childbirth". "Vampires," Barber also notes, " tend to be those who have died 'before their time'". These examples clearly apply to Heathcliff and Catherine, who dies in childbirth. Twitchell adds to the list: "Dying unbaptized, being buried in unconsecrated ground, being excommunicated, copulating with a witch or demon, being the seventh child of the same sex, being born on Christmas day being born with precocious teeth, being unruly during Lent ". Twitchell divides the taboo categories into "sins against the church" (here Bertha would certainly qualify, as would Rochester himself and Heathcliff); and "any social peculiarity might be a sign of diabolical propensities. So in dark-eyed cultures the blue-eyed were suspect; in dark-haired societies the blond was exiled [and] persons suffering from epilepsy or anorexia were obvious choices in all societies".

From the above description, it is obvious that Heathcliff and Bertha qualify as potential vampires, if not actual ones. Heathcliff's difference is emphasized from the time Mr. Earnshaw brings him to Wuthering Heights, a boy he found in Liverpool starving and homeless, whom even Earnshaw calls "it": "you must e'en take it as a gift of God, though it's as dark almost as if it came from the devil". Mrs. Earnshaw calls Heathcliff a "gipsy brat", and her son, Hindley, calls him a "dog" and an "imp of Satan".

Hindley's son, after only ten months' separation from Nelly Dean and now under the adult Heathcliff's care, calls the latter "Devil daddy", an example of Emily Brontë's grim humour. Isabella refers also to Heathcliff's "sharp cannibal teeth", a description that clearly could apply to a vampire. Indeed, Isabella's obsession with Heathcliff is itself an example of what Jung calls possession by an archetype. Here the trickster element of the vampire triumphs. After she succumbs to him, she realizes, as she tells Nelly, Heathcliff is a "'fiend, a monster, and not a human being!'".

Like the woman who lived on the moon, she could not resist the beauty—as she saw it—of the vampiric Heathcliff. Finally, note Nelly's description of Heathcliff as Catherine lies dying: "he gnashed at me, and foamed like a mad dog, and gathered her [Catherine] to him with greedy jealousy. I did not feel as if I were in the company of a creature of my own species ". By making Heathcliff the hero of her novel Emily Brontë compensates for Victorian prejudice against outsiders, such as gypsies and beggars, as well as prejudice against the supernatural. Jane's sympathy for Bertha does the same.

As for Bertha, her description is even more in line with that of vampires of the scapegoat variety and with the folkloric tradition. An outsider like Heathcliff, she comes from even further away—Spanish Town, Jamaica. Her mother, a Creole, "'was both a mad woman and a drunkard [... and] Bertha, like a dutiful child, copied her parent in both points,'" according to Rochester. Her hideous laugh may have been inspired by Lord Ruthven's "loud laugh" in John Polidori's The Vampyre. Before she knows who Bertha is, Jane describes her to Rochester: "'a woman, tall and large, with thick and dark hair hanging long down her back. I know not what dress she had on: it was white and straight; but whether gown, sheet, or shroud, I cannot tell'". Bertha's face, Jane tells Rochester, "was a discoloured face—it was a savage face. I wish I could forget the roll of the red eyes and the fearful blackened inflation of the lineaments."

"Ghosts are usually pale, Jane."

"This, sir, was purple: the lips were swelled and dark; the brow furrowed; the black eyebrows widely raised over the bloodshot eyes."

In folklore, Barber notes, the vampire "is never pale, as one would expect of a corpse: his face commonly is described as florid, or of a healthy colour, or dark, and this may be attributed to his habit of drinking blood"; also, the body tends to be swollen. Should the reader have any doubt as to what creature Charlotte Brontë is alluding to, Jane removes that doubt. "'Shall I tell you of what it reminded me?'" she asks Rochester. "'You may,'" he replies, to which she answers: "'Of the foul German spectre—the Vampyre'".

The use of the actual word, "Vampyre," indicates Charlotte was aware of the concept of vampires. Emily too uses the word in Wuthering Heights. Near the end of his life, when Heathcliff in effect commits suicide, as had Catherine, by refusing to eat, Nelly asks him: "'Tell me why you are so queer, Mr. Heathcliff?'". She alludes to his "deep black eyes", which, like Bertha's, are "blood-shot".

He looks like a "goblin", and Nelly wonders, "Is he a ghoul, or a vampire?". We know that, despite their isolation in the parsonage at Haworth, the Brontë children were well read and had access to the leading magazines of the day. Winifred Gérin, a major biographer of Charlotte, writes: "With Byron's works Charlotte was fully acquainted at 13". Byron had dealt with the vampire in "The Giaour," and had inspired his physician, John Polidori, to write the first vampire fiction in English prose, "The Vampyre: A Tale", after that memorable night in June 1816 in Geneva when Byron challenged himself, Polidori, Percy Bysshe Shelley, and Mary Wollstonecraft Shelley to each write a ghost story (Bleiler xxxiii).

Matthew Bunson writes: "Polidori took the framework of the tale that Byron had begun in the Villa Diodati and authored 'The Vampyre'". Quite probably Emily and Charlotte read Polidori's story, for the author was widely believed to be Byron, not Polidori. The story was particularly popular in France, where it inspired several plays. Since both Emily and Charlotte lived in French-speaking Brussels it is entirely possible they would have been exposed to the story there. In any case, the sisters' novels are evidence enough to show their awareness of the archetype.

Although Emily's poetry doesn't explicitly utilize the archetype, there are anticipations of its use in Wuthering Heights. Like Emily Dickinson and Christina Rossetti, contemporary poets superior to her, Brontë often writes about death and the afterlife, favourite Victorian preoccupations. In a poem that anticipates the situation of Cathy and Heathcliff (only reverses it, for the male dies first in the poem), the speaker suggests that the dead male might return for love of the other:

And if he came not for her woe
He would not now return;
He would not leave his sleep below
When she had ceased to mourn— (Complete Poems 139)

Polidori had made the literary vampire into a Byronic type, with his mysterious, scary brooding and strange attraction to male and female alike. In another poem Emily describes a similar character:

there was something in his face
Some nameless thing they could not trace
And something in his voice's tone
Which turned their blood as chill as stone
The ringlets of his long black hair
Fell o'er a cheek most ghastly fair
Youthful he seemed—but worn as they
Who spent too soon their youthful day
When his glance drooped 'twas hard to quell
Unbidden feelings sudden swell

The person the speaker describes could well be Heathcliff, or Rochester for that matter, another Byronic hero. In a Gothic poem called "Written in Aspin Castle," Brontë portrays an actual revenant—a returning spirit:

For around their hearths they'll tell the tale
And every listener swears it true
How wanders there a phantom pale
With spirit-eyes of dream blue—

Like the vampire, this spirit is "unforgiven." He "Wanders unsheltered shut from heaven / An outcast for eternity". Nevertheless, poems such as Number 138 (with the line "I know our souls are all divine," Complete Poems 150) and the well-known one that begins, "No coward soul is mine", a favourite of Emily Dickinson, with lines like "O God within my breast" and "Vain are the thousand creeds / That move men's hearts, unutterably vain",—these poems suggest Emily Brontë does not literally (or consciously) believe in the existence of vampires.

Nevertheless, as Twitchell has shown, Emily and her sister use vampire imagery in their novels to characterize Heathcliff and Bertha Rochester, and to some extent, I believe, Catherine Earnshaw and Rochester himself. Twitchell writes:

Emily Brontë resuscitated the vampire in the poetic characterization of Heathcliff while her sister was doing the same with Bertha Rochester. For Heathcliff (at least according to Nelly Dean) acts as if he were a vampire, devouring both Earnshaws and Lintons for his own vivification, while Bertha has to be sequestered in the attic lest her libidinal desires destroy the men-folk.

Of the four main characters in the two novels (Catherine/ Heathcliff, Jane/Rochester), only Jane is exempt from vampire characterization, but she has her shadow figure, her "dark double" as Gilbert and Gubar call her, in Bertha.8

In folklore, vampires are made—discovered if you will—after death, although people may in life suspect they will become vampires. Heathcliff is made into a creature resembling one by the way others treat him—by their making him a scapegoat. Besides "gipsy" and "vagabond", Heathcliff is called (here by the elder Mr. Linton) "'a little Lascar, or an American or Spanish castaway'". Hindley's treatment of Heathcliff, Nelly says, "was enough to make a fiend of a saint," and he seems "possessed of something diabolical" as he plans his revenge. Shamed by Catherine's transformation into a young lady after five weeks at Thrushcross Grange and jealous of the attention and affection she receives from Edgar Linton, Heathcliff develops what today we'd call a poor self image.

To Nelly he says: "I wish I had light hair and a fair skin, and was dressed and behaved as well, and had a chance of being as rich as he [Edgar] will be!" (44). Of course he does go away after overhearing Catherine tell Nelly "it would degrade her to marry him [Heathcliff]" but without hearing Catherine's declaration "Nelly, I am Heathcliff". Ironically, Heathcliff does get the money and gentleman status he longs for, but as we know he returns too late, for Catherine has already married Linton. Like Oscar Wilde's Dorian Gray (who shares vampiric traits with Heathcliff; see Hort 156-203), Heathcliff has become possessed by the vampire archetype, a victim of what Jung calls "psychic inflation".

Catherine, although not an outsider, shares vampiric traits with Heathcliff. As children, they scheme "naughty plan [s] of revenge". In a fit of anger at Nelly, Catherine pinches her violently. She is highly strung and difficult—just the sort of person who according to folklore would be a candidate for vampirism. In Literature and Evil, Georges Bataille speculates that Catherine and Heathcliff's "love can be reduced to the refusal to give up an infantile freedom which had not been amended by the laws of society or of conventional politeness". Catherine not only refuses to relinquish "infantile freedom"; she also quests for the power she's denied as a female. To this extent she, like Heathcliff, is a scapegoat. Jungian analyst Julia McAfee's comments are apropos here: "The vampire describes a psychological process where the struggle into being through love has gone awry. Vampirism is a paradigm of a blood-sucking, life-sucking love, a fatal possession". Catherine and Heathcliff are together possessed by the same archetype projected onto each other.

In her search for power in a patriarchal culture, she has failed to understand the only power she has is in herself—in Heathcliff, a projection of herself. She is as mean-spirited and self-centered, as evil if you will, as any vampire, but unlike Heathcliff she has no power over others, no power to turn them into vampiric creatures like herself—exactly what Heathcliff does to Isabella, his son Linton, Hareton, and the younger Catherine. For in a patriarchal society such as that in which Catherine lives, the power lies in the hands of men. After all, it is Mr. Rochester who controls Bertha, not the other way round. Thus it is ironic that the only power Catherine can exercise is her emotional power over Edgar and Heathcliff.

Heathcliff's vampiric power to affect others extends to Edgar Linton. Catherine's legal husband has no real power over Heathcliff, who declares vampirically, "The moment her [Catherine's] regard ceased, I would have torn his heart out, and drank his blood!". Speaking of hearts, Heathcliff accuses Catherine of betraying her own heart by rejecting him and marrying Linton. Further evidence that Emily Brontë has the vampire in mind in her characterization of Heathcliff is Heathcliff's threat to Nelly that if she neglects to have him buried in the way he demands, no minister at the service and his coffin laid next to Catherine's, Nelly "shall prove practically, that the dead are not annihilated!". Heathcliff wants no minister to say anything over him because "I have nearly attained my heaven, and that of others is altogether unvalued and uncoveted by me!".

Catherine herself once dreamt that she had gone to heaven, and as she tells Nelly: "heaven did not seem to be my home; and I broke my heart with weeping to come back to earth; and the angels were so angry that they flung me out, into the middle of the heath on the top of Wuthering Heights; where I woke sobbing for joy". Catherine and Heathcliff prefer their own self-made heaven to the traditional Christian one. Their depictions as vampiric creatures constitute an inversion of Christian conversion—instead of the cleansing, healing blood of Christ, they figuratively convert each other by sucking the blood from each other. Possessed by the vampire archetype, a combination of the contrasexual/shadow/ trickster archetypes, they fed on each other in a co-dependent relationship that can only lead to their mutual destruction.

Other vampiric actions of Heathcliff include digging up Catherine's grave. Just after she is buried, he digs down to her coffin, only to apprehend Cathy's presence above him. Relieved with the assurance she is with him, he refills the grave. One way to interpret this is to see her as having become a vampire—if not literally, then figuratively, as in the early scene with Lockwood when she tries to get into Wuthering Heights.

Yet it is the child Cathy in Lockwood's nightmare and it is her blood he sheds on the broken windowpane. She is a child in Lockwood's dream because her emotional growth has matured no further than the childhood companionship she shared with Heathcliff. Marigny observes the following: "A young man who commits the transgression of opening a tomb to see once more the face of his beloved runs the risk of discovering a grimacing devil, or even a vampire". Seventeen and a half years later Heathcliff again digs up Catherine's grave—or rather the sexton who's digging Edgar Linton's grave next to hers does it for him. This time he sees her face still preserved—a sign that she is a vampire according to folklore.

However we interpret these events, the imagery is clearly that of vampirism, and another conclusion can be drawn: there is no psychic unity, no individuation for this pair. To become individuated one must mature into a fully adult personality. Catherine and Heathcliff never mature beyond their childish bond: they remain puerile to their respective ends. This is not entirely their fault, of course. A heartless, prudish, stratified, patriarchal culture has interfered with the would-be lovers (they are never physically lovers) and their psychic growth has been stunted so that they never grow beyond a stage in which they can only identify with ego gratification. The anima and the animus are archetypes one accommodates in mature, adult life, if one accommodates them at all. Catherine and Heathcliff never mature; they never grow up.

If there is no individuation in Wuthering Heights, Jane Eyre is quite another story. It is a realistic novel with improbable, as well as Gothic elements, of which the vampire motif is a part. Tamar Heller interprets the novel as a combination of "two traditional plot lines":

> The tale of the woman alone—a female bildungsroman whose independent heroine is a significant innovation in a nineteenth-century context—and the tale of the woman and man, represented by the romance between Jane and Rochester.

Tom Winnifrith also recognizes the originality of Jane Eyre, whose author he calls "a pioneer in breaking away from the conventionalities of the Silver Fork School into a frank first-person narrative with the narrator giving full rein to her feelings". Like Wuthering Heights,Jane Eyre's continuing popularity, including the several film versions of both novels, attests to its archetypal appeal. Western civilization has produced far more heroes than heroines, and Jane Eyre is probably the first serious work of fiction in the West that creates a heroine who achieves individuation. Unlike Heathcliff and Catherine, Jane avoids possession by any negative archetype. If she is possessed by an archetype, it is the archetype of love, and this possession empowers her to become her own self—a whole woman.

Like Heathcliff, she enters the story a scapegoat, a ten-year-old orphan in the family of her widowed aunt by marriage, Mrs. Reed. Bullied by her fourteen-year-old cousin, John Reed, Jane is "the scapegoat of the nursery", confined to the "red-room" unjustly. Moglen correctly identifies the red-room as "a terrifying womb-world from which she is born into a new state of being". Adrienne Rich writes of Jane at this period of her life: "the temptation of victimization is never far away". That the room is red, the colour of blood, is significant from my point of view, for like Heathcliff and Bertha, the temptation Jane faces is to become the vampire-like creature people would be only too ready to see her as.

The scapegoatism that confronts Jane, not to mention Heathcliff and Bertha, says as much about the people who do the scapegoating as it does about the victims. As Jungian analyst Erich Neumann notes in Depth Psychology and a New Ethic, scapegoatism is "projection of the shadow," a method of displacing guilt and other unwelcome psychic components. Aliens and other outsiders are particularly apt victims: "The fight against heretics, political opponents and national enemies is actually the fight against our own religious doubts, the insecurity of our own political position, and the one-sidedness of our own national viewpoint".

The Reeds project their fear of poverty and dependency onto Jane, just as fears of contamination, stigmatization, sexual excess, and a host of unknown components of the shadow archetype are projected onto Heathcliff and Bertha. As a governess, Jane is also treated shabbily by Rochester's haughty aristocratic friends. How one reacts to being scapegoated is a measure of character. Heathcliff and Bertha incorporate the projections into themselves to their psychic (and physical) destruction. Although he may look like a gentleman and own property, at heart Heathcliff remains the ostracized demon-gypsy, the vampire-like creature almost everyone labels him, relying for self worth only on his impossible "love" (obsession would be a more appropriate term) for Catherine. Bertha has been driven insane. Only Jane among these scapegoats survives to become, in Rich's words, "a person determined to live, and to choose her life with dignity, integrity, and pride".

As a child and later an adolescent at Lowood, Jane grows into an independently-minded young woman, ready to begin the individuation process. She has accomplished the adolescent tasks of ego affirmation, confirmation of her dominant attitude type, introversion, and selection of a persona. She is a teacher and becomes the governess of Mr. Rochester, hired to teach his ward, and probable love child, Adèle Varens.

In Jungian psychology, the encounter with the shadow comes first in the adult individuation process.Although Jane has had to deal with many shadow figures (Mr. Brocklehurst comes immediately to mind along with all the Reeds; though technically the shadow is symbolized by a figure of the same gender, no one would deny Brocklehurst is a villain, full of shadow traits), Bertha is obviously the most prominent shadow figure with whom she has to deal. Those who, like Linda Peterson, may scoff at the vampiric interpretation of the Brontë novels I am discussing can hardly deny that Bertha is meant to be interpreted as, if not an actual vampire, a creature like a vampire. Moglen accepts this simple fact and links it with "fear of the female":

> The fear of the female is common among civilized as well as primitive men. Since it is a crucial product and cause of Victorian repression, we are not surprised that Berthe [sic] is a vampire: one of those who haunted the Victorian imagination. Jane identifies her in this way in describing the

nighttime visitation and Berthe [sic] does, in fact, suck Mason's [her brother's] blood as she tries to suck her husband's. She would deprive him, Rochester knows, of his energy, his vitality, his manhood.

We are reminded here that the vampire's first victims are those he or she knew and loved in life. Also, note that Rochester calls Bertha a "hideous demon" who "allured" him in typical vampire fashion. Even Jane describes her as a "clothed hyena). Earlier Bertha had actually bitten her brother, Richard Mason: "'She sucked the blood: she said she'd drain my heart'). Significantly, Bertha's attack takes place under a full moon, for, as Twitchell notes, the vampire is "energized" by moonligh). During the session after Jane and Rochester's aborted wedding Bertha's attack on Rochester is described thus: "the lunatic sprang and grappled his throat viciously and laid her teeth to his cheek", but he escapes and ties her up. The imagery is clearly straight out of vampire lore.

Jane runs the risk, in Brontë's and the typical Victorians' view, of becoming a Bertha were she to give into her libidinous desires for Rochester, never mind that the Victorians' attitudes toward women and sex were, speaking generally, twisted. Bertha, as the symbol of the shadow for Jane, represents both negative and positive possibilities, for by definition all archetypes are bipolar—both positive and negative or else neutral. The sexual empowerment of the archetype of love and passion (of Eros and Dionysus) is what Bertha represents. As Barbara Birge says in her discussion of Bram Stoker's Dracula, "potency is a sexual, generative, Dionysian, and healing kind of power. Such power is the potency Persephone, Eve, and Mina [in the film] sought to regain through their relationships". To this list I add Jane.

To preserve her psychic integrity, to incorporate the shadow qualities—negative and positive, Jane must acknowledge her kinship with Bertha, yet "save" her sexual fulfillment for matrimony. Otherwise she risks becoming that most forlorn of Victorian persons: the "fallen woman." She does the former by expressing sympathy for the woman whose existence has robbed her of her hopes for happiness in marriage. "'Sir,' she says to Rochester, "' you are inexorable for that unfortunate lady: you speak of her with hate—with vindictive antipathy. It is cruel—she cannot help being mad'" (265). Jane must now return to earth, so to speak, from the fantasy—her projected bliss with Rochester—she has been living. She must leave Rochester and Thornfield secretly and strike out on her own with virtually nothing of material value in her possession.

Having accommodated the shadow, Jane must accommodate the animus if she is to become a whole person. First, however, in a section that is rich with symbolism she must harrow hell as it were. The moon in the form of a mother had urged her to "flee temptation!". If the moon had a negative power over the vampiric Bertha, it has benevolent power over Jane. She finds herself at a crossroads, "where four roads meet", a place symbolizing choice. An "outcast" now, her heart "impotent as a bird with both wings broken", her only relation is "the universal mother, Nature". Mother Nature is all right for one night. Jane even has a sort of spiritual awakening with a masculine God: "Looking up, I, with tear-dimmed eyes, saw the mighty Milky Way. Remembering what it was—what countless systems there swept space like a soft trace of light—I felt the might and strength of God. Sure was I of His efficiency to save what He had made " (285). However, the following day, appropriately using capitalized nouns to personify abstractions, a method that harks back to the Age of Enlightenment, Want and Necessity rear their heads; and she realizes not only the negative side of the Earth Mother, but also of her fellow human beings, none of whom help her until, suffering from terrible despair and physical exhaustion, she is rescued from a rainstorm by St. John, Diana, and Mary Rivers—a remarkable example of what Jung calls synchronicity, for these three are her cousins, a fact they discover only much later (339).11

The local parson, St. John is planning to go to India as a missionary. He eventually finds work for Jane as a schoolmistress and offers to take her to India as his working wife, although he has no passion for her. Like Dr. John Graham

Bretton in Charlotte Brontë's Villette, St. John has a "Grecian" profile: he is fair, youthful, good looking. Yet Jane does not love him; she is still in love with Rochester. Here Jane is about the same age, "near nineteen", Catherine Earnshaw Linton was when she died, yet the contrast between the two could not be more vivid. Whereas Jane has acted throughout with intelligence and integrity under harsh circumstances, Catherine had acted with self interest alone and under relatively easy circumstances, marrying a man she didn't really love simply because she desired money, property, and social position.

Jane, in her own way just as passionate as Catherine (albeit she is introverted and Catherine is extraverted), is now tempted to do what society would expect of her—to marry a man of the cloth, closer to her own age than is Rochester (St. John is about ten years older than Jane; Rochester about twenty). As a symbol of the animus, St. John would be a man of the word, the logos, but Jane is herself a scholar, like St. John an introverted-thinking type, already familiar with the word. Her personal myth requires someone more her opposite—more physically active, wild, passionate, experienced in the larger world, an extraverted-sensation type such as Rochester. He is the senex, the older partner in terms of age and experience; she is the puella, the young woman who is stronger in terms of character and values. Together they would make a whole. What Jane does not want is a vampire, yet Rochester has some vampiric traits. She describes him thus upon first running into him: I traced the general points of middle height, and considerable breadth of chest. He had a dark face, with stern features and a heavy brow; his eyes and gathered eyebrows looked ireful and thwarted...

He is neither "handsome" nor "heroic-looking". All this suits her accurate image of herself as a "plain Jane." But it also could describe a Heathcliff or a vampire. It is a given in Brontë scholarship that both Heathcliff and Rochester are Byronic types. Given the Gothic features of both Wuthering Heights and Jane Eyre, the Byronic characteristics of Polidori's vampire, Lord Ruthven, and the popularity of Varney the

Vampire, published serially seven years earlier than Wuthering Heights and Jane Eyre, the character of any Byronic hero would likely resonate with vampiric implications.

Polidori, in fact, deliberately chose to make Ruthven Byronic in order to get revenge on Byron, with whom he had not got along. So he makes the vampire an aristocrat, an innovation from folklore, in which virtually anybody could be a vampire. Ruthven has "irresistible powers of seduction" for both men and women, very much like Byron.

Furthermore, Ruthven takes delight in ruining his female victims, so that they fall "from the pinnacle of unsullied virtue, down to the lowest abyss of infamy and degradation" (. Although she is not an adulteress, this is a fairly apt description of what Heathcliff does to Isabella, who was so irresistibly drawn to him. Whether or not Bertha was virtuous before her marriage to Edward Rochester, Rochester makes it clear she commits adultery after the wedding.

Perhaps this is a case where the victim is made into the villain. If she seduced him into marriage in the first place, he becomes a seducer or allows himself to be seduced again on the Continent once Bertha has gone mad and been incarcerated at Thornfield. Perhaps Bertha has turned Rochester into a potential vampire. Perhaps W. H. Auden's famous lines, "Those to whom evil is done / Do evil in return", apply to both Rochester and Bertha. Additionally Byronic is the fact Rochester has a big secret—the very existence of Bertha. Both Heathcliff and Rochester are exceedingly moody, another Byronic trait.

My point is not that Rochester is depicted as a vampire as are Bertha and Heathcliff, but that like Catherine he has some vampiric traits. Had Jane married him before his injuries he would have dragged her down, so to speak, whether Bertha lived or not, for as a wealthy Victorian aristocrat, he had all the power. Vampiric relationships are about power, about controlling the weaker person, sucking his or her blood and vitiating him or her. That is why a healthy relationship between Heathcliff and Catherine was impossible, and that is why before the destruction of Thornfield a healthy relationship between Edward Rochester and Jane Eyre would have been impossible. Bertha, who is almost literally a vampire, must be destroyed for two reasons. First, psychically she symbolizes the shadow for Jane and must disappear from her conscious life once Jane has accommodated the shadow. Second, she is obviously a legal impediment. Because she is mad, Rochester cannot divorce her. Everyone knows the way to kill a vampire is to drive a stake through his or her heart and cut off his or her head. Perhaps not so well known is that cremation is just as acceptable a method. Bertha dies aflame, falling from Thornfield, "her brains and blood... scattered". The important thing is to "render the body inert", and that's exactly what Brontë does with Bertha.

Rochester, never having become a full-blown vampire, does not have to die. Losing his sight is enough to deprive him of his power. Early in their relationship, Jane describes Rochester's eyes as "dark, irate, and piercing"; "he had great, dark eyes, and very fine eyes too". Do I go too far to say she is entranced by those eyes? I think not. It is with his "trance," remember, that the vampire "will put the victim under his power". Without his eyes, Rochester's sinister power is gone. It is as if the dregs of his psyche have been destroyed; only the valuable parts are left, the parts that with Jane will create a whole. Now she can unite with him as the positive animus, fully conscious and equal to each other.

Because of his infirmity, Jane is forced to become more extraverted, to become his eyes. ("Literally, I was the apple of his eye" 397.) Her thinking and feeling functions have long been developed, for she has always been a scholar and felt instinctively what was right and what was wrong. When St. John proposes to her, her intuition function is sufficiently developed to tell her such a union would be wrong; indeed, she intuits moving to India would kill her. When she intercepts Rochester's telepathic message, another example of synchronicity, her intuition is perhaps most keen. She finally develops her weakest function, sensation, by becoming her husband's eyes and by physically uniting with him (together they produce a son).

Having developed all four functions of consciousness, having accommodated the shadow and overcome scapegoating, having been united with the contrasexual, she has become a whole person, and with the legacy from her uncle, an "independent woman" financially, who chooses to join with another:

> for with him I was at perfect ease, because I knew I suited him; all I said or did seemed either to console or revive him. Delightful consciousness! It brought to life and light my whole nature: in his presence I thoroughly lived; and he lived in mine.

Jane Eyre has realized her personal myth.

Chapter 12

Study Questions and Answers

Q. The romantic novel,romanticism, and wuthering heights. Discuss?

Or

Q. Discuss the Romantic Element in Wuthering Heights?

The Romantic Novel

Robert Kiely raises the question, in The Romantic Novel in England, Is there actually an English romantic novel? He skirts answering his own question by suggesting that some novels are influenced by Romanticism and incorporate the same style and themes that appear in Romantic poetry and drama. In his discussion, the term romantic novel is often equated with the romance, with the Gothic novel, and with the romantic elements in a novel. Kiely regards Wuthering Heights as a model of romantic fiction; it contains these romantic/Gothic elements which charterize the romantic novel:

The dynamic antagonism or antithesis in the novel tends to subvert, if not to reject literary conventions; often a novel verges on turning into something else, like poetry or drama. In Wuthering Heights, realism in presenting Yorkshire landscape and life and the historical precision of season, dates, and hours co-exist with the dreamlike and the unhistorical; Brontë refuses to be confined by conventional classifications.

The protagonists' wanderings are motivated by flight from previously-chosen goals, so that often there is a pattern of escape and pursuit. Consider Catherine's marriage for social position, stability, and wealth, her efforts to evade the consequences of her marriage, the demands of Heathcliff and

Edgar, and her final mental wandering. The protagonists are driven by irresistible passion–lust, curiosity, ambition, intellectual pride, envy. The emphasis is on their desire for transcendence, to overcome the limitations of the body, of society, of time rather than their moral transgressions. They yearn to escape the limitations inherent to life and may find that the only escape is death. The longings of a Heathcliff cannot be fulfilled in life.

Death is not only a literal happening or plot device, but also and primarily a psychological concern. For the protagonists, death originates in the imagination, becomes a "tendency of mind," and may develop into an obsession.

As in Gothic fiction, buildings are central to meaning; the supernatural, wild nature, dream and madness, physical violence, and perverse sexuality are set off against social conventions and institutions. Initially, this may create the impression that the novel is two books in one, but finally Thrushcross Grange and Wuthering Heights fuse.

Endings are disquieting and unsatisfactory because the writer resists a definitive conclusion, one which accounts for all loose ends and explains away any ambiguities or uncertainties. The preference for open-endedness is, ultimately, an effort to resist the limits of time and of place That effort helps explain the importance of dreams and memories of other times and location, like Catherine's delirious memories of childhood at Wuthering Heights and rambles on the moors.

Romanticism and the Brontës

Romanticism, the literary movement traditionally dated 1798 to 1832 in England, affected all the arts through the nineteenth century. The Brontës were familiar with the writings of the major romantic poets and the novels of Sir Walter Scott. When Charlotte Brontë, for instance, wanted an evaluation of her writing, she sent a sample to the romantic poet Southey. The romantic elements in the Brontës' writings are obvious. Walter Pater saw in Wuthering Heights the characteristic spirit of romanticism, particularly in "the figures of Hareton Earnshaw, of Catherine Linton, and of Heathcliff–tearing open Catherine's grave, removing one side of her coffin, that he may really lie beside her in death–figures so passionate, yet woven on a background of delicately beautiful, moorland scenery, being typical examples of that spirit."

As the details of their lives became generally known and as Jane Eyre and Wuthering Heights received increasingly favorable critical attention, Charlotte, Emily, and Anne were cast in the role of Romantic Rebels. Contributing to the Romantic Rebels Myth was the association of Romanticism and early death; Shelley having died at 29, Byron at 36, and Keats at 24. Branwell died at the age of 31, Emily at 30, and Anne at 29; to add to the emotional impact, Branwell, Emily, and Anne died in the space of nine months. The Romantic predilection for early death appears in Wuthering Heights; Linton is 17 when he dies; Catherine, 18; Hindley, 27; Isabella, 31; Edgar, 39; Heathcliff, perhaps 37 or 38.

Romantic Elements in Wuthering Heights

The major characteristics of Romanticism could be extrapolated from a reading of Wuthering Heights:

The imagination is unleashed to explore extreme states of being and experiences. The love of nature is not presented just in its tranquil and smiling aspects but also appears in its wild, stormy moods, Nature is a living, vitalizing force and offers a refuge from the constraints of civilization, The passion driving Catherine and Heathcliff and their obsessive love for each other are the centre of their being and transcend death, So great a focus is placed on the individual that society is pushed to the periphery of the action and the reader's consciousness, The concern with identity and the creation of the self are a primary concern, Childhood and the adult's developing from childhood experiences are presented realistically, Heathcliff is the Byronic hero; both are rebellious, passionate, misanthropic, isolated, and wilful, have mysterious origins, lack family ties, reject external restrictions and control, and seek to resolve their isolation by fusing with a love object,

Hareton is the noble savage and, depending on your

reading of the novel, so is Heathcliff, Brontë experiments with the narrative structure (the Chinese-box structure in which Lockwood narrates what Nelly tells him, who repeats what others told her), the taste for local colour shows in the portrayal of Yorkshire, its landscape, its folklore, and its people, the supernatural or the possibility of the supernatural appears repeatedly.

Describe the Romantic Love in Wuthering Heights

Romantic Love in Wuthering Heights

Romantic love takes many forms in Wuthering Heights: the grand passion of Heathcliff and Catherine, the insipid sentimental languishing of Lockwood, the coupleism of Hindley and Frances, the tame indulgence of Edgar, the romantic infatuation of Isabella, the puppy love of Cathy and Linton, and the flirtatious sexual attraction of Cathy and Hareton. These lovers, with the possible exception of Hareton and Cathy, are self-centered and ignore the needs, feelings, and claims of others; what matters is the lovers' own feelings and needs.

Nevertheless, it is the passion of Heathcliff and Catherine that most readers respond to and remember and that has made this novel one of the great love stories not merely of English literature but of European literature as well. Simone de Beauvois cites Catherine's cry, "I am Heathcliff," in her discussion of romantic love, and movie adaptations of the novel include a Mexican and a French version. In addition, their love has passed into popular culture; Kate Bush and Pat Benetar both recorded "Wuthering Heights," a song which Bush wrote, and MTV showcased the lovers in a musical version.

The love-relationship of Heathcliff and Catherine, but not that of the other lovers, has become an archetype; it expresses the passionate longing to be whole, to give oneself unreservedly to another and gain a whole self or sense of identity back, to be all-in-all for each other, so that nothing else in the world matters, and to be loved in this way forever.

This type of passion-love can be summed up in the phrase more—and still more, for it is insatiable, unfulfillable, and unrelenting in its demands upon both lovers.

Heathcliff and Catherine: True Lovers?

Despite the generally accepted view that Heathcliff and Catherine are deeply in love with each other, the question of whether they really love each other has to be addressed. This question raises another; what kind of love—or feeling—is Emily Brontë depicting? Her sister Charlotte, for example, called Heathcliff's feelings "perverted passion and passionate perversity."

I list below a number of interpretations of their love/ ostensible love. Soulmates. Their love exists on a higher or spiritual plane; they are soul mates, two people who have an affinity for each other which draws them togehter irresistibly. Heathcliff repeatedly calls Catherine his soul. Such a love is not necessarily fortunate or happy. For C. Day Lewis, Heathcliff and Catherine "represent the essential isolation of the soul, the agony of two souls–or rather, shall we say? two halves of a single soul–forever sundered and struggling to unite."

A life-force relationship. Clifford Collins calls their love a life-force relationship, a principle that is not conditioned by anything but itself. It is a principle because the relationship is of an ideal nature; it does not exist in life, though as in many statements of an ideal this principle has implications of a profound living significance. Catherine's conventional feelings for Edgar Linton and his superficial appeal contrast with her profound love for Heathcliff, which is "an acceptance of identity below the level of consciousness." Their relationship expresses "the impersonal essence of personal existence," an essence which Collins calls the life-force. This fact explains why Catherine and Heathcliff several times describe their love in impersonal terms. Because such feelings cannot be fulfilled in an actual relationship, Brontë provides the relationship of Hareton and Cathy to integrate the principle into everyday life.

Creating meaning. Are Catherine and Heathcliff rejecting the emptiness of the universe, social institutions, and their relationships with others by finding meaning in their relationship with each other, by a desperate assertion of identity based on the other? Catherine explains to Nelly:

Surely you and everybody have a notion that there is, or should be, an existence of yours beyond you. What were the use of my creation if I were entirely contained here? My great miseries in this world have been Heathcliff's miseries, and I watched and felt each from the beginning; my great thought in living is himself. If all else perished, and he remained, I should still continue to be; and, if all else remained, and he were annihilated, the Universe would turn to a mighty stranger. I should not seem part of it" (Ch. ix, p. 64).

Dying, Catherine again confides to Nelly her feelings about the emptiness and torment of living in this world and her belief in a fulfilling alternative: "I'm tired, tired of being enclosed here. I'm wearying to escape into that glorious world, and to be always there; not seeing it dimly through tears, and yearning for it through the walls of an aching heart; but really with it, and in it" (Ch. xv, p. 125).

Transcending isolation. Their love is an attempt to break the boundaries of self and to fuse with another to transcend the inherent separateness of the human condition; fusion with another will by uniting two incomplete individuals create a whole and achieve new sense of identity, a complete and unified identity. This need for fusion motivates Heathcliff's determination to "absorb" Catherine's corpse into his and for them to "dissolve" into each other so thoroughly that Edgar will not be able to distinguish Catherine from him.

Freud explained this urge as an inherent part of love: "At the height of being in love the boundary between ego and object threatens to melt away. Against all the evidence of his senses, a man who is in love declares 'I' and 'you' are one, and is prepared to behave as if it were a fact."

Love as religion. Love has become a religion in Wuthering Heights, providing a shield against the fear of death and the annihilation of personal identity or consciousness. This use of love would explain the inexorable connection between love and death in the characters' speeches and actions. Robert M. Polhemus sees Brontë's religion of love as individualistic and capitalistic:

> Wuthering Heights is filled with a religious urgency–unprecedented in British novels–to imagine a faith that might replace the old. Cathy's "secret" is blasphemous, and Emily Brontë's secret, in the novel, is the raging heresy that has become common in modern life: redemption, if it is possible, lies in personal desire, imaginative power, and love. Nobody else's heaven is good enough. Echoing Cathy, Heathdiff says late in the book, "I have nearly attained my heaven; and that of others is altogether unvalued and uncoveted by me!"...The hope for salvation becomes a matter of eroticized private enterprise.
>
> Catherine and Heathcliff have faith in their vocation of being in love with one another.... They both believe that they have their being in the other, as Christians, Jews, and Moslems believe that they have their being in God. Look at the mystical passion of these two: devotion to shared experience and intimacy with the other; willingness to suffer anything, up to, and including, death, for the sake of this connection; ecstatic expression; mutilation of both social custom and the flesh; and mania for self-transcendence through the other, That passion is a way of overcoming the threat of death and the separateness of existence. Their calling is to be the other; and that calling, mad and destructive as it sometimes seems, is religious.

The desire for transcendence takes the form of crossing boundaries and rejecting conventions; this is the source of the torment of being imprisoned in a body and in this life, the uncontrolled passion expressed in extreme and violent ways, the usurpation of property, the literal and figurative imprisonments, the necrophilia, the hints of incest and adultery, the ghosts of Catherine and Heathcliff–all, in other words, that has shocked readers from the novel's first publication. Each has replaced God for the other, and they anticipate being reunited in love after death, just as Christians anticipate being reunited with God after death. Nevertheless,

Catherine and Heatcliff are inconsistent in their attitude toward death, which both unites and separates. After crying "Heathcliff! I only wish us never to be parted," Catherine goes on to say, "I'm wearying to escape into that glorious world," a wish which necessarily involves separation (Ch. xv, p. 125).

Conventional religion is presented negatively in the novel. The abandoned church at Gimmerton is decaying; the minister stops visiting Wuthering Heights because of Hindley's degeneracy. Catherine and Heathcliff reject Joseph's religion, which is narrow, self-righteous, and punitive. Is conventional religion replaced by the religion of love, and does the fulfillment of Heathcliff and Catherine's love after death affect the love of Hareton and Cathy in any way? Does the redemptive power of love, which is obvious in Cathy's civilizing Hareton, relate to love-as-religion experienced by Heathcliff and Catherine?

Love as addiction. Is what Catherine and Heathcliff call love and generations of readers have accepted as Ideal Love really an addiction? Stanton Peele argues that romantic or passion love is in itself an addiction. What exactly does he mean by addiction?

An addiction exists when a person's attachment to a sensation, an object, or another person is such as to lessen his appreciation of and ability to deal with other things in his environment, or in himself, so that he has become increasingly dependent on that experience as his only source of gratification.

Individuals who lack direction and commitment, who are emotionally unstable, or who are isolated and have few interests are especially vulnerable to addictions. An addictive love wants to break down the boundaries of identity and merge with the lover into one identity. Lacking inner resources, love addicts look outside themselves for meaning and purpose, usually in people similar to themselves. Even if the initial pleasure and sense of fulfillment or satisfaction does not last, the love-addict is driven by need and clings desperately to the relationship and the lover. Catherine, for example, calls her relationship "a source of little visible delight, but necessary."

The loss of the lover, whether through rejection or death, causes the addict withdrawal symptoms, often extreme ones like illness, not eating, and faintness. The addict wants possession of the lover regardless of the consequences to the loved one; a healthy love, on the other hand, is capable of putting the needs of the beloved first.

Q. Explain Wuthering Heights as a social economic novel, along with its psychological interpretations.

Or

Q. Is Wuthering Heights a Socio Economic Novel?

WUTHERING HEIGHTS AS SOCIO-ECONOMIC NOVEL

The novel opens in 1801, a date Q.D. Leavis believes Brontë chose in order "to fix its happenings at a time when the old rough farming culture based on a naturally patriarchal family life, was to be challenged, tamed and routed by social and cultural changes that were to produce the Victorian class consciousness and 'unnatural' ideal of gentility." In 1801 the Industrial Revolution was under way in England; when Emily Brontë was writing in 1847, it was a dominant force in English economy and society, and the traditional relationship of social classes was being disrupted by mushroom-new fortunes and an upwardly-aspiring middle class. The criterion for defining a gentleman was shifting to money, from character, breeding, or family. This social-economic reality provides the context for socio-economic readings of the novel.

Is Brontë supporting the status quo and upholding conventional values? Initially the answer would seem to be "no." The reader sympathizes with Heathcliff, the gypsy oppressed by a rigid class system and denigrated as "imp" or "fiend." But as Heathcliff pursues his revenge and tyrannical persecution of the innocent, the danger posed by the uncontrolled individual to the community becomes apparent. Like other novels of the 1830s and 40s which reveal the abuses of industrialism and overbearing individualism, Wuthering Heights may really suggest the necessity of preserving traditional ways.

This is not the way Marxist critics see the novel. For Arnold Kettle the basic conflict and motive force of the novel are social in origin. He locates the source of Catherine and Heatcliff's affinity in the (class) rebellion forced on them by the injustice of Hindley and his wife Frances.

He, the outcast slummy, turns to the lively, spirited, fearless girl who alone offers him human understanding and comradeship. And she, born into the world of Wuthering Heights, senses that to achieve a full humanity, to be true to herself as a human being, she must associate herself totally with him in his rebellion against the tyranny of the Earnshaws and all that tyranny involves.

Catherine's death inverts the common standards of bourgeois morality and so has "revolutionary force." Heathcliff is morally ruthless with his brutal analysis of the significance of Catherine's choosing Edgar and her rejecting the finer humanity he represents. Despite Heathcliff's implacable revenge, we continue to sympathize with him because he is using the weapons and values (arranged marriages, accumulating money, and expropriating property) of Victorian society against those with power; his ruthlessness strips them of any romantic veneer. As a result, he, too, betrays his humanity. Through the continuity of life and the aspirations expressed in the love of Cathy and Hareton, Heathcliff recognizes some of the quality of his love for Catherine and the unimportance of revenge and property; he thereby is enabled to regain his humanity and to achieve union with Catherine. "Wutherng Heights then," Kettle concludes, "is an expression in the imaginative terms of art of the stresses and tensions and conflicts, personal and spiritual, of nineteenth-century capitalist society."

Writing nearly twenty-five years later, Marxist Terry Eagleton posits a complex and contradictory relationship between the landed gentry and aristocracy, the traditional power-holders, and the capitalist, industrial middle classes, who were pushing for social acceptance and political power. Simultaneously with the struggle among these groups, an accommodation was developing based on economic interests

Though the landed gentry and aristocracy resisted marrying into first-generation capitalist wealth, they were willing to mix socially and to form economic alliances with the manufacturers and industrialists. The area that the Brontës lived in, the town of Haworth in West Riding, was particularly affected by these social and economic conditions because of the concentration of large estates and industrial centers in West Riding.

Proceeding from this view of mid-nineteenth century society, Eagleton sees both class struggle and class accommodation in Wutheirng Heights. Heathcliff, the outsider, has no social or biological place in the existing social structure; he offers Catherine a non-social or pre-social relationship, an escape from the conventional restrictions and material comforts of the upper classes, represented by the genteel Lintons. This relationship outside society is "the only authentic form of living in a world of exploitation and inequality." It is Heathcliff's expression of a natural non-social mode of being which gives the relationship its impersonal quality and makes the conflict one of nature versus society. Heathcliff's connection with nature is manifested in his running wild as a child and in Hindley's reducing him to a farm laborer. But Catherine's marriage and Hindley's abuse transform Heathcliff and his meaning in the social system, a transformation which reflects a reality about nature–nature is not really "outside" society because its conflicts are expressed in society.

However, Heathcliff the adult becomes a capitalist, an expropriator, and a predator, turning the ruling class's weapons of property accumulation and acquisitive marriage against them. Society's need to tame/civilize the unbridled capitalist is handled in the civilizing of Hareton. Hareton represents the yeoman class, which was being degraded. In adopting the behaviour of the exploiting middle classes, Heathcliff works in common with the capitalist landowner Edgar Linton to suppress the yeoman class; having been raised in the yeoman class and having acquired his fortune outside it, he joins "spiritual forces" against the squirearchy. Thus, he represents both rapacious capitalism and the rejection of capitalist society. However, because the capitalist class is no longer revolutionary, it cannot provide expression for Heathcliff's rejection of society for a pre-social freedom from society's restraints. From this impossibility comes what Eagleton calls Heathcliff's personal tragedy: his conflictive unity consisting of spiritual rejection and social integration. Heathcliff relentlessly pursues his goal of possessing Catherine, an obsession that is unaffected by social realities. In other words, the novel does not fully succeed in reconciling or finding a way to express all Heathcliff's meanings.

Eagleton acknowledges that ultimately the values of Thrushcross Grange prevail, but that Brontë's sympathies lie with the more democratic, cozy Wuthering Heights. The capitalist victory over the yeomanry is symbolized by the displacement of Joseph's beloved currant bushes for Catherine's flowers, which are in Marxist terms "surplus value." With Heathcliff's death a richer life than that of Thrushcross Grange also dies; it may be a regrettable death–but it is a necessary death because the future requires a fusion of gentry and capitalist middle class, not continued conflict.

Psychological Interpretations of Wuthering Heights

Psychological analyses of Wuthering Heights abound as critics apply modern psychological theories to the characters and their relationships,

A Freudian Interpretation

The most common psychological readings are Freudian interpretations. Typical of Freudian readings of the novel is Linda Gold's interpretation. She sees in the symbiosis of Catherine, Heathcliff, and Edgar the relationship of Freud's id, ego, and superego. At a psychological level, they merge into one personality with Heathcliff's image of the three of them buried (the unconscious) in what is essentially one coffin. Heathcliff, the id, expresses the most primitive drives (like sex), seeks pleasure, and avoids pain; the id is not affected by time and remains in the unconscious (appropriately, Heathcliff's origins are unknown, he is dark, he runs wild and is primitive as a child, and his three year absence remains a mystery). Catherine, the ego, relates to other people and society, tests the impulses of the id against reality, and controls the energetic id until there is a reasonable chance of its urges being fulfilled. Edgar, the superego, represents the rules of proper behaviour and morality inculcated by teachers, family, and society; he is civilized and cultured. As conscience, he compels Catherine to choose between Heathcliff and himself.

In Freud's analysis, the ego must be male to deal successfully with the world; to survive, a female ego would have to live through males. This Catherine does by identifying egotistically with Heathcliff and Edgar, according to Gold. Catherine rejects Heathcliff because a realistic assessment of her future with him makes clear the material and social advantages of marrying Edgar and the degradation of yielding to her unconscious self. Her stay at Thrushcross Grange occurs at a crucial stage in her development; she is moving through puberty toward womanhood. She expects Edgar to accept Heathcliff in their household and to raise him from his degraded state; this would result in the integration of the disparate parts of her personality–id, ego, and superego–into one unified personality. Confronted by the hopelessness of psychological integration or wholeness and agonized by her fragmentation, she dies.

Gold carries her Freudian scrutiny to the second generation; the whole history of both generations of Earnshaws, Lintons, and Heathcliffs may be read as the development of one personality, beginning with Catherine Earnshaw and ending with Catherine Linton Heathcliff Earnshaw. The second Cathy has assimilated and consolidated the id/Heathcliff and the superego/Edgar through marriages with Hareton and Linton.

Jungian Interpretations

Jungian readings also interpret the relationship of Catherine and Heathcliff as aspects of one person; those aspects may be the archetype of the shadow and the individual or the archetypes of the animus/anima and the persona. These interpretations are derived from Jung's distinction between the collective unconscious and the personal unconscious. The collective unconscious is inherited, impersonal, and universal. The content of the collective unconscious is mainly archetypes; some archetypes are the same in a particular society or time period, others are the same in all societies and times. The archetypes may find expression in myth and fairy tales. The most common and influential archetypes are the shadow, the animus, and the anima. Every human being also has a personal unconscious, in which material is stored that was once conscious but has been forgotten or repressed. The personal unconscious adapts archetypes based on the individual's experiences. The personal unconscious finds expression in dreams and metaphor.

The shadow. In the collective unconscious, the shadow is absolute evil. In the personal unconscious, the shadow consists of those desires, feelings, etc. which are unacceptable, perhaps for emotional or for moral reasons. The shadow is generally equated with the dark side of human nature. The shadow is emotional, seems autonomous because uncontrollable, and hence becomes obsessive or possessive. Heathcliff, then, can be seen as Catherine's shadow–he represents the darkest side of her, with his vindictiveness, his sullenness, his wildness, and his detachment from social connections. She rejects this part of herself by marrying Edgar, thereby explaining Heathcliff's mysterious disappearance. But Heathcliff, the shadow, refuses to be suppressed permanently; Jung explains that even if self-knowledge or insight enables the individual to integrate the shadow, the shadow still resists moral control and can rarely be changed. Cathy's efforts to integrate Heathcliff into her life with Edgar are doomed; her inability to affect Heathcliff's behaviour can be seen in his ignoring her prohibition about Isabella. The resurfaced Heathcliff obsessively seeks possession of Catherine to insure his own survival.

The animus and the anima. What Jung calls the persona is the outer or social self that faces the world. The animus is the archetype that completes women, that is, it contains the male qualities which the persona lacks. The animus generally represents reflection, deliberation, and ability for self-knowledge and is male. The anima represents the female traits that a man's persona lacks, generally the ability to form relationship and be related, and it is female. The relationship of the anima/animus to the individual is always emotional and has its own dynamic, because, as archetypes, the anima and animus are impersonal forces.

The individual is rarely aware of his anima/her animus. In some of its aspects, Jung says, the animus is the "demon-familiar." The animus of a woman and the anima of a man take the form of a "soul-image" in the personal unconscious; this soul-image may be transferred to a real person who naturally becomes the object of intense feeling, which may be passionate love or passionate hate. "Wherever an impassioned, almost magical, relationship exists between the sexes, it is invariably a question of a projected soul-image." When a man projects his anima onto a real women or a woman projects her animus onto a man, a triad arises, which includes a transcendent part. The triad consists of the man, the woman, and the transcendent anima/animus. Not surprisingly, the object of the projection will be unable to live out the lover's animus or anima permanently.

Now to apply Jung's theory to Catherine, for whom Heathcliff.is the animus, and to Heathcliff, for whom Catherine is the anima. For Catherine, Heathcliff expresses anger and hostility, freedom, command, irresponsibility, rebellion, and spontaneity. For Heathcliff, Catherine is beauty, love, status, and belonging. The projection of their soul-images explains their profound sense of connection or identity with each other, e.g., Catherine's "I am Heathcliff" speech and Heathcliff's references to Catherine as his soul and his life. The element of transcendence in the projection is expressed in Catherine's vision of something, some life, beyond this one, in her view of existence after death, in Heathcliff's longing to see Catherine's ghost, and their life together after death. And is there any question about Heathcliff's being a "demon-familiar"?

MONOMANIA: A nineteenth Century Theory

An entirely different approach is taken by Graeme Tytler, who applies nineteenth-century psychological theory to the novel. In Brontë's day, an obvious label for Heathcliff would have been monomaniac, a term which is today equated with obsession but was in the nineteenth century a specific disorder with clearly defined symptoms and progression. Graeme Tytler theorizes that Heathcliff fits the contemporary medical diagnosis of monomania, as defined by Jean Etienne Dominique Esquirol, one of the founders of modern psychiatry. Esquirol defined monomania as "the disease of going to extremes, of singularization, of one-sidedness." The application of this definition to Heathcliff is too obvious to need further comment; equally relevant to a diagnosis of Heathcliff is Esquirol's listing of the causes of monomania:

Monomania is essentially a disease of the sensibility. It reposes altogether upon the affections, and its study is inseparable from a knowledge of the passions. Its seat is in the heart of man, and it is there that we must search for it, in order to possess ourselves of all its peculiarities. How many are the cases of monomania caused by thwarted love, by fear, vanity, wounded self-love, or disappointed ambition.

Tytler distinguishes stages in the development of Heathcliff's monomania. Heathcliff shows a predisposition to monomania up to and slightly after Catherine's death in such behaviour as his single-minded determination to be connected to her after her death. It is, however, not until eighteen years or so after her death that he shows signs of insanity. Much of what he says and does after Chapter xxix is symptomatic of monomania–hallucinations, insomnia, talking to himself or to Catherine's ghost, his preoccupation at meals and in conversation, his sighs and moans, his harsh treatment of Cathy and Hareton, and his being haunted by Catherine's image.

Classify Wuthering Heights On The Basis of Religion, Metaphysics, and Mysticism.

The passionate yearning of Catherine and Heathcliff for each other, their desperate striving for union, and their intransigence in pursuing that quest suggest transcendent meanings; as a result, the novel has been read as a religious novel and as a metaphysical novel and Emily Brontë has been called a mystic. Brontë's reputation as a mystic is also based on her poetry.

Wuthering Heights as a Religious Novel

Wuthering Heights is not a religious novel in the sense that it supports a particular religion (Christianity), or a particular branch of Christianity (Protestantism), a particular Protestant denomination (Church of England). Rather, religion in this novel takes the form of the awareness of or conviction of the existence of a supreme being or spirit-afterlife.

An overwhelming sense of the presence of a larger reality moved Rudolph Otto to call Wuthering Heights a supreme example of "the daemonic" in literature. Otto was concerned with identifying the non-rational mystery behind all religion and all religious experiences; he called this basic element or mystery the numinous. The numinous grips or stirs the mind so powerfully that one of the responses it produces is numinous dread, which consists of awe or awe-fullness. Numinous dread implies three qualities of the numinous: its absolute unapproachability, its power, and. its urgency or energy. A misunderstanding of these qualities and of numinous dread by primitive people gives rise to daemonic dread, which Otto identifies as the first stage in religious development.

At the same time that they feel dread, they are drawn by the fascinating power of the numinous. Otto explains, "The daemonic-divine object may appear to the mind an object of horror and dread, but at the same time it is no less something that allures with a potent charm, and the creature, who trembles before it, utterly cowed and cast down, has always at the same time the impulse to turn to it, nay even to make it somehow his own." Still, acknowledgment of the "daemonic" is a genuine religious experience, and from it arise the gods and demons of later religions. It has been suggested that Gothic fiction originated primarily as a quest for numinous dread, which Otto also calls the mysterium tremendum. For Derek Traversi the motive force of Brontë's novel is "a thirst for religious experience," which is not Christian. It is this spirit which moves Catherine to exclaim, "surely you and everybody have a notion that there is, or should be, an existence of yours beyond you. What were the use of my creation if I were entirely contained here? (Ch. ix, p. 64).

Out of her–and Brontë's–awareness of the finiteness of human nature comes the yearning for a higher reality, permanent, infinite, eternal; a higher reality which would enable the self to become whole and complete and would also replace the feeling of the emptiness of this world with feelings of the fullness of being (fullness of being is a phrase used by and about mystics to describe the aftermath of a direct experience of God).

Brontë's religious inspiration turns a discussion of the best way to spend an idle summer's day into a dispute about the nature of heaven. Her religious view encompasses both Cathy's and Linton's views of heaven and of life, for she sees a world of contending forces which are contained within her own nature. She seeks to unite them in this novel, though, Traversi admits, the emphasis on passion and death tends to overshadow the drive for unity. Even Heathcliff's approaching death, when he cries out "My soul's bliss kills my body, but does not satisfy itself" (Ch. xxxiv, p. 254), has a religious resonance.

Thomas John Winnifrith also sees religious meaning in the novel: salvation is won by suffering, as an analysis of references to heaven and hell reveals. For Heathcliff, the loss of Catherine is literally hell; there is no metaphoric meaning in his claim "existence after losing her would be hell" (Ch. xiv, p. 117). In their last interview, Catherine and Heathcliff both suffer agonies at the prospect of separation, she to suffer "the same distress underground" and he to "writhe in the torments of hell" (XV, p. 124). Heathcliff is tortured by his obsession for the dead/absent Catherine. Suffering through an earthly hell leads Healthcliff finally to his heaven, which is union with Catherine as a spirit. The views of Nelly and Joseph about heaven and hell are conventional and do not represent Brontë's views, according to Winnifrith.

Wuthering Heights as a Metaphysical Novel

Metaphysics is the "branch of speculative inquiry which treats of the first principles of things, including such concepts as being, substance, essence, time, space, cause, identity, etc.; theoretical philosophy as the ultimate science of Being and Knowing" (OED). Dorothy Van Ghent finds evidence, at one level of Wuthering Heights, of metaphysical exploration: the book seizes, at the point where the soul feels itself cleft within and in cleavage from the universe, the first germs of philosophic thought, the thought of the duality of human and nonhuman existence, and the thought of the cognate duality of the psyche.

The novel presents the collision between two types of reality, restrictive civilization and anonymous unrestrained natural energies or forces. This collision takes the form of inside/domestic versus outside/nature, human versus the "other," the light versus the dark within the soul. The novel repeatedly shows efforts to break through or cross the boundary of separation of the various dualities, like Lockwood's breaking the window in his dream or the figure of two children who struggle for union (Catherine and Heathcliff, Cathy and Linton, Cathy and Hareton).

The two kinds of realities are, in Van Ghent's reading, both opposed and continuous There is a continuous movement to break through the constraint of civilization and personal consciousness and also a movement toward "passionate fulfillment of consciousness by deeper ingress into the matrix of its own and all energy." In other words, the impetus of life is toward unifying the dark and the light, the unknown and the known, the elemental and the human.

Catherine and Heathcliff, Van Ghent explains, are violent elementals who express the flux of nature; they struggle to be human and assume human character in their passion, confusions, and torment, but their inhuman appetites and energy can only bring chaos and self-destruction. The second generation presents the childish romance of Cathy and Linton and the healthy, culturally viable love of Cathy and Hareton. The adult love of Cathy and Hareton involves a sense of social and moral responsibilities in contrast to the asocial, amoral, irresponsible, and impulsive child's love of Catherine and Heathcliff. Van Ghent calls their love a "mythological romance" because "the astonishingly ravenous and possessive, perfectly amoral love of Catherine and Heathcliff belongs to that realm of the imagination where myths are created"; a primary function of myth being to explain origins, practices, basic human behaviour, and natural phenomena. The two kinds of love (childish and adult) and the two generations are connected by Heathcliff in his role first as demon-lover and finally as ogre-father and by the two children figure.

Emily Brontë as a Mystic

Though the word mysticism is often used vaguely to indicate occultism or spiritualism, it has a very specific meaning in Christianity and Western culture. Evelyn Underhill defines mysticism as "the direct intuition or experience of God" or "the life which aims at union with God" and a mystic as "a person who has, to a greater or less degree, such a direct experience–one whose religion and life are centered, not merely on an accepted belief or practice, but on that which he regards as first-hand personal knowledge." If her use of "God" is expanded to include a higher presence or force and spiritual reality, her definition includes most discussions of Brontë as a mystic. The mystic traditionally goes through three stages–(1) purgation, or a purification of the individual and disengagement from worldly affairs; (2) illumination, or the conviction of God's power and surrender to His will; and (3) union with God. Typically mystics experience oceanic feelings during union with God. Ellen Moers defines oceanic feelings as "the sensation of selflessness and release from the flesh and to the comprehension of the universal Oneness that are often experienced on the open seas." Moers believes that for Brontë the expanse of the moors created oceanic feelings, as can be seen in her poems and novel.

Claims that Brontë is a mystic are often based primarily–and even entirely–on her poems. Lines like these from "High waving heather, 'neath stormy blasts" are cited to prove her mysticism or at least her mystical leanings:

Earth rising to heaven and heaven descending,
Man's spirit away form its drear dungeon sending,
Bursting the fetters and breaking the bars.

Relying entirely on the poems, Caroline F.E. Spurgeon identifies Emily Brontë as an unusual type of mystic:

In her poems her mysticism is seen principally in two ways: in her unerring apprehension of values, of the illusory quality of material things, even of the nature she so loved, together with the certain vision of the one Reality behind all forms. This, and her description of ecstasy, of the all-sufficing joy of the inner life of one who has tasted this experience, mark her out as being among those who have seen, and who know. In The Prisoner, the speaker, a woman, is "confined in triple walls," yet in spite of bolts and bars and dungeon gloom she holds within herself an inextinguishable joy and unmeasured freedom brought to her every night by a 'messenger'.

Other ideas that also qualify her, in Spurgeon's eyes, as a mystic are the fact that Brontë knows that ordinary things hold the secret of the universe and that she has a sense of the continuousness of life and the oneness of God and man, as expressed in "No coward soul is mine":

O God within my breast
Almighty ever-present Deity
Life, that in me hast rest
As I Undying Life, have power in Thee!...
With wide-embracing love
Thy spirit animates eternal years
Pervades and broods above,
Changes, sustains, dissolves, creates and rears
Though Earth and moon were gone
And suns and universes ceased to be
And thou wert left alone
Every Existence would exist in thee

Similarly, Winifred Gerin reads "On a sunny brae alone I

lay" as a description of a mystical experience in which every detail is sharply defined in terms of sight, sensation, and hearing. The "glittering spirits," who sing to the poet of the ecstasy of being, reveal that death, far from being the tragedy of life, is its one certain bliss. Some of the mystical ideas that Spurgeon and Gerin identify can also be found in Wuthering Heights, particularly in the speeches of Catherine and Heathcliff, and critics regularly support claims of mysticism in the novel by referring to the poems.

Q. Discuss the Gothic Elements of Wuthering Heights.

Or

Q. What makes Wuthering Heights a Gothic Novel.

The English Gothic Novel: A Brief Overview

The English Gothic novel began with Horace Walpole's The Castle of Otranto (1765), which was enormously popular and quickly imitated by other novelists and soon became a recognizable genre. To most modern readers, however, The Castle of Otranto is dull reading; except for the villain Manfred, the characters are insipid and flat; the action moves at a fast clip with no emphasis or suspense, despite the supernatural manifestations and a young maiden's flight through dark vaults. But contemporary readers found the novel electrifyingly original and thrillingly suspenseful, with its remote setting, its use of the supernatural, and its medieval trappings, all of which have been so frequently imitated and so poorly imitated that they have become stereotypes. The genre takes its name from Otranto's medieval–or Gothic–setting; early Gothic novelists tended to set their novels in remote times like the Middle Ages and in remote places like Italy (Matthew Lewis's The Monk, 1796) or the Middle East (William Beckford's Vathek, 1786).

What Makes a Work Gothic is a Combination of at Least Some of these Elements

A castle, ruined or intact, haunted or not (the castle plays such a key role that it has been called the main character of the Gothic novel), ruined buildings which are sinister or which arouse a pleasing melancholy, dungeons, underground passages, crypts, and catacombs which, in modern houses, become spooky basements or attics, labyrinths, dark corridors, and winding stairs, shadows, a beam of moonlight in the blackness, a flickering candle, or the only source of light failing (a candle blown out or, today, an electric failure), extreme landscapes, like rugged mountains, thick forests, or icy wastes, and extreme weather, omens and ancestral curses, magic, supernatural manifestations, or the suggestion of the supernatural, a passion-driven, wilful villain-hero or villain, a curious heroine with a tendency to faint and a need to be rescued–frequently, a hero whose true identity is revealed by the end of the novel, horrifying (or terrifying) events or the threat of such happenings.

The Gothic creates feelings of gloom, mystery, and suspense and tends to the dramatic and the sensational, like incest, diabolism, necrophilia, and nameless terrors. It crosses boundaries, daylight and the dark side, life and death, consciousness and unconsciousness. Sometimes covertly, sometimes explicitly, it presents transgression, taboos, and fears–fears of violation, of imprisonment, of social chaos, and of emotional collapse. Most of us immediately recognize the Gothic (even if we don't know the name) when we encounter it in novels, poetry, plays, movies, and TV series. For some of us–and I include myself– safely experiencing dread or horror is thrilling and enjoyable.

Elements of the Gothic have made their way into mainstream writing. They are found in Sir Walter Scott's novels, Charlotte Brontë's Jane Eyre, and Emily Brontë's Wuthering Heights and in Romantic poetry like Samuel Coleridge's "Christabel," Lord Byron's "The Giaour," and John Keats's "The Eve of St. Agnes." A tendency to the macabre and bizarre which appears in writers like William Faulkner, Truman Capote, and Flannery O'Connor has been called Southern Gothic.

The Gothic and Wuthering Heights

Whether or not Wuthering Heights should be classified

as a Gothic novel (certainly it is not merley a Gothic novel), it undeniably contains Gothic elements.

In true Gothic fashion, boundaries are trespassed, specifically love crossing the boundary between life and death and Heathcliff's transgressing social class and family ties. Brontë follows Walpole and Radcliffe in portraying the tyrannies of the father and the cruelties of the patriarchal family and in reconstituting the family on non-patriarchal lines, even though no counterbalancing matriarch or matriarchal family is presented. Brontë has incorporated the Gothic trappings of imprisonment and escape, flight, the persecuted heroine, the heroine wooed by a dangerous and a good suitor, ghosts, necrophilia, a mysterious foundling, and revenge.

The weather-buffeted Wuthering Heights is the traditional castle, and Catherine resembles Ann Radcliffe's heroines in her appreciation of nature. Like the conventional Gothic hero-villain, Heathcliff is a mysterious figure who destroys the beautiful woman he pursues and who usurps inheritances, and with typical Gothic excess he batters his head against a tree. There is the hint of necrophilia in Heathcliff's viewings of Catherine's corpse and his plans to be buried next to her and a hint of incest in their being raised as brother and sister or, as a few critics have suggested, in Heathcliff's being Catherine's illegitimate half-brother.

A Feminist Theory of The Gothic and Wuthering Heights

Ellen Moers has propounded a feminist theory that relates women writers in general and Emily Brontë in particular to the Gothic. Middle-class women who wanted to write were hampered by the conventional image of ladies as submissive, pious, gentle, loving, serene, domestic angels; they had to overcome the conventional patronizing, smug, unempowering, contemptuous sentimentalizing of women by reviewers like George Henry Lewes, who looked down on women writers:

Women's proper sphere of activity is elsewhere [than writing]. Are there no husbands, lovers, brothers, friends to coddle and console? Are there no stockings to darn, no purses to make, no braces to embroider? My idea of a perfect woman is one who can write but won't (1850).

Those women who overcame the limitations of their social roles and did write found it more difficult to challenge or reject society's assumptions and expectations than their male counterparts. Ellen Moers identifies heroinism, a form of literary feminism, as one way women circumvented this difficulty. (Literary feminism and feminism may overlap but they are not the same, and a woman writer who adopts heroinism is not necessarily a feminist.) Heroinism takes many forms, such as the intellectual or thinking heroine, the passionate or woman-in-love heroine, and the traveling heroine. Clearly all the Brontë sisters utilize the passionate heroine, whether knowingly or not, to express subversive values and taboo experiences covertly.

What subversive values and taboo experiences does Emily Brontë express with her passionate heroine Catherine? Moers sees subversion in Brontë's acceptance of the cruel as a normal, almost an energizing part of life and in her portrayal of the erotic in childhood. The cruelty connects this novel to the Gothic tradition, which has been associated with women writers since Anne Radcliffe. The connection was, in fact, recognized by Brontë's contemporaries; the Athenaeum reviewer labeled the Gothic elements in Wuthering Heights "the eccentricities of 'woman's fantasy'" (1847). Moers thinks a more accurate word than eccentricities would be perversities. These perversities may have originated in "fantasies derived from the night side of the Victorian nursery–a world where childish cruelty and childish sexuality come to the fore." Of particular importance for intellectual middle-class women who never matured sexually was the brother-sister relationship. In childhood, sisters were the equal of their brothers, played just as hard, and felt the same pleasures and pains; girls clung to this early freedom and equality, which their brothers outgrew, and displaced them into their writing:

Women writers of Gothic fantasies appear to testify that the physical teasing they received from their brothers–the pinching, mauling, and scratching we dismiss as the unimportant of children's games–took on outsize proportions and powerful erotic overtones in their adult imaginations. (Again, the poverty of their physical experience may have caused these disproportions, for it was not only sexual play but any kind of physical play for middle-class women that fell under the Victorian ban.)

Moers applies this principle to the Brontës' chronicles of Angria and Gondal, which the sisters collaborated on with their brother. Their turbulent sagas are filled with unbridled passions, imprisonment, adultery, incest, murder, revenge, and warfare. Thus the uncensored fantasies of Angria and Gondal, whose imaginative hold Emily never outgrew, may have provided an outlet for the sisters' imaginations, passions, and aspirations; fostered their intellectual and artistic equality with their brother; and provided the model for Emily's impassioned Heathcliff and Catherine as well as for Charlotte's Rochester.

Emily Jane Brontë: Poet and Novelist (1818-48)

Sealed in her art-world, the moor strategically placed for escape above the house, no domesticating and limiting mother to weaken her capacity for identification with whatever sex she chose to impersonate at a particular moment, polite society at a safe distance, and a father who seems to have selected her as an honorary boy to be trusted with fire-arms in defence of the weak, Emily Brontë's life exemplifies a rough joy in itself, its war-games, its word games and its power to extend its own structuring vision out upon the given world. [Davies, 9]

Emily Brontë was born at Thornton, Bradford, Yorkshire, and just after the birth of her sister Anne (20 April 1820), she moved with her family to Haworth, near Keighley, Yorkshire, where she spent most of her life. Today remembered chiefly as the author of the eighteenth-century romance Wuthering Heights (1847), set in her native Yorkshire, Emily Brontë was the second surviving daughter and fifth child of Cornishwoman Maria Brontë and the Ulsterman Reverend Patrick Brontë (1777-1861), "perpetual curate" (rector) of the remote village of Haworth on the Yorkshire Moors from 1820 until his death in 1861. Maria died on 15 September 1821, survived by her husband, five daughters, and a son, Branwell (1817-48).

Emily and her sisters (except Anne) attended Cowan Bridge School, a Church of England clergymen's daughters' boarding school (the original of Lowood in Charlotte's Jane Eyre). Emily spent a total of just six months there: 25 November 1824 to 1 June 1825. The eldest sisters, Maria and Elizabeth, became so ill that they had to be taken home, and died shortly after their return, the former on 6 May and the latter on 15 June 1825. From then until 1830 the surviving children remained at Haworth. From 29 July through October 1835 Emily taught at Miss Wooler's School at Roe Head, where Charlotte had taught in 1831-32.

The girls' real education, however, was at the Haworth parsonage, where they had the run of their father's books, and were thus nurtured on the Bible, Homer, Virgil, Shakespeare, Milton, Byron, Sir Walter Scott and many others. They enthusiastically read articles on current affairs, lengthy reviews and intellectual disputes in Blackwood's Edinburgh Magazine and The Edinburgh Review. They also ranged freely in Aesop and in the colourfully bizarre world of The Arabian Nights' Entertainments.... [Cambridge Guide, 118

After service as a governess in Halifax, Yorkshire (the second half of the year 1838), in 1842 Emily accompanied her surviving sisters, Anne and Charlotte, to Brussels, where from mid-February through the beginning of November they attended the Pensionnat Héger with the goal of improving their proficiency in French in order to start their own school. Their 1844 plans for their own school, however, foundered, and the sisters were reunited at Haworth in August 1845. When in the autumn of 1845 Charlotte accidentally discovered the manuscript of Emily's Gondal verses, she initiated the publication of a volume of poems by all three sisters, who as a clergyman's daughters thought it advisable to adopt the noms des plumes Currer (Charlotte), Ellis (Emily), and Acton (Anne) Bell (probably with a pun on "Belle"). In the preface to the 1850 edition of the poems, Charlotte herself recalls the moment of discovery:

Of course, I was not surprised, knowing that she could and did write verse: I looked it over, and something more than surprise seized me, — a deep conviction that these were not common effusions, not at all like the poetry women generally write. I thought them condensed and terse, vigorous and genuine. To my ear, they had also a peculiar music — wild, melancholy, and elevating.

A year after the publication by Thomas Cautley Newby, London, of Wuthering Heights (December 1847), Emily died of tuberculosis. On 19 December 1848, she suddenly expired as she stood with one hand on the mantlepiece of the living room in the Haworth parsonage. She was just 30 years old but had already produced a romantic tragedy in novel form, written over the course of 1845-46, yet to be surpassed in the English language. As Paul Lieder points out,

Emily Brontë wrote so little in her short life that it is difficult to appraise her work with any surety. One point is generally agreed upon: that in both her prose and poetry there is, in spite of minor faults, a rare power.

In her poetry, Emily Brontë achieves a remarkable effect by the energy and sincerity, and often by the music, with which she portrays her stoicism, independence, and compassion in stanzas which in many instances are the commonplace vehicles used by mere rimers. It is as though she were brought up to feel that certain forms of verse were the patterns, and had, with dogged acceptance, poured into them her emotions with an honesty that made the outward form seem negligible.

Q. Discuss Heathcliff as a revenger in Wuthering Heights.

Or

Q. Classify the major trait of Healthcliff.

Heathcliff the Revenger

The first indication of Heathcliff's savage personality is found in the opening chapter when the dogs - "A brood of tigers", "fiends" are represented and Heathcliff growls in unison with them. He informs Lockwood that the bitch is not kept for a pet. Catherine's diary provides a clue to the cause of Heathcliff's savagery and hatred, "Poor Heathcliff! Hindley calls him a vagabond, and won't let him sit with us and eat with us anymore... and swears that he will reduce him to his right place". Mr. Earnshaw first describes him thus - "though its as dark almost as if it came from the devil".

Heathcliff's dominant personality quickly becomes evident - "You must exchange horses with me, I don't like mine". This incident demonstrates the extent to which Heathcliff has already been hardened and brutalised. The ragged new-comer to Wuthering Heights is an image of a human creature reduced to its bare animal essence, the naked will to live. Nelly's comments about Heathcliff's ability to withstand pain supports this point of view, "He would withstand Hindley's blows without winking or shedding a tear". Heathcliff's dominant will was being fed by Mr. Earnshaw's favouritism, when he dies this changes, Heathcliff then suffers the tyranny of Hindley. From this point on, the revenge theme begins in the novel. Heathcliff's recollection of the Grange in Chapter 6 is tied this first inkling of revenge, "If I might have the privilege of flinging Joseph off the highest gale and painting the housefront with Hindley's blood".

Heathcliff's language at the Grange, indicated a malevolent attitude, "I've vociferated curses enough to annihilate any fiend in Christendom". Heathcliff's hatred for the Linton family is traceable to this moment - "Yet the villain scowls so plainly in his face, would it not be a kindness to the country to hang him at once before he shows his nature in acts as well as in features". Catherine's stay at the Grange precipitates a further decline in Heathcliff's behaviour. When she returns he is dirtier than before - "I shall be as dirty as I please and I like to be dirty and I will be dirty". Later he confides to Nelly the purpose of his meditations, "I am trying to be settle how I shall pay Hindley back. I don't care how long I wait if I can only do it at last" - "I only wish I new the best way. Let me alone and I'll plan it out, while I'm thinking of that, I don't feel pain". Now the novel's counter-theme to the love story becomes clear - Heathcliff's long premeditated ruthless revenge gradually increasing in scope with all the force of Heathcliff's primitive unchanging will behind it. From this point on, there is in Heathcliff a subordination of all other feelings except revenge.

Now the prince-in-disguise is destined to become a demon, taking on in fact the fiendishness that Nelly had seen lurking in his eyes as a child. Heathcliff's development in this light is traced to Hindley - "His treatment of the latter was enough to make a fiend of a saint". Truly it appeared that Heathcliff was possessed of something diabolical at that stage, he delighted to see Hindley degrading himself past redemption and became daily more noticeable for savage sullenness and ferocity. His disappearance follows his learning of Catherine's engagement - further disappointment - thus widening the scope for revenge.

The returning Heathcliff, despite his outwardly civilised facade, was still demonic in air, "A half civilised ferocity lurked yet in the depressed brows and the eyes full of black fire". In describing Heathcliff to Isabella, Catherine sees him "as a fierce pitiless wolfish man... and he'd crush you like a sparrow". Catherine marks the change in him, his speech has acquired a new hammerblow rhythm, "What new phase in his character is this", ponders Catherine. She sees beneath his unreclaimed nature something of his diabolism, and she compares Heathcliff to Hindley, "It is as bad as offering Satan a bad soul. Your bliss like his lies in inflicting misery". The marriage to Isabella and his pursuit of ugliness helped to strip the mask of civilisation and releases the central characters in their raw animal states.

From here on the plot is dominated by the demonic revenge - from here on Heathcliff strips all others of all the trappings of personality except passion. Sadism now replaces love, and violence is a necessary part if we are to experience this hellish world. In Chapter 14, we see the real Heathcliff and his preoccupation with Catherine leads him into a torrential harangue, "2 words will comprehend my future - death and hell". To Isabella he says, "She degenerates into a mere slut". His talk here is insistent and driven home by a cruel logic. His violent images and use of hyperbole, express an impetuous will, that cannot accept opposition and his rhetoric hardens as it gathers momentum to a language of absolute imperatives, "The nuisance of her presence outweighs the gratification to be derived from tormenting her". His logic depends on a refusal to admit any compromise with passion, any form of mediocrity.

This leads us to the completion of his revenge against Hindley and his becoming master of the Heights. The fight between them is described by Isabella with violent language, Heathcliff is described in demonic terms, "sharp cannibal, teeth, basilisk eyes". Now with victory over Hindley achieved and Edgar retreated in sorrow, the violent aspect of revenge gives way to patience and legalistic guile. To complete his revenge over the Lintons, Heathcliff employs these latter tactics - the marriage between Linton and Catherine is patiently contrived. The question of succession, shrewdly investigated, his guardianship over his son, the decisive cotosill to the inheritance of the Grange. Heathcliff's final thirst for revenge is quenched however by his failure to remain passionate. In the final chapters of the novel, he is torn between two competing passions, that for revenge and that for sympathy and fondness for Hareton. Finally he possesses no ability to prevent the future happiness of the younger generation and deprived of his passion, dies.

Write Down the Metaphor and Theme Analysis in Wuthering Heights.

Metaphor Analysis

Wind - The home of the Earnshaws and then Heathcliff is called 'Wuthering Heights,' and in the first chapter Mr. Lockwood says that 'wuthering' is a significant adjective, as it is "descriptive of the atmospheric tumult to which its station is exposed in stormy weather. Pure, bracing ventilation they must have up there at all times, indeed; one may guess the power of the north wind blowing over the edge, by the excessive slant of a few stunted firs at the end of the house; and by a range of gaunt thorns all stretching their limbs one way, as if craving alms of the sun".

Indeed the wind is an important symbol for change in the novel. It is present during many of the significant events in the lives of the characters. When Mr. Earnshaw dies there is a 'high wind,' and the weather is described as 'wild and stormy.' On the night that Heathcliff leaves Wuthering Heights there is a great storm with wind and rain. And on the morning that Ellen finds Heathcliff dead, the rain and wind are coming in through his window and beating his lattice back and forth.

Windows and Doors - Throughout the novel there are instances of locked or open windows and doors symbolizing imprisonment or freedom. In the very beginning Lockwood encounters locked doors and gates at Wuthering Heights, and he sees the ghost of Catherine trying to get in a window. Ellen leaves a window open for Heathcliff to come in and see Catherine in her coffin. Most of the examples come later in the novel when Heathcliff has Isabella and then Catherine locked up in Wuthering Heights.

Catherine cannot leave the house or her room because of locked doors, and Ellen cannot leave either because she has been locked in. It is only when Zillah lets her out of the room that she is able to leave. Catherine is only able to leave the house when Linton unlocks the door for her, and she escapes though the window in her mother's old room. By the end of the novel when everyone is free of revenge, Lockwood goes to Wuthering Heights to find the gate unlocked and the doors open.

The hair in the locket - A symbol that shows up only once in the novel is one for the intertwined lives and destinies of Edgar and Heathcliff because they both love Catherine. When Heathcliff comes in to view Catherine in her coffin, he takes the lock of Edgar's hair out of her locket and throws it to the ground, replacing it with his own. Ellen takes both locks, winds the yellow and black locks together, and puts them both in the locket.

Theme Analysis

Race/Class/Education - Throughout the novel characters are prejudged by their race, class or education. When

Heathcliff is first introduced he is described as a dark skinned boy with dark hair, and because of this people are prejudiced against him. He is called a 'gypsy' numerous times, and the Lintons treat him badly and send him away from their house because of his appearance. Heathcliff also quickly dislikes his son because of his light skin and hair.

Class is also an issue. There was a class hierarchy in Bronte's England, and this can be seen in the novel as well. The residents of Wuthering Heights seem to be of a lower class than the Lintons at Thrushcross Grange. Even though she loves him, Catherine will not marry Heathcliff after he has been degraded, and instead marries into the rich Linton family, causing all of the major conflict in the novel. The Lintons are of a higher class both because they have more money and don't seem to have to work, and because they are better educated.

Catherine tries to better her station both by marrying Edgar Linton and by her constant reading. She laughs at Hareton because of his lack of education. Heathcliff admits that Hareton is smarter than Linton, yet because of how they are raised and what they will inherit, Linton will be the more upgraded while Hareton will remain a servant. It is only when Catherine and Hareton become friends and she begins to educate him that Hareton turns into a gentleman and loses his crude behaviour.

Revenge - Revenge is a major theme of the novel. Early in the novel Heathcliff is described as plotting revenge, and the second half of the novel is dominated by Heathcliff's revenge against Hindley and his descendants for his mistreatment of him and against Edgar and his descendants for Catherine's death. Heathcliff's revenge affects everyone in the novel, and he seems to think that if he can revenge Catherine's death, he can be with her. He has been looking for her since her death, as he has been sensing her near him. However, it is only at the end of the novel, when he has given up his plans for revenge, that he is able to see Catherine and that he is reunited with her.

Supernatural - Supernatural events happen in the very beginning of the novel and continue until the very end. In chapter three Lockwood is grabbed and pleaded to by Catherine's ghost through a window, and in the last chapter Ellen talks about people seeing the ghosts of Heathcliff and Catherine walking on the moors. In between Heathcliff tells Ellen about hearing Catherine sighing in the graveyard and sensing her nearby, and when he gives up his plans of revenge he even seems to sees her ghost.

Ellen also once sees Heathcliff as a goblin, and wonders if he is a vampire or a ghoul, although she realizes she is being silly. These themes and instances are tied to a spirituality and life-after-death theme in the novel. Edgar and Heathcliff both want to be with Catherine after she has died. Edgar does not want her to haunt him, but he does look forward to a time when they can be together again. Heathcliff does want Catherine to haunt him, and she indeed seems to, and he also looks forward to spending eternity with her after death.

Q. Discuss the significance of symbolism and Muse in Wuthering Heights.

Or

Q. Emily Bronte's Muse and Symbolism.

Emily Brontë was the daughter of a strict Evangelical minister, but the symbolism in her poetry frequently reflects the processes of doubt permeating Victorian society. The alter ego she constructed in her poetry was a princess called A.G. Almeda who was brave and powerful, but who also possessed a degree of tyranny and selfishness and who later became the Queen of Gondal, the Brontë sisters' fantastical and imaginary land. Gilbert and Gubar claim that A.G.A brought 'all men to her feet' and tragedy 'to all who loved her' hinting at darker aspects and deep desires within Brontë's psyche.

Emily Brontë became a 'reclusive and anti-social character' who 'lived inside herself' and whose imagination was fed by her beloved Yorkshire moors. One of her early formative experiences involved a narrow escape from death on the moors which shaped her view of the moors as beautiful and compelling. The moors appeared to combine death and desire, and Emily incorporated this into the unusual religious and spiritual symbolism which is integral to her work.

Other Victorian female poets entered into a unique discourse with one another, but Emily Brontë clung to her distinctly male identity. Brontë's alter ego may have been a wealthy and commanding female, but her muse was a masculine one and Homans suggests Brontë had 'masculine visitants' creating a 'visionary experience' which was comparable to a 'masculine poet's muse'. The personal tone in 'My Comforter' describes the thoughts she has 'concealed' within her soul in the 'light that lies hid from men' and its 'gentle ray' cannot be controlled by a patriarchal system or by a male God. She sees Christians as 'wretches', 'howling' empty praise in a 'Brotherhood of misery' and their 'madness daily maddening' her.

Brontë claims she stood in the glow of heaven and the 'glare' of hell and forged her own path between 'scraph's song and demon's groan'. Only 'thy soul alone' can know the truth, and her appeal to 'My thoughtful Comforter' is not an appeal to God, but to her enigmatic male muse which governs her spiritual belief. He is epitomised by the life-giving 'soft air' and 'thawwind melting quietly' and lovingly around her. She is grateful that her 'visitants' allow her 'savage heart' to grow 'meek' and allow her to conform to the role she is forced to play within an ordered Christian and patriarchal system. Her poetry focuses on the betrayals of mind and body, as she seeks to find answers to questions that her society does not permit her to ask. Brontë's religious symbolism and unique spirituality show a form of pantheistic atheism, although she continued to attend a church 'whilst sitting as motionless as a statue' and it seems that this careful passivity is juxtaposed with uncontained anger and frustrated passions.

Brontë's male muse is intrinsically linked to the moors and attached to the eastern wind blowing across them. The wind is tied to the spiritual essence of a god, and often involves a 'retelling of Milton's and Western culture's central tale of the fall of women' so integral to the Catholicism of Gerald Manley Hopkins and Coventry Patmore. Her sensual relationship with her muse appears to have been 'threatening as well as inspiring' and enveloped her poetry with deep longing and a desire for fulfilment. Brontë's spiritual belief and secular spiritualism is symbolised by her love of nature and typified by 'shadows of the dead' which she sees around her. Gilbert and Gubar see Emily Brontë's poetry and beliefs as threatening the rigidly hierarchical state of heaven and hell, and Brontë believed that the dead remained on the earth and moved around her.

She also saw dead friends and family watching her at night, and this dream-like sleepy other reality has some similarities with Christina Rossetti's 'soul-sleep'. Brontë's religious symbolism shows no hope for everlasting life and her spirit languishes in 'dead despair'. Her poem 'I'll not weep' echoes Gerard Manley Hopkins sonnet 'No Worst' however, as she claims the 'summer's day' will end 'in gloom' and that life ends with the 'tomb'. Hopkins's and Brontë's diverse beliefs required different types of religious symbolism, but both experienced deep feelings of anguish and isolation. Brontë believes in the 'soul' which is 'sighing' but believes death releases to peaceful oblivion rather than everlasting life. She desires freedom and 'liberty' for an unconfined and 'chainless soul'.

The religious symbolism in 'The Philosopher' highlights the sounds of the soul as she chastises herself for 'dreaming/ unlightened'. Outside the world is 'white' and there is room and light for 'space-sweeping soul'. The next stanza is italicised and articulates forbidden desires, while the italics simultaneously highlight and apologise for the defiance. She yearns to sleep 'without identity' with imagination and thought annulled as earthly woes disappear. Emily Brontë's derisive view of patriarchal heaven suggests that it cannot contain or even 'half-fulfil' the 'wild desires' she experiences. She does not fear 'threatened hell' or its 'quenchless fires' because her 'will' is stronger.

The next stanza is written alliteratively in the first person and states her strength of purpose. She has 'three gods within' which are 'warring night and day', showing her frustration and secular spirituality, blended uniquely with Evangelist doctrine. The three gods symbolise the trinity, but form a unique triumvirate stronger than orthodox spirituality because they are all 'held' within her until death or re-birth. This unique form of individualised pantheistic ideology and spirituality is revealed through her religious symbolism in her work.

Brontë longs to 'rest' in oblivion rather than immortality. Her muse in the form of a male 'spirit' stands over her and channels her spiritual ideology. The 'golden stream' signifies the soul rather than wealth and the blood suggests flowing life. The 'sapphire' stream in the colour of the skies over the moors, suggesting virginal purity and innocence as well as cleansing water. The streams flow into the dark sea of eternity, offering an endless peaceful rest. The 'spirit' kindles 'all with sudden blaze' which is 'white as the sun', and signifies innocent and uncorrupted soul-fire. The poet states that she has searched and 'sought' her 'spirit' and 'seer' in 'Heaven, Hell, Earth and Air' but all prove inadequate. She yearns for a spiritual state which would prevent her seeking 'oblivion' or 'stretching eager hands to Death'. Her spirit muse embodies soul, spirituality and 'living breath' and she wishes to vanquish 'Power and Will and the 'cruel strife' on god's earth and be 'lost in one repose', and suggests that Christianity is a prime cause of her subjection.

The moors and nature are intrinsically tied to her spiritual beliefs, but her adoration of nature differs from that of Hopkins. Hopkins's sees nature as an essential part of God's glory, while Brontë focuses on the mystical aspect of nature and the moods produced, rather than on precision and detail. Her poetry reflects changes in faith and belief within her society, as Victorians increasingly saw a separation of the 'moral sense from the religious institutions that had once expressed it'. The religious symbolism in her poetry shows that Brontë believed that a god or celestial being resided in nature, but orthodox religion and its hierarchical structure had no meaning for her. Emily Brontë considered the imagination to be more important than the word of God, while the romantic aspects of her nature generated a powerful male muse, and the 'favourite characters' incorporated into romantic situations were manifestations of aspects of Brontë herself. Brontë's individual spiritual mysticism highlights her deep longing to create new forms in thought and writing, while her masculine muse encapsulates her deep yearnings and desires. She remains aware of the presence of the soul, but cannot accept the patriarchal and ordered concept of Christianity, reflecting some of the processes of doubt in Victorian Britain.

Q. Write a brief passage on Family-Systems Theory, Addiction, and Emily Brontës Wuthering Heights.

Or

Q. Family-Systems Theory, Addiction, and Emily Brontës Wuthering Heights. Classify

Critic informed by the family systems theory derived from the treatment of chemical dependence can add many insights to standard crticism of Wuthering Heights. He or she would emphasize that as soon as Lockwood asks that he be told their stories by Nellie, the novel becomes the histories of several family systems and all the characters in the systems, male as well as female, living and dead. Focusing on the family as a unit at Wuthering Heights we discover one of the best illustrations of a closed system in literature. They are not merely extremely isolated from others, they are actively hostile: instead of welcoming the protoreader, Lockwood, they refuse to come to his aid as six dogs attack him inside the house. Even the reader is excluded from some of the activity at the Heights, for at times it is presented in a dialect almost unintelligible to all but those raised in the neighborhood. Even members of the family at times find Joseph's "speech difficult to understand" when he got excited and "his jaws worked like those of a cow chewing its cud."

When Lockwood does manage to get past some of the rigid boundaries, Hareton Earnshaw is instantly angry at him and "Mrs. Heathcliff" at first won't even speak to him. Many readers no doubt identify with Lockwood's sarcastic understatement, "I began to feel unmistakably out of place in that pleasant family circle." When Lockwood tries to escape from the system, a dog prevents him, as in the Leary household. In his case, two dogs attack and pin him to the ground and a servant asks, "Are we going to murder folk on our very door-stones?" The family motto, "Every man's hand was against his neighbour," appears to Lockwood in a dream and he adopts it has his own. When one of the ancestors, a recently dead family member. comes to him as a child in the dream, crying "Let me in.... I'm come home," Lockwood, already imitating the others, slashes her wrists on the broken window and replies, as the blood stains his bed, "I'll never let you in."

Lockwood proclaims to the family, "I'm not going to endure the persecutions of your hospitable ancestors," but as soon as one enters a family system of any age one is in the presence of ancestors. "Before passing the threshold" for the first time" Lockwood looked up and "detected the date `1500' and the name `Hareton Earnshaw'." He then confronted the latest incarnation of that name who, when he was learning to read, began by reading his own name carved on the door. This is an example of transgenerational repetition in the same house for centuries almost beyond the imagination of readers in America, which had just been discovered in 1500. At Wuthering Heights names are simply repeated, as if there were little difference between the generations, as if they kept adopting the same roles and following the same script century after century.

When we add to name repetition the habit of cousins marrying cousins in a complicated genealogy, we can see why readers of the novel are as confused as Lockwood was when he first entered the family. Readers get to feel exclusion from a closed system as they wonder which Catherine, for example, is being discussed. Because of "the thousand forms of past associations, and ideas" a family member "awakens, or embodies," even the inmates become bewildered: Heathcliff, for example, at times believed that Catherine II was Catherine I and often "Hareton seemed a personification of my youth, not a human being; I felt to him in such a variety of ways, that it would have been impossible to have accosted him rationally."

Thus, as Lockwood put it, "Time stagnates here," not only in choice of names but also in repetition of abuse and addiction.

After Hindley's funeral Heathcliff went to Hareton, "lifted the unfortunate child on to the table and muttered, with peculiar gusto — 'Now, my bonny lad, you are mine! And we'll see if one tree won't grow as crooked as another, with the same wind to twist it." Heathcliff says later, "I can sympathize with all his feelings, having felt them myself.

I know what he suffers now, for instance, exactly — it is a mere beginning of what he shall suffer, though. And he'll never be able to emerge from his bathos of coarseness and ignorance. I've got him faster than his scoundrel of a father served me, and lower.... And the best of it is, Hareton is damnably fond of me! You'll own I've outmatched Hindley there." As family systems histories document so often, the habit of abuse binds the victim to the abuser: Hareton "took the master's reputation home to himself, and was attached by ties stronger than reason could break — chains, forged by habit." One of those habits was patrolling the boundaries of the closed system like a guard dog: Hareton stones even his old nurse Nelly when she tries to return to the Heights.

The law of repetition compulsion in this kind of a patriarchal family system is, in Heathcliff's words, that "The tyrant grinds down his slaves and they don't turn against him; they crush those beneath them." When Heathcliff elopes with Isabella he hangs her dog to prevent its barking; when Isabella finally escapes from him she passed by "Hareton, who was hanging a litter of puppies." Heathcliff's next student of sadism, Linton, learns the same lesson: "He'll undertake to torture any number of cats." Sadism infects all who enter that system, whether or not they come under Heathcliff's direct tutelage. The second Catherine, for example, comes from a different family system but soon "seemed to have made up her mind to enter into the spirit of her future family, and draw pleasure from the griefs of her enemies."

A chemical dependency family systems theorist would focus on the addictions that result from these abuses. Like Lockwood, such a critic would say to Nelly Dean, "I am interested in every character you have mentioned." Hindley, for example, an apparently minor character, emerges as an important father figure. He has a process addiction — gambling — and eventually mortgages all of his land, but his drug of choice is alcohol. In the habit of coming "home rabid drunk," he is often in a murderous rage. Nelly tries to control his drinking, but Heathcliff exclaims "It is a pity [Hindley] cannot kill himself with drink.

He' s doing his very utmost but his constitution defies him." Hindley is a true alcoholic, unable to stop even when he wants to. For example, "he kept himself sobre" in order to attend his sister's funeral but he "rose in suicidal low spirits, as fit for the church as for a dance; and instead, he sat down by the fire and swallowed gin or brandy by the tumberful." Like many alcoholics, he was apparently trying to medicate depression with alcohol. Alcohol is his way out of a depressing family system. When he dies at the age of 27 we learn that "he has spent the night in drinking himself to death deliberately."

This novel reminds us that in such family systems, women are not the only victims of split loyalties, triangulation, scapegoating, invalidism, and anorexia. The story proper begins with one of the patriarchs named Earnshaw bringing Heathcliff into the system. He is named him after a child who died in childhood, but like Jane Eyre he is an outsider and the tension is intense.

Absorbing that tension, Mr. Earnshaw soon succumbs to invalidism and death. Nelly says, "It hurt me to think the master should be made uncomfortable by his own good deed. I fancied the discontent of age and disease arose from his family disagreements, as he would have it that it did." Nor are women the only ones who manipulate illness to control others: Linton Heathcliff does so even more consistently than Catherine does and, like her, ends up a victim of the family dynamics he tries to control.

A critic oriented to process dependencies such as addictions to control and to rage can identify Catherine's personality as addictive before she succumbs to anorexia. Catherine tries to enlist Nelly in her means of control, asking her to communicate to others the peril of provoking her, reminding them "of my passionate temper, verging, when kindled, on frenzy." When Nelly calls her bluff Catherine turns to anorexia. Nor are rage and fasting the only ways we see her control others: "I have such faith in Linton's love, that I believe I might kill him, and he wouldn't wish to retaliate."

Of course, the most obvious process addiction in the novel is the "love" of Heathcliff and Catherine, one of the most famous examples in literature of pure enmeshment, a total loss of boundaries that seems to triumph over death, sustaining the myth that romantic love is a viable form of spirituality. A family systems critic oriented to addictions can explore parts of this pattern that are often overlooked.

Catherine is not the only character to choose anorexia as a means of self-destruction. Early in their relationship, like an aspiring saint in the courtly school of love, "fasting and reflection seemed to have brought" Heathcliff to the point where he could ask Catherine to "make me decent." After he loses Catherine to anorexia, Heathcliff finds himself also unable to eat until finally, after swallowing nothing for four days, he manages to die. Despite, or perhaps because of, this conclusion to their relationship, this half of the novel remains popular, often the only half made into movies.

Movie versions rarely show what we now call functional behaviour. Yet some of the children at Wuthering Heights are able to stand up for themselves against abuse. Heathcliff defends himself against Cathy's laughter, and Cathy confronts her father. Nelly defends herself against Catherine's physical abuse: "You have no right to nip me, and I'm not going to bear it." And Edgar Linton follows her example, complaining to Catherine, "You've made me afraid and shamed of you.... I'll not come here again."

These defenses do not stop the abuse, but readers' childhood memories of similar instances of courage may be positively reinforced in such passages. Longing for a healthier family is better satisfied by the second generation. Closed family systems change usually only in response to their almost complete disintegration and/or to intervention from the outside. In this case, the influence of Catherine Earnshaw's husband, Edgar Linton, seems to be the key.

His daughter, Catherine Linton, seems much "healthier" than her mother and thus some readers may perceive that transgenerational repetition is not inevitable. After a considerable struggle she manages to transplant some flowers from Thrushcross Grange to Wuthering Heights.

They become the symbol of the change. She makes amends to Hareton for her sadistic behaviour and helps him to read. Hareton is then able to give the lie to Heathcliff's assertion, "I've got him faster than his scoundrel of a father served me, and lower." Ultimately, they transform Wuthering Heights into an open system. The protoreader, Lockwood, recounts, "I had neither to climb the gate, nor to knock — it yielded to my hand. That is an improvement! I thought.... Both doors and lattices were open." Many readers, like orphans, seek such functional family systems in life but find them only in fiction.

Q. Suicides in Wuthering Heights.Discuss

Or

Q. Write a passage on the significance of Suicides in Wuthering Heights.

Brontë's Wuthering Heights, set in 1771-18O3 but published in 1847, alludes both to pre-1823 burial customs and to those of 1823. Brontë seems to have felt free to use both the laws in effect during the time of her story and those governing early Victorian times. 14 In narrating the details surrounding Hindley Earnshaw's death (1784), for example, she draws upon the earlier statutes. Although the exact cause of Hindley's death is never determined, all who saw him at the end claim that he died in a state of drunkenness.

Mr. Kenneth, who tells Nelly about the death, says that he "died true to his character, drunk as a lord". And Heathcliff, when Nelly asks if she may proceed with suitable arrangements for Hindley's funeral. retorts that "correctly... that fool's body should be buried at the cross-roads, without ceremony of any kind. I happened to leave him ten minutes, yesterday afternoon; and, in that interval, he fastened the two doors of the house against me, and he has spent the night in drinking himself to death deliberately!"

The precise circumstances of Hindley's death, which are

reported in considerable detail, have important implications for the course of Brontë's novel. For if Hindley did die drunk and debauched, as both Kenneth and Heathcliff indicate he did, in the eighteenth century he would automatically have been considered a suicide, exactly as Heathcliff suggests.

Even more importantly, in that case his property could legally have been forfeited to the Crown, with nothing left for Hareton arid hence nothing left for Heathcliff to employ as a tool in his revenge. It is probably for this reason that Heathcliff allows Nelly to perform proper burial rights for Hindley, thus relinquishing a more immediate revenge upon Hindley's dead body while gaining a long-term hold on the entire Earnshaw family.

Earlier, just before coming to the Heights, Nelly had consulted with Linton's lawyer about Hindley's death and had requested that the lawyer come to the Heights with her. His refusal is telling, for he advises that "Heathcliff be let alone, affirming that if the truth were known, Hareton would be found little else than a beggar". The "truth" here may be that Heathcliff is Hareton's only hope because he is Hindley's creditor; or that the lawyer, probably Mr. Green, is already under Heathcliff's influence. But it may also be that Hindley's death as a suicide is better left ignored, primarily because of the possibility of forfeiture.

Catherine Earnshaw's death precedes her brother's by only half a year, and it too can be considered suicidal. There is little doubt that Catherine knows how to induce her own ill health, even though she does not intend suicide when she first embarks upon her fast in Chapter II. At this point, totally breaking her own body and heart is, for Catherine, still "a deed to be reserved for a forlorn hope". What happens, however, is that Catherine's body only partially cooperates with her will, and Nelly's assumption that Catherine is in total control of her situation is a tragic miscalculation. After only three days' fast, Catherine is already past saving. When she realizes that neither Linton nor Heathcliff has become genuinely alarmed and then chooses not to die, she cannot reverse her headlong journey toward destruction.

The important scene before her mirror already spells this doom for Catherine, as Q. D. Leavis has realized. Catherine is shocked when she sees her own reflection because she seems to understand what Yorkshire folklore dictates: that sick people should never look at themselves in a mirror. If they do, their souls may take flight from their weak bodies by being projected into the mirror, and this can cause their death. In accordance with this belief, immediately after she sees her reflection in the mirror, Catherine is convinced that she really will die.

Leavis suggests that this realization replaces Catherine's fear of ghosts, anxiously expressed just before: "I hope it will not come out when you are gone! Oh! Nelly, the room is haunted!". I believe, however, that the realization and the fear are even more closely related. For Catherine actually seems to consider herself to be the ghost once she recognizes that the face in the mirror is her own. " 'Myself,' she gasped, 'and the clock is striking twelve! It's true then; that's dreadful!' "). Catherine's utter horror here stems from her superstitious belief that suicides become restless ghosts.. She now assumes herself to be a suicide, and it is this aspect of Catherine's unnerving realization before the mirror that incites her subsequent raving about the ghosts at Gimmerton Kirkyard.

After this scene, there is only one more meeting between Catherine and Heathcliff before her actual death. On that occasion their dialogue is flied with allusions to Catherine's suicide and her would-be haunting of Heathcliff. Catherine now feels that she will never be at peace; while Heathcliff repeatedly expresses regret over what he feels is Catherine's self-murder and his relationship to it. In desperation, Heathcliff can forgive Catherine her murder of him but not her own willed death, which she in turn blames on him. All this seemingly metaphorical talk of murder reflects suicide law. Any accomplice of a suicide was legally considered his/her murderer, so that, ironically, the protagonists' accusations of one another could, were they true, carry the weight of law, as well as of guilt.

Catherine is not, however, buried as a suicide. Nelly

wonders "after the wayward and impatient existence she had led, whether she merited a haven of peace at last" (WH 137-38), but after looking at her in death, decides that she probably does, Instead, Catherine is interred in the corner of the Kirkyard under the wall, "to the surprise of the villagers". Because the local people did not know of the means of Catherine's death, they might have expected that she would lie either in the chapel with the Lintons or by the tombs of the Earnshaws.

Their wonderment is understandable when one recalls another folk belief about suicides. Particularly after the 1823 law, when suicides could legally be buried in churchyards, it became customary in parts of northern Britain for their bodies to be laid below the churchyard wall, so that no one would be likely to walk over their graves (. The place of Catherine's burial would thus have had particular significance for the folk of Gimmerton, who would no doubt have inferred the nature of her death from the location of her grave.

Unquestionably the place of Catherine's burial determines Heathcliffs own choice of a burial site and consequently his own need not to become discovered as a suicide. Because of his reputation and his doubtful place in the Gimmerton community, it is far less likely that Heathcliff would be extended the kind of pity that had allowed for the churchyard burials of Hindley and Catherine.

He knows this and knows too of the possibility of interment in the public highway and is therefore scrupulous about not appearing suicidal. This accounts for the long delay of his own death, which continues to trouble the novel's critics; recent examples include Mitchell, 1973. Unfortunately for Heathcliff's union with Catherine, Linton dies before Heathcliff does and is the one to be buried in the grave next to hers. Lawyer Green, now the tool of Heathcliff, does suggest that Linton be buried appropriately in the chapel. Linton's death is of natural causes and his family all lie there. But Green, though under Heathcliff's influence,] must abide by the stipulations of Linton's will, which states Linton's desire to be buried with Catherine. Nelly, for one, issues "loud protestations against any infringement of its directions". Less than a year elapses between Linton's death and Heathcliffs, the year in which Heathcliff and Wuthering Heights are so intensely haunted by Catherine that even the prosaic Lockwood is influenced to dream of her. Toward the end of this time, Nelly observes how isolated and peculiar Heathcliff has become and warns him against taking his own life.

As she notes, he undergoes his most dramatic set of changes from the time of his curious hunting accident, when "his gun burst" while he was "out on the hills by himself". Finding himself still alive after the accident, Heathcliff forces himself to reach home, despite a heavy loss of blood, Detained by this accident, lie is brought into closer contact with Cathy and Haremn. Now, however, as his tormentings of them only serve to remind him of Catherine, he becomes affected by the strange tedium vitae that was considered the cause of so many nineteenth-century suicides.

Uotations from Wuthering Heights "I cannot continue in this condition," he tells Nelly. "I have to remind myself to breathe — almost to remind my heart to beat!". He also forgets to eat but makes the attempt when Nelly urges him and then takes great care to tell her that "It is not my fault, that I cannot eat or rest. I assure you it is through no settled designs".

As he begins to fail, the one thing uppermost in Heathcliff's mind is his burial. To Nelly he gives detailed instructions for its procedures: "..you remind me of the manner that I desire to be buried in. It is to be carried to the churchyard, in the evening.. No minister need come; nor need anything be said over me"). Each of Heathcliff's requests is in accord with the 1823 statute governing the burial of suicides: the hour, the place, and the lack of a Christian burial service. Nelly seems to) realise their significance. In a moment of insight she brings up the fear that has haunted Heathdiff ever since the day of Catherine's death: "And supposing you persevered in your obstinate fast, and died by that means, and they refused to bury you in the precinct of the Kirk?"

Heathcliff's only means of recourse now are to charge Nelly with the business of moving his body, so that he can be with Catherine, and directly to threaten Nelly with haunting should she fail to comply. The threat seems sufficient to frighten the superstitious servant, and the next evening when Heathcliff does die, Nelly conceals her suspicions about his death from Kenneth: "Kenneth was perplexed to pronounce of what disorder the master died, I concealed the fact of his having swallowed nothing for four days, fearing it might lead to trouble, and then, I am persuaded he did not abstain on purpose; it was the consequence of his strange illness, not the cause".

Her actions now free Nelly to carry out Heathcliff's instructions to the letter and "to the scandal of the whole neighbourhood" Shocked by Heathcliff's interment side by side with the married Lintons, the people also appear to know the meaning of Heatincliff's burial without Christian rites.

It is not long afterward that under the Nab the local shepherd boy sees the ghosts of what he must now consider as two suicides, Heathcliff and Catherine. In the end, Lockwood's much-discussed final words in Wuthering Heights take on added irony in light of the folklore of suicide. Referring to the gravesites of Catherine, Linton, and Heathcliff, Lockwood wonders "how anyone could ever imagine unquiet slumbers for the sleepers in that quiet earth". But anyone knowing the customs surrounding suicide in eighteenth- and nineteenth-century Britain — as Emily Brontë did — could, on the contrary, hardly imagine quiet slumbers for them.

Q. Discuss the significance of dreams in Wuthering Heights.

Or

Q. Write an essay on Dreams in Wuthering Heights.

Lockwood dreams at the site of textual stimulus and production. Taken by chance to the inner sanctum of the novel, he immediately finds himself dealing with books, diaries, carved writing, and fearful dreams that come to him from his idle reading. His very first experience, his reading of the carved initials, confers on the whole scene a provocative correspondence between the interior of the paneled bed and the interior of a text. The initials Lockwood reads return to him, in his semiconscious state, as a "glare of white letters" that stare from the dark "as vivid as spectres." Frank Kermode has shown that the sequence of letters encodes the novel's double plot structure so that Lockwood has, in effect, already read the tale Nelly will tell him. It is as though Lockwood has passed like a microbe into the brain of the text and is shown, in eerie disguise, the primitive formation of signifiers that will "plot" the passions and actions of Nelly's story.

The enigmatic quality of the story is also suggested by Lockwood's hallucination. The staring white letters, aligned across a black page of psychic space, produce a maximum of narrative gaps and missing pieces. And yet it is also the case that Lockwood's presence in the "penetralium" hints at the text's desire to captivate its reader. In a novel that concentrates on the building and breaking of barriers, what we see in the ensuing dreams of Lockwood is the naked action of the text's massed energies breaking across the hopelessly anomic and emotionally pallid being of the intruder. The dreams signal the flickering trace of responsive life that even Mr. Lockwood harbors within him and, in doing so, the dreams become equipment for reading.

The key to the dreams is their instigating source in a commercially printed text whose margins are overwritten by a secret manuscript diary. Lockwood's hallucination has led him to knock his candle over and singe one of "the antique volumes" that rests on the ledge. As he examines "the injured tome" and the other pious books, he discovers Catherine Earnshaw's personal memoir. The dominant symbol in the paneled bed episode thus becomes the doubled text that juxtaposes a discourse in print with a discourse in manuscript: the printed text is culturally based and rhetorically directed to a public, socially coded world; the manuscript text is based in the secrecy of selfhood and is directed only to the undisclosable identity of its own author. Lockwood's two dreams plumb the nature of each kind of discourse and the problem of reading that each kind inherently possesses.

His instinct with the printed book is to attach himself to the forward thrust of the discourse; his instinct with the diary is to backtrack from the handwriting to its originating subject. With both texts situated for him within the same margins, his "eye wander[s] from manuscript to print". As this happens, the dreams descend, each engaging him at a substrate of consciousness and each making profound the instinctive and casual orientations he had adopted in his waking state. In the process, the dreams penetrate Lockwood and turn his reading into a performative action in spite of all his ordinary preferences for reading as a dilatory habit.

The first dream ushers Lockwood to a local house of worship that, we have already learned, is down on its institutional luck because of the congregation's parsimony. But this condition is exactly reversed in the dream, for it is the profligacy of discourse by Jabes Branderham rather than the parsimony of the audience that wrecks the chapel's public function. The Croesian profusion of utterance that Jabes invests in his sermon on forgiveness makes discourse intolerable; all solicitude for the audience is missing. Jabes founds his text on the authority of another text. Textual authority then becomes for him a gateway to discursive license at both the thematic and performative levels of his sermon. The charity of the Word is thematized as a hounding moral quantum, while the quantitative limits of discourse are shattered by a moralistic tyrant. Throughout the sermon we follow not Jabes' utterance but its punishing effect on Lockwood.

Oh, how weary I grew. How I writhed, and yawned, and nodded, and revivedl How I pinched and pricked myself, and rubbed my eyes, and stood up, and sat down again, and nudged Joseph to inform me if he would ever have done!

Then, in a "sudden inspiration," Lockwood attempts condign retribution by exposing the extravagance of Jabes' polemic as, intrinsically, a social crime. " 'Sir... I have endured and forgiven the four hundred and ninety heads of your discourse.... The four hundred and ninety first is too much. Fellow martyrs, have at him!"' But Jabes climaxes his sermon, maddeningly, by fusing his theme and his performance: Lockwood's harrowed reception of Jabes' discourse becomes itself the unforgivable sin:

Thou art the man!... Seventy times seven didst thou gapingly contort thy visage seventy times seven did I take counsel with my soul.... The First of the Seventy-First is come. Brethren, execute upon him the judgment written!

With this final appeal to the text as autocrat Jabes turns Lockwood's parallel appeal to the congregation against him. Anarchy breaks loose: "the whole chapel resounded with rappings and counterrappings. Every man's hand was against his neighbour". The first dream thus discloses a condition of public strife and moral confusion when discourse mounts to power by abrogating the social contract on which communication depends. The little chapel beyond Gimmerton becomes a parable of life in Gesellschaft where divisiveness is contagious. With dense and deliberate irony Brontë uses a printed book as the symbol of connection between contaminated discourse and Gesellschaft power-mongering. The printed book, the very artifact she has produced, is always to some degree an official tool of Gesellschaft life and an instance of its homogenizations of human expression

In the second dream, Lockwood is prompted by "hieroglyphics" rather than public writing, and instead of journeying abroad in public space, where he had encountered a savage surplus of text, he now remains in the secret recess of the paneled bed where he encounters a bewildering barrenness of text-a ghost. Catherine is an illegible mystery. She is not threateningly behind her text, like Jabes, but threateningly beyond her text. She appears as the radical realization of the living Catherine's desire to reach her private, impenetrable essence.

It is this figure o f imponderable mystery, devoid of any other's etching, who asks Lockwood to carry out the deed of admission. Instead, Lockwood's terror rouses in him the still flickering core of his own presocial self:

finding it useless to attempt shaking the creature off, I pulled its wrist on the broken pane, and rubbed it to and fro till the blood ran down.

What Lockwood has encountered in this dream is what Carlyle called "the world out of clothes," and Lockwood's reaction duplicates Carlyle's: "Imagination, choked as in mephitic air, recoils on itself, and will not forward with the picture". The panicked Lockwood must retreat to the world-in-clothes, the textualized world, that links our sense of identity to the presence of signs:

he fingers relaxed, I snatched mine through the hole, hurriedly piled the books up in a pyramid against it, and stopped my ears to exclude its lamentable prayer.

The pyramid of books restores, at a crude level, the textualized world in which Lockwood, or any social being, must function.

The dreams do for Lockwood what the novel does for us. They outline the cognitive and performative boundaries within which discourse must fit its hazardous project. The text is always obstruction. It can be read only if the reader is neither bullied by the text nor left choking in mephitic air. The reverse is also true: the reader can neither bully the text nor disappear, like a wayward mist, from its reach. What the dreams manifest about reading, the story of the novel extends to social being. Social being can flourish neither in the power structures of Gesellschaft relations nor in the wild moors of Romantic subjectivity. The remorseless harangue and the remote hieroglyph are both of them the enemies of solidarity and significance.

There is a third space. It is the space of narrative or, rather, travelings. The difficult road located by Wuthering Heights winds its way between the text as tyrant and the text as enigma. Ultimately, as Cathy and Hareton will show, the text must be a gift, an exchange of presences, an inscription of Gemeinschaft.

Chapter 13

Some Interesting Weather Quotations in Wuthering Heights

Weather Quotations

"Atmospheric Tumult"

"One may guess the power of the north wind blowing over the edge by the excessive slant of a few stunted firs at the end of the house, and by a range of gaunt thorns all stretching their limbs one way, as if craving alms of the sun."

"The power of the north wind"

"All the day had been flooding with rain."

"Linton is as different as a moonbeam from lightning, or frost from fire."

"The storm came rattling over the Heights in full fury. There was a violent wind as well as thunder."

"In the evening the weather broke; the wind shifted from south to north-east, and brought rain first, and then sleet and snow."

"She was the most winning thing that ever brought sunshine in to a desolate house."

"I found plenty of entertainment in listening to the larks singing far and near, and enjoying the sweet warm sunshine." "Her eyes radiant with cloudless pleasure."

"Catherine's face was just like the landscape - shadows and sunshine flitting over it in rapid succession; but the shadows rested longer, and the sunshine was more transient."

"In every cloud, in every tree - filling the air at night, and caught by glimpses in every object by day - I am surrounded with her image!"

Bibliography

Allen, Walter. The English Novel. New York: E. P. Dutton, 1955.

Benvenuto, Richard. Emily Brontë. Boston: Twayne Publishers, 1982.

Brontë, Charlotte. "Editor's Preface to the New [1850] Edition of Wuthering Heights." In Wuthering Heights, edited by David Daiches. Penguin, 1965, pp. 37-41.

Brontë, Emily. Wuthering Heights. New York, NY: Modern Library, 1950.

Crailic, W. A. The Brontë Novels. London: Methuen, 1968.

Daiches, David, ed. In the introduction to Wuthering Heights. Penguin, 1965,